A SHEARWATER BOOK

THE LAND WE SHARE

THE LAND WE SHARE

Private Property

AND THE

Common Good

ERIC T. FREYFOGLE

ISLAND PRESS / SHEARWATER BOOKS

Washington / Covelo / London

A SHEARWATER BOOK
Published by Island Press

Shearwater Books is a trademark of The Center for Resource Economics.

Library of Congress Cataloging-in-Publication Data
Freyfogle, Eric T.
The land we share : private property and the common good / Eric T. Freyfogle.
     p.   cm.
"A Shearwater book."
Includes bibliographical references and index.
ISBN 1-55963-890-7 (cloth : alk. paper)
1. Land tenure—United States. 2. Land use—Environmental aspects—United States.
3. Land use—Economic aspects—United States. 4. Landowner—United States.
5. Right of property—United States. 6. Common good. I. Title.
HD205.F74 2003
333.3′0973—dc21
2003009612

Design by Jeff Clark at Wilsted & Taylor Publishing Services

Printed on recycled, acid-free paper

British Cataloguing-in-Publication data available.

Manufactured in the United States of America

10   9   8   7   6   5   4   3   2   1

To the reader of open mind

who cares about homeland health

CONTENTS

THE LAND WE SHARE

INTRODUCTION

Few ideas have bred more mischief in recent times, for the beauty and health of landscapes and communities, than the belief that privately owned land is first and foremost a market commodity that its owner can use in whatever way earns the most money. The appeal of this extravagant yet familiar idea—at least for developers and mining companies and the politicians they support—is easy to perceive. What is harder to see and what very much needs to be seen is how costly, unfair, and disruptive the idea is, especially to people who care for their communities and natural surroundings and who yearn to live peaceably at home.

As a public issue, private property has enjoyed more attention lately than it has at any time since the 1930s. Public debates at that time centered on corporate powers and whether corporations should enjoy the same property rights as morally responsible humans. (Corporations largely won.) Today's discussions have more to do with land use and conservation and with the rights and responsibilities that attach to the ownership of land, water, and other resources of nature. What rights should private owners enjoy, and what duties might society reasonably impose on them, given the problems of urban sprawl, decayed cities, and environmental decline? Can private development and resource-use practices continue as in the past, or have the complexities of modern life brought us to the point where a new approach is needed, some new understanding of how the private owner fits with the surrounding community? These are the questions that now confront us, and with mounting urgency.

The most vocal participants in current debates have been the leaders of "wise use" and "property rights" organizations. In their view, landowners possess inherent rights to use their lands intensively, free of restraint, so long as they avoid visibly harming anyone else. Indeed, these advocates commonly assert, landowners have always possessed these rights—or they have, that is, until recent decades, when regulatory agencies began trampling upon their rights and threatening property as an institution.[1]

Such claims, however, rest upon a poor understanding of how the law has defined landowner rights over the course of America's history. They also reflect muddled thinking about how the rights of one owner are restrained by the rights of neighbors and about how private rights fit with pursuit of the public's well-being. Private property is made possible by law, police, and courts: it is a social institution in which public and private are necessarily joined.

The recent extravagant claims about property rights have arisen mostly in response to the conservation movement and its demands for change. That movement has pursued many goals, from the preservation of historic structures, older neighborhoods, and family farms to the protection of waterways, open spaces, the atmosphere, and endangered species. Fueling these varied efforts has been a conviction that uncoordinated development too often produces landscapes that are ecologically degraded, unpleasant to be in, and ultimately damaging to human life. Sprawling development in the United States consumes a full square mile of land every two and one-half hours, day and night, while core cities grapple with crumbling neighborhoods and vacant properties (Philadelphia alone has 60,000). Year by year, valuable topsoil erodes (on cornfields, about two bushels for every bushel of crop); mountaintops are lopped off by cost-cutting mining companies (with residues left to clog rivers); and commercial forests lose diversity and ecological functioning as owners convert them to monocultural plantations. For many people these land-use practices are simply intolerable. Communities need to assert greater control over their landscapes if waterways are to recover, if wild species are to survive, and if people are to enjoy healthy lives in harmonious surroundings.[2]

Inevitably, this conservation impulse has collided with widely held ideas about private ownership, worrying people who see merit on both sides of the clash. Yes, we would like healthier, more pleasing surroundings, but can we obtain them without undercutting the cultural values and economic growth that private property promotes? Can private property and conservation coexist? To address such questions, we need to dig beneath the surface of the familiar yet complex institution of private property to see why it exists, how it functions, and how it might change to better serve our collective needs.

Today's discussions about private property carry forward and are illuminated by a long history of impassioned debate over landowner rights. In his popular "Letters from an American Farmer," penned during the Revolution, French immigrant J. Hector St. John de Crevecoeur could hardly contain his delight over his exalted status as a private landowner:

> The instant I enter on my own land, the bright idea of property, of exclusive right, of independence exalt my mind. Precious soil, I say to myself, by what singular custom of law is it that thou wast made to constitute the riches of the freeholder?[3]

Crevecoeur's contemporary and former countryman, Jean-Jacques Rousseau, embraced a decidedly different view of the institution in his much-read study of economic inequality:

The first person who, having fenced off a plot of ground, took it into his head to say *this is mine* and found people simple enough to believe him, was the true founder of civil society. What crimes, wars, murders, what miseries and horrors would the human race have been spared by someone who, uprooting the stakes or filling in the ditch, had shouted to his fellow-men: Beware of listening to this imposter; you are lost if you forget that the fruits belong to all and the earth to no one![4]

In the seventeenth century, English philosopher John Locke countered King Charles II's aggressive claims to control all English land by spinning a state-of-nature tale that showed how private property arose independently of any law or government action. Private property was a natural right of individuals, Locke proclaimed, arising out of the mists of time. Government was the sworn protector of private property, not its creator. Locke's tale struck responsive chords on both sides of the Atlantic and proved enormously influential, and yet Benjamin Franklin was hardly alone in challenging it. Far from arising from God or nature, private property was a "creature of society," Franklin confidently asserted. As such, it was "subject to the calls of that society, whenever its necessities shall require it, even to its last farthing."[5] Save for those few items "absolutely necessary" for subsistence—"the savage's temporary cabin, his matchcoat, and other little acquisitions"—all property was the product of "public convention," with the public holding full power to limit "the quantity and uses of it."[6] British utilitarian philosopher Jeremy Bentham would later put Franklin's point more firmly: "Property and law are born together, and die together. Before laws were made there was no property; take away laws and property ceases."[7]

Thomas Jefferson was among many who took a more intermediate view, mixing Locke's natural-rights reasoning with Franklin's view of property as social convention.[8] Jefferson spoke often of property as a vital individual right, even as he revised Locke's phrase "life, liberty, and property" to his now-familiar "life, liberty, and the pursuit of happiness." The right of property for him chiefly had to do with a man's ability to acquire land for subsistence living, at little or no cost: It was a right of opportunity, a right to gain land, not a right to hoard it or to resist public demands that owners act responsibly. Jefferson was hostile to speculators and land barons who tied up vast tracts of land while other citizens went landless. Government should break up large landholdings, he urged, and otherwise take every chance to make land freely available. He wondered openly whether private property would remain fair and just once the vast American continent filled up:

> Whenever there is in any country, uncultivated lands and unemployed poor, it is clear that the laws of property have been so far extended as to violate natural right. The earth is given as a common stock for man to labour and live on. If, for the encouragement of industry we allow it to be appropriated, we must take care that other employment be furnished to those excluded from the appropriation. If we do not the fundamental right to labour the earth returns to the unemployed.[9]

Once the new nation began to function under the Constitution, private property was constrained less by moral concerns and natural-rights reasoning than by the legal powers held by the people collectively (the *demos*). Courts agreed that legislatures possessed broad powers to control how private land was used. Even for Chief Justice Roger Taney, a Southern conservative and author of the proslavery Dred Scott decision, private desires were properly subordinated to public need:

> While the rights of private property are sacredly guarded, we must not forget that the community also have rights, and that the happiness and well being of every citizen depends on their faithful preservation.[10]

For antebellum jurists of all persuasions, landowner rights were limited by the longstanding rule that an owner should cause no harm, either to immediate neighbors or to the surrounding region (the doctrine *sic utere tuo ut alienum non laedas*, or "use your own so as not to injure another"). They were also constrained by the overarching common law principle *salus populi suprema lex est*: "the good of the people is the supreme law."[11] These were potent legal constraints on ownership, though not potent enough for radical democrats such as Thomas Skidmore, who insisted that the law fully recognize the rights of all Americans to have access to land. Skidmore's plan, set forth in his popular text, *Rights of Man to Property!* (1829), would have given each citizen at birth an equal share of the earth's natural bounty. To make the scheme work, property rights would end when each owner died, with the land then reverting to the state for reallocation. Skidmore's specific scheme was unworkable and wisely ignored. But some of his ideas would resurface in more practical form in 1879 with the appearance of Henry George's best-selling treatise, *Progress and Poverty*. George would pose fundamental, enduring questions about the fair reach of private rights: When a growing community causes vacant land to rise in value—as was happening in city after city—should not that value accrue to the community that created it, rather than to the landowner who had done nothing in particular to bring it about? Why should a private landowner get rich from a bounty that nature alone provided, when nature was the common heritage of all?

If these various questions over the generations have received answers, they have been temporary answers, valid only so long as society did not change. Yet society would not stop changing. New conditions, new values, rising populations and technology, new scientific understandings, refined senses of justice and beauty—all have combined to keep alive the fundamental property questions. Together they have pushed the rights and responsibilities of private ownership to take on new forms.

This book explores the institution of private property and how it might be changed to respond to today's needs. Necessarily, the inquiry roams widely, wandering into history, attending to law as well as philosophy, taking up economics, and probing the links between private rights and the common good. My particular interest lies in the private ownership of land, water flows, timber, and nature's other parts—though much of what is said also applies to private rights in historic buildings, retail malls, and the like.

A number of specific issues resurface regularly in the chapters that follow. One has to do with the mismatch between the way private land is portrayed in law and culture and the way it exists in the real world of nature. Private land in the law is an abstract human construct; a bundle of legal rights and responsibilities typically defined without regard for the land's natural features. Property in the law has clear legal boundaries that crisply divide one parcel from the next. In nature, the situation is starkly different. Nature is an interconnected whole, one parcel fully linked with the next. Even a seemingly slight action on one tract of land can trigger far-spreading ecological ripples. Much of today's conflict about property rights has arisen precisely because land is so different in law and in nature.

A second recurring issue has to do with another mismatch—this one between the popular view of private property as a relatively static, stable bundle of legal rights and the historical reality, which records significant changes in what landowners have been allowed to do. Private property, in fact, has been an evolving, organic institution with ownership rights that have varied greatly from era to era and place to place. The vast potential for further change of this institution very much needs exploring.

The third issue relates to the recurring tension within property law between one landowner's desire to develop land intensively and the desires of neighbors and community members to remain free of annoying if not damaging disturbances. When development would undercut the settled life, which interest should the law favor? Should the law favor those who want stability and calm, or should it favor instead the more restless owners who yearn to build and reshape?

Fourth is the issue of whether private property, at root, should be considered an individual entitlement or is better understood as a tool that governments use to foster the collective well-being of all.

Finally, there is the pressing question of whether good land use should be an obligation of private ownership or instead be viewed as a more praiseworthy act, deserving of compensation when the good activity benefits the community. For instance, when land is best used as wildlife habitat and left substantially unaltered—rather than being turned into a golf course—should the public pay the owner to keep it that way, or would payment be unfair to other taxpayers?

Private ownership, I believe, is in need of fundamental change if it is going to serve America well in the twenty-first century. The public must regain its legitimate interest in private land. I say regain because it once had a relatively clear grasp of that interest, only to lose it over the course of the nineteenth century. Far more than it has, property law needs to pay attention to nature and to tailor the rights and responsibilities of ownership so as to protect the land's natural functioning. It needs to steer development away from ecologically sensitive areas and find ways to limit uses that overload the land's natural capacity to sustain them. Developers need to be told, clearly and firmly, to shape their visions to the land, not the land to their visions. And this needs to happen—it can happen—while retaining private property's ability to protect privacy, promote enterprise, and keep society stable. Paradoxically, many of the ideas I propose here contain distinct echoes of property law as it existed late in the eighteenth century, before industrialism so powerfully reshaped the institution.

A good many of the ideas needed to reform private property reside in America's rich land-use past.

Today, many property disputes reach the courts (and hence the newspaper front pages) in the form of arguments about whether a particular land-use regulation has or has not interfered with private rights so severely as to amount to an unconstitutional "taking" of private property in violation of the just-compensation clause of the Constitution. I turn to the just-compensation clause in the final chapter, where I explore ways of improving how government regulates land. It is possible, I believe, for the Constitution to give lawmakers substantial power to redefine the rights of landowners, bringing them up to date and promoting conservation, while at the same time heightening the protections landowners enjoy against unfair government treatment.

CHAPTER ONE

The

MANY ELEMENTS

of

OWNING LAND

Iowa, 1998

In 1993, the owners of 960 acres of farmland in Kossuth County, Iowa, petitioned the county board of supervisors to designate their property as a protected "agricultural area" under the laws of the state of Iowa. The legal designation, if granted, would allow them to engage in any agricultural activity they wanted, without having to worry that their activities could legally be deemed a nuisance. The landowners apparently sought the legal designation in order to set up the latest technology in meat production: a Confined Animal Feeding Operation (CAFO), which harbors in one place thousands or tens of thousands of animals along with their attendant odors, wastes, flies, and rodents. So long as the owners complied with the specific rules that regulated CAFOs, an "agricultural area" designation would insulate them from the risk that annoyed neighbors might sue to halt the operation. After balking at first, the county board voted by a narrow margin to grant the landowners' request.[1]

Two couples living nearby, Clarence and Caroline Bormann and

Leonard and Cecelia McGuire—fearing that the planned livestock operation would seriously disrupt their lives and adversely affect the value of their own properties—filed suit in April 1995 to challenge the county's decision. The effect of the board's action, they asserted, was to strip them, as landowners, of their legal rights to protect themselves against activities that disrupted their own land uses. Without the designation, they could challenge a CAFO as a nuisance if the odors, pests, and pollution threats were sufficiently annoying; with the designation, that right was taken away. So severe was this curtailment of their legal rights, they claimed, that it amounted to an unlawful "taking" of their private property within the meaning of the federal and Iowa constitutions. Either the government should pay them for this taking or the "agricultural area" designation should be struck down.

Three years later, in *Bormann v. Board of Supervisors*, the Iowa Supreme Court resolved the dispute, agreeing in full with the Bormanns' and McGuires' allegations. The county designation did indeed strip them of a valuable property right when it effectively gave the owners of the 960 acres license to commit a nuisance. Because the CAFO had not yet been built, no one knew for sure whether or not it would amount to a legal nuisance; that is, an activity that imposes substantial, unreasonable harm on neighbors. But the "agricultural area" designation made the CAFO immune to suit based on nuisance and therefore improperly interfered with the Bormanns' and McGuires' property rights. As protector of the rights of Iowa citizens, property rights included, the court would invalidate the offending legal action.

The Iowa court's ruling in *Bormann* provides a good beginning point to make sense of contemporary discussions about what it means to own land and about how far government can go in regulating a landowner's rights. Those discussions, although long present on the public scene, have become more heated and politically potent over the past two decades. Elevating the issue to prominence have been a variety of development interests, extractive industries, and free-enterprise think tanks, which have expressed alarm about the ways governments have restrained what landowners can do. These groups have condemned many land-use laws not just as bad public policy but as violations of constitutionally protected rights that individual landowners enjoy. Governments, they acknowledge, have legitimate powers to regulate land uses that are plainly harmful. But many recent laws, they assert, have gone far beyond that narrow function and have compelled landowners to devote their private lands to uses that affirmatively promote public goals, such as historic preservation, nature conservation, and the control of sprawl. However worthy these goals, they urge, land-use regulations that yield benefits for the public as a whole should be accompanied by the payment of compensation to landowners whose land values are reduced as a consequence.[2]

For generations, land-use laws such as those affecting the Bormanns have emanated chiefly from local and state governments, and that pattern continues today. Drawing the most fire recently, however, have been a handful of statutes enacted at the federal level, two above all: the provision in the Clean Water Act that bars landowners from putting fill material into wetlands without a permit (which may be either denied or granted with costly conditions),[3] and the provision in the Endangered Species Act that prohibits landowners from altering critical wildlife habitat on their lands whenever the alteration would injure or kill a protected species.[4] The wetlands law has broad coverage; it applies not just to obvious wetlands with standing water and cattails but to lands that merely include wet soils and water-tolerant plants. The endangered species provision affects fewer landowners, but when it does apply it sometimes severely limits even ordinary land uses, such as timber harvesting and homebuilding. Less talked about than these two federal laws are the

many state and local laws that ban construction on ecologically fragile lands such as floodplains and barrier islands or that impose construction moratoria or designate open-space greenbelts to control
urban sprawl. When such laws apply, landowners often can build
nothing, for a temporary period or even permanently.

Rising up to defend these various laws have been government
agencies and an array of public interest groups concerned about such
matters as ecological degradation, declining communities, urban
sprawl, and the loss of open spaces. On the surface, the resulting
debates have swirled around specific policy issues. Do "isolated
wetlands" provide significant ecological benefits? Do the aesthetic
and psychological benefits of greenbelts around communities justify
their costs? Beneath the surface, however, lie fundamental questions
about private property and how private rights fit with the common
good. What rights do landowners have to use their lands, and when
can they reasonably complain about legal constraints? What does
land ownership entail, and how far can government legitimately go
in frustrating landowner expectations?

Extractive industries and development interests have found the
private property issue useful in their efforts to ward off limits on their
activities. Laws that severely curtail what owners can do, they claim,
interfere with their private rights and are therefore unconstitutional
unless those landowners are compensated. In the simple, easily
grasped way that such groups present the issue, government is the
force that interferes with landowner activities, and private property
is the shield that landowners use to keep government at bay.

Having successfully elevated the issue to national prominence,
many advocates of private property rights have taken the offensive.
They have lobbied Congress and state legislatures to enact statutes
requiring compensation for landowners whenever a law reduces
the market value of a land parcel by some specified percentage (often

50 percent).[5] Few laws requiring such compensation have been enacted—and none to date at the federal level—but the threat of enactment has nonetheless deterred land-use regulators at all levels of government.

This debate was at its peak when the *Bormann* decision was handed down. Many observers hardly knew what to make of the ruling. The case was about property rights (those of the Bormanns and their neighbors) that government had allegedly invaded. And in the end the court protected those rights by striking down the law responsible for their invasion. But the facts of *Bormann* were far different from the simplistic case trotted out in public debates. In the hypothetical dispute widely viewed as the norm, an individual landowner desires to engage in a particular land use, only to be frustrated by an overbearing regulatory agency. *Bormann*, in contrast, involved a dispute between adjacent landowners, with government and state law called upon to reconcile their conflict. In addition, the Iowa court's ruling, although nominally protecting property rights, directly challenged the understandings and economic interests of some of the most ardent advocates of the property rights cause, particularly industrial agriculture. In *Bormann*, private property rights had been used as a sword to attack intensive land uses, not as a shield to protect them.

As property disputes go, *Bormann* was not especially complicated. It seemed complicated only in contrast to the rhetoric of the day, which portrayed the private property issue so simplistically. In truth, private property is a more complex and more social institution than it seems. Property is widely viewed as an individual right, and appropriately so, yet it is an individual right that is curiously dependent upon laws enacted by the majority for public aims. Because the actions of one landowner inevitably affect neighboring landowners, visibly and invisibly, the rights of one owner need tailoring to fit with the rights of other owners. Many times, how property is employed also affects the surrounding community—socially, economically, and ecologically—so the community and its interests must be taken into account. Finally, we need to consider the interests of future generations and the wisdom of conserving the land for their use. Consideration of the long-term future necessarily limits the powers and increases the responsibilities of present-day owners.

To make sense of the contemporary concerns about private property—that its original formulation is being corrupted, as some believe, or that landowner rights are too extensive, as others contend —one needs to start at the beginning and probe the fundamental elements of this commonplace yet poorly understood institution. A good way to undertake such an exploration is to examine a number of important or representative legal cases, from the past as well as the present, and see how they portray private property. Once the basic elements of private ownership are clear, we can make better sense of property's past, see how the institution has evolved, and uncover its underlying justifications. We can also better address the critical issue of land conservation and how we might accomplish it while adequately respecting the essential attributes of ownership. Leading American conservationists have repeatedly offered a stern warning: because private land is so extensive, we are unlikely to achieve conservation goals or halt the processes of degradation unless the country revises (yet again, as we shall see) what it means to own nature.

What, then, are the fundamental elements of private property? A basic one, illustrated by the *Bormann* decision in Iowa, is that the rights of one landowner are necessarily constrained by the rights of neighbors. Landownership includes more than just the right to put land to use; it also includes the indispensable right to complain when other landowners materially interfere with one's quiet enjoyment. Inevitably, these rights are relative: one owner's right to use land is tempered by his neighbor's right to remain undisturbed. Nuisance law incorporates this ownership element by providing vital protection for land uses, ordinary as well as sensitive, yet it does so by restricting the ability of all landowners to conduct activities that cause harm. Nuisance law enhances and protects property rights at the same time as it limits them.

To recognize this practical fact is to see why "absolute ownership" —viewed by some as the baseline of private property—literally makes no sense. What could absolute ownership mean when ownership necessarily includes both a right to use land and a right to complain about interferences by neighbors? Would an owner possess absolute rights if the law allowed him to engage in any land use, without regard to consequences? Such a scheme would indeed maximize an owner's right to use land, but the law could fairly grant one owner that right only if it granted the same right to all others—thus stripping all owners of the right to halt interferences by neighbors. It would be equally apt to claim that absolute ownership exists when the mix of rights is just the opposite: when a landowner is legally able to halt *any* disruption of her activities but then faces severe limits on her own ability to use land intensively.

Property law itself has rarely employed the term *absolute ownership*, except in the important and revealing instance of groundwater law. For generations, hydrogeology was a mystery to landowners and lawmakers alike. Knowing so little about water tables, courts were reluctant to conclude that groundwater withdrawals by one landowner caused another owner's well to go dry. Many states thus embraced a legal rule on groundwater that they labeled "absolute ownership." Under the rule, landowners possessed an unlimited right to withdraw water from beneath their private lands without regard to the effects on others. As we now know, water does not stay in one place underground: a strong pump beneath one parcel pulls water from beneath adjacent lands. But all was fair under the absolute ownership rule: if neighbors disliked the loss, they could pump harder themselves.

With a bit of reflection, we can see that this now largely discarded groundwater rule differs little from its ostensible opposite: the "no ownership" doctrine, or the rule that groundwater below private land is unowned until someone brings it to the surface. Under both legal regimes, landowners can take as much water as they are able to in the race with their neighbors to extract. Under neither system can a landowner complain if her well goes dry. Below ground as well as above, in short, absolute ownership in practice resembles no ownership unless an owner's right to use enjoys some protection against competing actions by others. Oil and gas law has similar characteristics. Many states view oil and gas as unowned, free for any surface landowner to capture at will. Other states follow a rule that sounds much different: the surface owner holds secure title to all oil and gas beneath the surface. But states in the latter category freely allow surface owners to pump from their lands as much as they please, even if the oil or gas is drawn from neighboring lands. Under both legal approaches, then, the practical outcome is the same: oil and gas go to whomever is first to extract it from the ground, so long as a pumper is not trespassing on someone else's land surface.

The lesson here—a second, related element of private ownership —is that a world in which landowners can do as they please is a world in which property rights are in fact tenuous. Ownership without protection is insecure, yet security can come only by limiting one's rights to use land as one pleases. Thus, a landowner's right to use water in a stream—to consider a final illustration—is highly uncertain so long as upstream landowners remain free to consume or pollute the stream without regard for downstream effects.

Related to the image of ownership as absolute is another, more sophisticated and popular image helpful in identifying further elements of owning nature: the metaphor of property as a bundle of rights or a bundle of sticks.[6] This simple image conveys the useful idea that private ownership entails a variety of distinct legal rights, such as the right to earn income from the property, the right to sell it, the right to bequeath it at death, the right to exclude others from it, the right to use water on or under it, and the right to pledge it as security. Long popular in legal writing, this image captures the notion that an owner's rights in property can vary in abundance, just as a bundle can contain more or fewer sticks. Ownership is not one aggregate right; it is many distinct rights, and a landowner can possess few or many of them.

Contemporary opponents of land-use regulation make regular use of this metaphor of ownership. Why they do so is easy to see, for it makes their critique of unwanted regulations seem more potent. When ownership is undifferentiated, a typical restriction on a landowner diminishes his rights only in small part. When ownership instead is a bundle of sticks, a given law might take away one stick in its entirety; it seems a more severe taking of a distinct landowner right. For instance, a law that bans an owner from withdrawing groundwater because of regional shortages is, in this view, a total deprivation of the groundwater stick in the bundle.

The bundle-of-sticks metaphor has pedagogical value for the law school classroom, but when it is used without care it sows confusion and mischaracterizes what laws do. For instance, how would one depict the *Bormann* ruling in terms of its effects on landowner sticks? The owners of the 960 acres might claim that the ruling cut severely or eliminated one of their sticks—a stick representing the right to use land intensively. But it is misleading to leave it at that, for it was the court's ruling that enabled the Bormanns and McGuires to vindicate a stick in their own bundles—the right to halt interferences by neighbors. If the court had ruled against the Bormanns, it would have effectively pruned that critical stick. In any fair-minded system, the right-to-protection and right-to-use sticks are necessarily relative. Other landowner rights are similarly reciprocal. Moreover, particular sticks come in a variety of shapes and sizes, a reality that the bundle metaphor distorts. The right to use water in a stream that runs through or beside one's land, for instance, can appear in widely different legal forms, from the right to consume and pollute the stream at will to the right (commonly recognized in America's early years) to use a stream only in ways that leave its waters undiminished in both quality and quantity. The typical land-use or environmental law neither adds to nor detracts from an owner's overall bundle; instead, it reconfigures the rights within the bundle.

The relativity of many sticks in an owner's bundle illuminates two further fundamental elements of private ownership. First, property law always expresses a policy position as to whether a given land use should or should not be allowed (the law, that is, is never neutral). Second, when the law is called upon to resolve land-use conflicts such as the one in *Bormann*, there is no "pro–private property" position that the law can take. Neighboring landowners often propose land uses that clash. Owners occasionally resolve their conflicts by cutting deals. Far more often, the law is used to resolve the dispute: landowners curtail their activities only when the law orders them to do so. When the law affirmatively constrains a particular land use—as nuisance law does, for instance—it openly favors one land use (the use being protected) at the expense of another (the use being constrained). Yet even when the law remains silent, allowing both competing land uses to proceed, it nonetheless resolves a land-use dispute and therefore also incorporates a policy judgment. When both land uses can proceed, the law implicitly favors the more intensive use by allowing it to win out in a physical sense. Had the Bormanns and McGuires lost their suit, Iowa law would have illustrated this possibility. The CAFO would then have been built, the Bormanns and McGuires would have suffered, and the law would have effectively resolved the dispute by favoring the CAFO. In all situations, then, the law provides an answer for land-use conflicts, either by allowing a particular land use or by restricting it. Either way, the law passes judgment as to what land uses are proper. A law that allows all activities to proceed, in short, is no more neutral or more pro-private property than a law that protects sensitive land uses: it merely accentuates the right to use land intensively at the expense of the right to complain about interferences.

When the Bormanns and the McGuires turned to Iowa's courts to regain their nuisance-law protections, they did what landowners all across the country have done: they drew upon a land-use law to protect the value of their property. This essential, value-protecting role of law is too often overlooked. Land-use laws enhance land values more often than they reduce them, which is why proponents of land-use rules are usually landowners themselves. To see the pervasiveness of this truth, one need only consider the typical residential subdivision in America today. The land-use options of subdivision owners are often so severely curtailed that they may do virtually nothing except continue existing residential uses. Of all possible uses of the land, all but one is banned—not by state or local laws but by restrictive covenants voluntarily accepted by a present or former owner. Covenants are widespread, detailed, and highly popular not because owners enjoy having their own options restricted but because they want their neighbors' options curtailed and are willing to limit their own in exchange.

To dig further into private property as an institution and identify more of its basic elements, we need to bring the public and its interests into the scene more vividly than they appear in *Bormann*. We need to recognize some of the ways that members of the broader public, not just immediate neighbors, are affected for good or ill by private land-use protection. To do that, and to tie the discussion to the conservation issue that is so important today, we can leave the farmlands of Iowa and head for the forests of the Northeast, journeying back a century to another time in America's history when the issue of private property blazed on the public scene.

The movement to conserve natural resources first gained national prominence during the tenure of President Theodore Roosevelt at the dawn of the twentieth century. Leading the conservation effort at the federal level was Roosevelt's chief forester, Gifford Pinchot. A lanky Pennsylvanian who had studied forestry in Germany, Pinchot had helped manage the Biltmore forests of George Washington Vanderbilt and labored with other sportsmen to protect populations of game species. Pinchot's work got results largely because it built upon earlier state and local conservation efforts aimed at halting land and waterway degradation and preserving local, land-based economies from the onslaught of industrialization. Conservationists met resistance, both from industries that were being criticized and from private landowners who claimed that conservation laws undercut their rights to alter nature. Specific debates swirled around polluted rivers, disrupted fish migrations, denuded hillsides, and scarce hunting prospects. Never far from the surface, though, were long-simmering questions about what it should mean to own land and how the prerogatives of individual owners should fit with the needs of their communities.[7]

One important installment of the early-twentieth-century conservation saga arose in the forests of Maine, which were enduring the same harvesting pressures that had caused Vermont and New Hampshire to lose most of their standing timber in preceding decades. Throughout New England, wild forests had been important communal assets since the first years of European settlement.

Settlement patterns in the Northeast (in contrast to much of the South) centered around distinct towns, which often owned and managed forests, marshes, pastures, and other lands for the shared use of community members. Town residents, however, typically used more than just town-owned lands and their own private tracts to sustain themselves. They regularly headed into the great surrounding woods and unenclosed fields to meet the needs of daily life—even when that land was owned by someone else. New Englanders endorsed the idea of private ownership as the exclusive right to use, but they applied that notion largely to homes and yards, gardens and tilled fields, working woodlots and fenced pastures. In the case of unworked or unenclosed lands, private rights were more limited. The public retained interests in such lands and could use them for their own gain so long as they did not disturb the owner.[8]

State law throughout New England implicitly and sometimes explicitly authorized the public's use of unenclosed private lands for hunting.[9] By law, wildlife was owned by the people collectively, not by the owner of the land where the wildlife lived. Public hunters, then, were merely harvesting public game wherever they hunted. So important was this right that Vermont incorporated it into its 1777 constitution: public hunters could enter and take game on any unenclosed land, without regard for the owner's wishes. The public also held legal rights to fish in navigable waterways, a right that in Massachusetts and Maine extended to all "great ponds" over 10 acres in size, even ponds entirely surrounded by private land. Beyond these rights to hunt, fish, and trap was the public's more general right to forage. Many settlers cut lumber and cordwood from the countryside; pastured animals; and gathered berries, wild fruits, and flowers. Herbs, seeds, roots, medicinal plants, nuts—all were widely viewed as the common bounty of nature, unless and until the owner either enclosed the land or tilled it.[10]

By the late nineteenth century, public rights in land had declined considerably. Rural landowners were reducing their traditional foraging. Instead, they spent more time producing specialized commodities for the market. Commercial farmers who did so began to resist and even belittle their neighbors who continued older, subsistence ways of life. Blueberry growers who supplied distant markets, for instance, increasingly opposed their poorer neighbors, who viewed unenclosed blueberry patches as an invitation to help themselves. Large-scale farmers, annoyed by the wandering livestock of their less prosperous neighbors, pushed state legislatures to rewrite laws that had required landowners to fence their crops if they wanted stray livestock to stay away. Thereafter, those who owned livestock were required by law to keep their animals under control or else pay for the damage they caused. Even with these gradual shifts, however, New Englanders still viewed their forests as a common inheritance. Woodlands, they believed, were freely and properly open for recreation, hunting, and other public uses that did not disrupt the owner's activities.[11]

Northern New Englanders had good reason to worry about the decline of their forests. Timber companies were amassing larger and larger landholdings. As operations grew and local regions were stripped of trees, local sawmills and timber-dependent industries lost their supplies and closed their doors. Timber-cutting and pulp-making operations degraded rivers and disrupted catches, upsetting fishermen. Joining the worried chorus by late century were resort owners and hunting guides who catered to the tourist trade. Deforestation marred the beauty of the countryside, rendering landscapes less appealing to vacationers. According to long-time residents, heavy timber cutting was also harming local climates, making winters colder and summers hotter and drier. Then there was the plentiful evidence connecting timber cutting to increasingly silt-laden rivers and alarming fluctuations in water flows.

During the 1890s, pressure mounted in Maine for the regulation of timber harvesting, particularly for limits on the removal by pulp companies of small-diameter trees that the lumber industry had previously left untouched. Waves of land speculation by outside investors further fueled the forest controversy. Yet even with widespread support for cutting regulations, lawmakers hesitated to proceed. Aside from the predictable political pressures exerted by the timber industry, many legislators were genuinely uncertain about how forestry regulation would affect the property rights of forest owners. Did the state have sufficient constitutional power to act? Would regulation improperly interfere with vested property rights?

Maine, 1907

To resolve the legal issues, the Maine senate approved a resolution on March 27, 1907, calling upon the state's highest court for an advisory judicial opinion. The federal constitution kept federal courts from issuing advisory opinions not based on actual cases or controversies, but Maine was among the states that allowed its own courts to do so. Taking advantage of the process, Maine's lawmakers posed their question: Did the legislature have the power under the constitution "to regulate or restrict the cutting or destruction of trees growing on wild or uncultivated land by the owners thereof without compensation therefor to such owner"?

To the surprise of many observers, the Maine Supreme Court unanimously upheld the state's power to regulate.[12] Indeed, so strongly worded was the court's ruling that it provided a ringing endorsement of the legislature's authority to curtail private rights whenever, in its judgment, the public's interest was served. That power extended to the regulation of private land uses, even when they did not amount to nuisances. Earlier decisions in Maine and elsewhere had long sustained the state's regulatory powers, so the

court's opinion was not without precedent. Still, pressure from timber interests had been strong, and the conservation impulse had
aroused widespread worries about threats to private property.

Just as remarkable as the court's views on legislative powers were
the many asides about private land that it interspersed with its legal
conclusions. As it described the proposed law, the court observed
that the law would apply only to "wild or uncultivated land," which
meant land that neither the current nor any former owner had developed to any significant degree. "Such property," the court noted, "is
not the result of productive labor, but is derived solely from the state
itself, the original owner."[13] Readers of the day would have had no
trouble understanding these comments, for they drew upon—and
reminded readers of—moral and natural-rights reasoning about
who could own land and how much. The guiding light of natural-
rights thought on property was John Locke and his labor theory
of property, under which a person could gain ownership of land
only by mixing his labor with it and creating value. Influenced by
this seventeenth-century philosopher, many New Englanders questioned whether a person could claim full property rights in vacant,
undeveloped land. Such land was not the same as other land, many
believed; until tilled or enclosed it remained a shared asset, subject
to public use and control. Wildness and lack of cultivation were also
evidence that a land parcel's owner did not need the land for subsistence. This, too, was an issue under natural-rights reasoning, for a
family could morally claim only as much land as it needed and could
use. Private claims in vast, little-used tracts were morally suspect,
particularly when the owner acquired title directly from the state at
trivial cost.

Politics being what they were, the legislature received the high
court's opinion but then decided not to use the broad powers the
court upheld. The forest-owners group, it turned out, was powerful
enough to resist overt legal restraint. Yet the owners were able to

avoid regulation only by giving their approval to some of the ways Maine residents had long used these private forests. Timber owners announced that the public could continue using their woodlands to support hunting and fishing camps, guide services, and nature outings. Private forests supported multiple uses, the owners argued, some private, some public. Forest owners would allow them all to continue on a de facto basis in exchange for their continued right to cut timber freely. Overall, the mix was balanced and sound, forest owners asserted successfully, and lawmakers should not upset it. Private owners could manage their forests as they saw fit, even clear-cutting when they liked, while the public would retain its de facto rights to use such lands for other purposes.[14]

From this story we can draw a number of important lessons. To begin with, public power is often needed to curtail private actions that conflict with the good of whole. That power is integral to property as an institution, just as integral as a landowner's right to halt trespassers and a landowner's power to halt nuisances committed by neighbors. A central element of ownership, then, is the obligation of landowners to refrain from activities that cause harm to public interests, an obligation that government implements by means of various land-related laws. The public is obviously harmed by negative effects of land uses that spill across land boundaries and affect entire landscapes, such as the silt that clogged Maine's waterways and killed its fish. Public harms, though, can occur without such visible, transboundary effects. A community has a far longer life than any human owner and therefore has concerns about future productivity and the land's lasting health that individual owners may not have. Thus, a landowner can harm the public interest simply by degrading the land that he owns or by interfering with important ecological processes.

Another link between private land and public good exists when the public has de facto rights to enter and use privately owned lands. The precise public rights in Maine were peculiar to that place and time, yet they illustrate well a further element of ownership: the fact that one owner's property rights are commonly limited by the existence of rights held by others (specific individuals or the public at large), either to make use of the same land (as in Maine) or to limit the ways that the owner can personally use the land. Sometimes other people can actually enter and use the private land. Sometimes the right takes forms that do not involve human entry but that are significant nonetheless—as the next case will illustrate. Recurring disputes arise when landownership is fragmented in this way, as when the main owner of the land proposes a use that conflicts with the rights that others have in the same land. One important role of property law is to resolve such disputes, just as it resolves disputes among neighboring landowners.

Finally, there is the reality, so evident in the Maine dispute, that private landownership is very much a contested concept, buffeted by economic and political forces. Out of that buffeting comes change over time in the rights and responsibilities of ownership (although in the Maine case, the outcome for the time being was to maintain the status quo). Ongoing change is itself an important element of private property considered as an institution. Far from being static, the rights and responsibilities of ownership form an evolving, organic institution. To understand private property fully, and particularly to make sense of current debates about it, we need to gain a sense of the path that private property has followed to get where it is today.

The opinion of the Maine justices hinted at yet another element of ownership—an amorphous one that we will take up later—having to do with the legitimacy of private property rights in a moral or philosophic sense. When property law gives a landowner extensive powers over a tract of land, putting police and courts at his disposal to protect those rights, it gives him authority over the lives of other people. A forest owner who can stop local residents from taking firewood has interfered with their subsistence economies. An owner who can clear-cut trees, polluting waterways and killing fish, similarly wields power to disrupt the lives of fishermen. Interferences of this type are an inherent part of private property, but they are not beyond moral scrutiny, particularly given the fact that public power stands ready to enforce them. In the Maine decision, the justices referred obliquely to long-standing natural-rights discussions when they spoke about how much land a person might rightfully own and about the propriety of people holding more resources than they need and can reasonably use. The court also mentioned an issue that would become nationally important soon thereafter: whether private corporations, drawing their powers entirely from the state, should possess the same property rights as flesh-and-blood, morally responsible individuals. Though these precise moral concerns are less lively today than in the past, the need to justify private property remains strong. To address that need is to shed particularly valuable light on how private rights are appropriately reconciled with the public's interests and conservation aims. We will examine property's justifications in a later chapter.

We can continue to explore private landownership by moving from the forests of Maine to the rivers of New York and shifting our focus from disputes about trees and tourism to one of the knottiest issues relating to private landownership, then and now: How does the private ownership of land fit with the public ownership of wild animals, including wild animals that reside upon the private land? The question is directly relevant because of contentious disputes about the federal Endangered Species Act, yet its importance extends well beyond that. Wildlife is emblematic of the many ways that land parcels are interconnected. It is emblematic, too, of the many parts of nature that are crucial to sustaining the well-being of landscapes and communities but that possess little or no value to landowners as individuals. Wildlife protection is often possible only when protective efforts are undertaken at a spatial scale well above that of the individual land parcel. In its dependence on such large-scale action, wildlife conservation is similar to many other public goals. In the twenty-first century, private land is likely to be subject to governance processes aimed at addressing a variety of landscape-level needs.

New York, 1917

A decade after the Maine dispute, the judges of New York's highest court were presented with a case that also involved conservation laws and private lands. This case, too, dealt with trees. But the central drama featured the animal depicted on the flag of colonial New York—an animal once widespread but by the early twentieth century so uncommon that measures were needed to protect it: the energetic and destructive beaver.[15]

Before 1900, New York had allowed residents to trap beaver during an open season, but so low had beaver numbers fallen that open seasons were suspended. Four years later, realizing that a ban on trapping would not suffice, the legislature enacted a law protecting all beavers. The law applied to private as well as public lands and prohibited interference not just with beavers but also with their dams and lodges. In 1906, the state restocked beaver in the Adirondacks by releasing 21 animals, including 4 at "Eagle Creek, an inlet of the Fourth Lake of the Fulton Chain." Predictably, the released beavers and their progeny began to cause trouble. And because of the 1904 statute, the affected landowners could do little about it.

One Barrett and other landowners not named brought suit challenging the statute. They had acquired their land as building sites, largely because of the attractive forest. Between 1910 and 1912, the

30

beavers felled 198 of their trees and girdled and destroyed others, resulting in a monetary loss of $1,900. The landowners wanted the state to pay for these losses and for the court to invalidate the beaver-protection law. In their initial argument they asserted that, although the state doubtless had power to protect some wild animals, it lacked the power to protect animals that were known to be destructive, such as the beavers. Their second argument was similar: the statute was an unreasonable exercise of the state's police power, given that it kept private landowners from protecting their property. Finally, they asserted, the state should pay for the destroyed trees because the state had intentionally released the beaver into the wild "knowing their propensity to destroy trees."

The New York Court of Appeals began its ruling by reviewing the general principles of wildlife law:

> The general right of the government to protect wild animals is too well established to be now called in question. Their ownership is in the state in its sovereign capacity, for the benefit of all the people. Their preservation is a matter of public interest. They are a species of natural wealth which without special protection would be destroyed.[16]

Wild animals located on private land did not belong to the landowner, even temporarily. The state owned them, though in a sovereign sense—on behalf of the people as a whole—rather than in a proprietary sense, as a private party might own a domesticated animal. As owner, the state had broad powers to protect wildlife. Yet even as it recognized that power, the court remained mindful that regulations entailed costs:

> Wherever protection is accorded, harm may be done to the individual. Deer or moose may browse on his crops; mink or skunks kill his chickens; robins eat his cherries. In certain cases the Legislature may be mistaken in its belief that more good than harm is occasioned. But this is clearly a

matter which is confided to its discretion. It exercises a governmental function for the benefit of the public at large, and no one can complain of the incidental injuries that may result.[17]

As for Barrett's claim that the state could not protect a dangerous or destructive animal, the court was prepared to let the legislature draw its own conclusions. The state's police power was not limited "to guarding merely the physical or material interests of the citizen. His moral, intellectual, and spiritual needs may also be considered." Beavers were not just important for their fur and food value; they were "in a class by themselves" because of their "curious instincts and intelligence," which were "a source of never-failing interest and instruction."

What made the beaver drama uncommon was not the ban on disturbing or molesting the wildlife but the fact that the state had acted affirmatively to reintroduce the species in habitat where it did not reside. On this issue also, it was the legislature's task to determine where the public interest lay:

> The attempt to introduce life into a new environment does not always result happily. The rabbit in Australia, the mongoose in the West Indies, have become pests. The English sparrow is no longer welcome. Certain of our most troublesome weeds are foreign flowers.
>
> Yet governments have made such experiments in the belief that the public good would be promoted. Sometimes they have been mistaken. Again, the attempt has succeeded. The English pheasant is a valuable addition to our stock of birds. But whether a success or failure, the attempt is well within governmental powers.

In the end, all of Barrett's arguments failed and the statute was upheld.[18]

Although not the first case to uphold the state's power to protect wildlife on private land, *Barrett* was a prominent national ruling because it provided such a ringing endorsement of that power. Nonetheless, the court's ruling left many property-law issues unresolved, issues that remain alive today: How far can the state go in protecting wildlife habitat on private land before its restrictions interfere too much with private rights? When a state acts, must it, like New York, enact a protection that is statewide, or can it protect a species and its habitat on some lands and not others? And what about wildlife habitat that is unoccupied at the time of protection but is needed for the successful propagation and restoration of a wild species? Can a state limit a landowner's destruction of such habitat when necessary to protect a species?

Like *Bormann* and the Maine forestry decision, *Barrett* helps to fill out the picture of private landownership in the United States. It, too, vividly illustrates the conflict between the private interests of a landowner and the interests of the surrounding community. If beaver and other roaming wild species are to thrive in private landscapes, coordination or protection is needed at the landscape level. Many other conservation challenges also require landscape-level planning or policies, from highway placement and retail mall planning to the control of residential development to protect lakes and rivers. In recognition of these needs, the private rights of individual owners are tempered by the existence of decision-making power at a spatial scale large enough to address the public's wide-ranging needs. The existence of such power is becoming—and needs to become even more—a visible, institutional element of private ownership.

A further element to glean from *Barrett* has to do with the special way in which private owners hold title to vital parts of nature, particularly parts that disregard property boundaries. Wildlife in America is owned by the state, not the private landowner, with the state as trustee obligated to manage wildlife on behalf of all residents. The same unusual rule applies with respect to water bodies and water flows, including groundwater aquifers. Landowners have rights to use water that flows over, along, or beneath their lands—even rights of absolute ownership, in the case of groundwater—but these rights are use rights alone and are clearly subordinate to the state's pre-eminent ownership of all water. These special rules on wildlife and water are hardly surprising, for both are mobile parts of nature that ignore property boundaries and both are essential to sustain human existence, indirectly if not directly. Yet as ecologists have now made clear, nature's healthy functioning depends upon other parts of nature as well. As nature's value becomes recognized, and particu-larly in landscapes that are declining in ecological health, the public might well seek to protect other parts of nature (topsoil, for instance). Similar reasoning has already been applied to assert a public interest in human-created parts of the landscape, such as historic structures. Private rights in them can also be subject to special limitations.

The idea that private property rights in nature might vary based on nature itself—the land's natural features or the wild species pre-sent on it—is not a new idea in property law, as our final case illustrates. But although this idea has been around in the past, it has only recently entered public debate strongly—strongly enough to account for much of today's conflict over private rights and govern-ment power.

Washington State, 1914

Plaintiffs in *Cawsey v. Brickey* had formed a gun club and leased cer-tain lands in Skagit County as a shooting preserve. In 1913, Wash-ington enacted a law authorizing county game commissions to promote game conservation by designating specified lands within each county as game preserves where hunting was banned. Skagit County's game commission used the power to designate no-hunting areas, including lands that the plaintiffs had leased specifically for hunting. The owners of the leased lands remained free to use them for other purposes, but the gun club—which had acquired only the right to hunt—was shut out from using the lands entirely and filed suit to have the restriction struck down.[19]

The gun club questioned first the state's general power to ban hunting on private land, but its argument was summarily rejected. In England and in the United States, the court responded, the "use of game was subject to absolute governmental control for the common good." The club's second, stronger argument was that the no-hunting ban applied to certain private lands but not to others. It bore unequally on landowners and thus ran afoul of the state's constitutional ban on special or class legislation. This was a more plausible legal claim, but the court nonetheless rejected it also. The game-protection law applied equally to all citizens, the court reasoned, even if it did not apply to all land within the state: All persons were prohibited from hunting in no-hunting areas, and thus no one received special favors. The fact that some land was covered by the ban and some was not made good sense, the court noted, for lands within the state were by no means the same in nature's terms. Lands varied in their natural features, so it was appropriate for landowner rights to vary as well:

> The owner of land which from its location and character is peculiarly suited for a game preserve is not situated similarly to other landowners with reference to the subject-matter and purpose of a law creating a preserve. The subject-matter and purpose is protection and preservation of game. It is so declared in the title of the act. One whose land is thus peculiarly suited to meet those purposes obviously occupies a different relation to the purpose of the law from that occupied by one whose land is not so suited.[20]

The words may have sounded commonplace, but their content was not. It was a powerful line of reasoning, with vast implications. The rights of ownership, the court implied, did not exist as an abstract bundle that all owners possessed equally. If some land was

35

naturally suited for wildlife conservation and some land was not, the rights of ownership could take the differences into account. What made this reasoning so potent was that it applied just as readily to many other lands and land uses, even to the building of factories, golf courses, and grocery stores. The rights of landowners to engage in such activities might similarly depend on their lands' natural suitability for them. Perhaps even the right to build a home on land might attach not to all land but only to land where a home could be built without ecological degradation.

As the twentieth century drew to a close, questions about property rights and nature would animate public debates more than any other. Should the rights of wetland owners be the same as the rights of those whose land is high and dry? Should the owners of rare wildlife habitat have the same right to cut timber or to build houses as they would if their lands were ecologically different? Property law did not need to give all landowners the same rights; therein was *Cawsey*'s lesson. But it was a lesson that would clash with conflicting understandings of ownership in which landowner rights were defined in the abstract, without regard either for nature or for the human social context. Even at the dawn of the twenty-first century, *Cawsey*'s lesson would be far from accepted.

As these various cases reveal, private property is a complicated but nonetheless comprehensible institution, very much a human creation and subject to many of the same tensions and forces that stimulate other social conflicts. Property is at root a legal institution, yet property laws themselves stem from the lawmaking community—that is, from a source that lies above and behind the law. To study property law is to gain insights into society as a whole: where it has been, what it values, and where it wants to go.

CHAPTER TWO

OWNERSHIP

in the

NEW NATION

To step back from the Iowa farm dispute in *Bormann* far enough to allow the details to fade is to see reenacted a human drama of mythic proportions. Set in the present and on a small scale, it is the oft-repeated saga of the machine that enters the garden, the bulldozer that invades the countryside. A quiet, settled, perhaps even ecologically sound occupation of land is disrupted by noisy industrial technology. Satisfied inhabitants of a place are confronted by carriers of the latest gadgets, out to intensify the domination of nature.

Viewed narrowly as a legal dispute, *Bormann* was a classic conflict, featuring the two long-dominant American images of owning land—the rival versions of what private dominion is all about. The Bormanns' claim tapped into an ownership image that has held high a landowner's right to live peaceably at home without significant disruption. To exercise dominion in this view is to be protected in one's quiet enjoyment of the land. Once termed the agrarian image of ownership, the Bormanns' view today might be called the community, or ecological, vision of private property, given that it protects lands and communities while encouraging lasting ties between

37

people and places. A more aggressive understanding of private ownership guided the owners of the 960 acres. Their vision emphasized
opportunity, a release of physical energy, and an owner's liberty to
act with little restraint. Dominion in this view is about exploiting the
land for personal gain. Long associated with the frontier and frontier
life, this aggressive view of ownership might now be termed the
industrial or developmental perspective because of its acceptance of
intensive land uses.

For generations, Americans have drawn upon these alternative
images when talking about private property and debating what ownership ought to mean. Sometimes we favor one over the other, sometimes we mix the two. These conflicting images, in turn, have played
parts in a larger cultural conflict between the ideal of the settled,
community-based life and the competing ideal of the energetic,
unconstrained individual: America as the land of harmony and
health versus America the land of restlessness and change. Restless
Americans have disrupted their home communities in various ways.
Some have initiated intensive land-use practices that physically affect
surrounding lands. Others have expressed their discontent by leaving their communities for new opportunities in less confining places.

A particularly effective embodiment of this cultural clash
appeared in Hamlin Garland's popular autobiography from 1917, *A
Son of the Middle Border*. Like writers before and after him, Garland
used the stuff of his particular life and the people he knew to drama-
tize the larger struggles of his day. Born in Wisconsin on the eve of
the Civil War, Garland witnessed the momentous era that stretched
from Lincoln's election to World War II. He spent his youth and
young manhood on the northern frontier, and as the frontier moved
west, his family went with it. No sooner had they settled a farm, built
a home, and formed ties with neighbors than short-term frustrations
prompted his father to pull up roots and try again elsewhere, break-
ing fresh ground on the west-moving edge. As Garland aged, he

could appreciate the urges that drove his father on. He could see, too, what a heavy toll the constant moving exacted from his submissive mother. In his father burned the dominant American urge to make a go of it alone and to tame nature in an endless quest to get rich. In his mother simmered the opposing, minority urge of American society: to sink roots in a place and, over time and with the help of friends and family, to make it bloom.

The first move that Garland remembered came when his father quit their Wisconsin farm to seek new land in Iowa. To his father, Garland later reported, "change was alluring. Iowa was now the place of the rainbow, and the pot of gold." Infused with visions of heading west, his father's "face shone with the light of the explorer, the pioneer"; the idea of the move expressing "all that was fine and hopeful and buoyant in American life." Mostly in retrospect, one suspects, Garland could sense that his mother's reaction was far different; in her "sweet face a wistful expression deepened and in her fine eyes a reflective shadow lay." To her, the westward moves from Wisconsin to Iowa and on to the Dakotas were about losing friends and relatives, not about acquiring new homes. "It seemed to me at the moment," Garland would later write, "as if all America were in process of change, all hurrying to overtake the vanishing line of the middle border, and the women at least were secretly or openly doubtful of the outcome."[1]

After time in Boston and a stint at lecturing, Garland returned west to visit his family. His vision now influenced by books and urban life, he could see frontier life and its hardships more clearly. New understandings welled up as he crossed the Mississippi River by rail into Iowa:

All that day I had studied the land, musing upon its distinctive qualities, and while I acknowledged the natural beauty of it, I revolted from the gracelessness of the human habitations. The lonely box-like farm-houses on the ridges suddenly appeared to me like the dens of wild animals. The lack of color, of charm in the lives of the people anguished me. I wondered why I had never before perceived the futility of woman's life on a farm.[2]

In the mid-1920s, soon after Garland's autobiography appeared, social critic Lewis Mumford explored these same themes in his studies of the ways Americans inhabited their lands. There were "two Americas," Mumford observed, "the America of the settlement and the America of the migrations."[3] In the initial wave of internal migration, Americans had headed west and away from settlement, just as the Garlands had done. Hard on the heels of this first wave was a second one, led by the industrial pioneers who brought "a new pattern of factories, railroads, and dingy industrial towns" to the pastoral countryside. Next came the migrants who flowed into America's financial centers, into "the cities where buildings and profits leap upward in riotous pyramids"; they too were driven by the restless urge to make the land anew. Finally there was the migratory wave just beginning to take place as Mumford wrote, driven by those who pushed the edges of burgeoning cities out into the countryside, thrusting aside the settled to make way for the next round of the new. A later generation would term this migration "urban sprawl." Writing with Mumford in the 1920s, forester and planner Benton MacKaye gave the phenomenon a more sinister name. It was the "iron glacier" of the metropolis, MacKaye declared in his classic *The New Exploration*, gradually reaching out, invading, and degrading the landscape:

> This invasion would take its start from the central community. Its movements here as elsewhere we may liken to a glacier. It is spreading, unthinking, ruthless. Its substance consists of tenements, bungalows, stores, factories, billboards, filling-stations, eating-stands, and other structures whose individual hideousness and collective haphazardness present that unmistakable environment which we call the "slum." Not the slum of poverty, but the slum of commerce.[4]

MacKaye's particular, prescient worry was about sprawl that extended along the highways just then connecting city to city. He warned that compact, self-aware communities, separated by open spaces that he termed "intertowns," would soon degenerate if this new wave was left unchecked. Displacing these open spaces would be a formless, characterless type of land occupation he called "road-town," or "a continuous tunnel of structures from one end of the State to another." For urban dwellers and travelers, the countryside would vanish from sight, overtaken by the relentless "metropolitan flood."

Despite his harsh words, MacKaye was no opponent of cities. What he sought was a countryside where people took charge of themselves and the land, occupying it in ways that allowed cities and urban culture to flourish while protecting the beauty, serenity, and fertility of the spaces between. Encouraged by the warm reception given to his pioneering proposal for an Appalachian Trail, MacKaye advocated strict planning along the nation's new highways. Stores and services should not be allowed to pop up at highway intersections and interchanges, where they would blur the line between metropolis and countryside, sap cities, and scar the land. Many people listened to him, but few would act.[5]

The clashing impulses so vividly portrayed by Garland and Mumford appeared again in poignant, fictional form in Wallace Stegner's classic novel of the 1930s, *The Big Rock Candy Mountain*. Like Garland, Stegner could see America's cultural impulses—those of the boomers and the stickers, he would term them—played out in the lives and fortunes of his parents as they journeyed from Iowa westward and northward to Canada, the Dakotas, Utah, and Nevada. Like Garland, Stegner came to side with his soft-spoken mother, whose life was disrupted even more than Garland's by his father's rebellion against the challenges of settled life. John Steinbeck, using drifting characters less able to chart their own destinies, would play on similar themes in his masterwork *The Grapes of Wrath,* set in the same Depression decade.

To carry this literary strand to the present, we can turn to *Jayber Crow*, a penetrating novel from 2000 by writer and farmer Wendell Berry. Set in a fictionalized version of Berry's home region along the Kentucky River, the narrative features a male character this time— Jayber Crow—in the role of the settler and sticker. Jayber grows up near Port William but wanders off as a youth to see the world. Impulses and spiritual uncertainties drive him onward while chance and nature guide his path. Jayber lands work at a horse trotting track, where speed is all but even the fastest seem to get nowhere. Repulsed and discontent, he takes over an empty chair in a local barbershop, learning the trade and observing life. When the urge to return home settles in, Jayber uses the river to get there—the river that so many boomers and migrants would use instead as an avenue of escape. Once home, he slips into the settled life of a declining town, laboring at low pay to satisfy basic human needs.

As Jayber expects, the ensuing decades bring challenges and sadness even as they yield contentment and spiritual growth. Much of his regret after World War II settles upon a brash young farmer, Troy Chatham, who "overflows with the impatience of the new" and who needs "to go headlong, day or night, and perform heroic feats." Troy casts aside the diverse, family-centered practices of the best local farmers. Instead, he specializes in a few cash crops, buys ever-bigger equipment, and embraces practices that ignore the land's sensitivities. Though his farming operations expand, Troy can barely stay ahead of creditors, even as his soil erodes. Outwardly confident, he is inwardly lonely and discontent:

> He was lonely because he could imagine himself as anything but himself and as anywhere but where he was. His competitiveness and self-centeredness cut him off from any thought of shared life. He wanted to

have more because he thought that having more would make him able to live more, and he was lonely because he never thought of the sources, the places, where he was going to get what he wanted to have, or of what his having it might cost others.[6]

To reach Berry's fictional Port William, Kentucky, with its contrasting figures of Troy Chatham and Jayber Crow, is to return to the time of the Bormanns and to their fears about how an industrial livestock facility might degrade their Iowa landscape. Troy Chatham did not have an industrial livestock plant in mind, but he was plainly the type to jump at the idea. And if Troy stayed in place physically—unlike the wandering parents of Hamlin Garland and Wallace Stegner—his roots in that place were shallow and his ties with neighbors weak.

Troy Chatham's view of the world translates into a particular understanding of private land ownership, an understanding that clashes with the perspective that arises out of Jayber Crow's far different set of values. For Troy, land was a commodity, best used when devoted to the activity that generated the most money. In Jayber's contrasting view, land was both more than that and other than that. The individual owner, to be sure, had a sizable claim on how the land should be used, but others also had claims—the surrounding landowners, the community at large, other resident life-forms, and other generations whose lives had been and would be linked to the land. For Troy, land was a tool for individual advancement; for Jayber, land undergirded communal life and was held by an owner in trust.

The tensions that animate these narratives have long inhabited private property as an institution. Over time, they have given rise to a wide variety of ownership regimes, some readily identifiable as private property, others much less so. During the nineteenth century, private property as a worldwide institution drew attention from historians and anthropologists, particularly in England and continental

Europe.[7] What most of them concluded from their scholarly studies was that property regimes evolve naturally over time in a distinct, predictable way, from rights held by people in common to rights that give extensive, exclusive powers to individuals. Many nineteenth-century scholars assumed that property's earliest form was true communism, in which individuals and families held no distinct ownership rights.[8] Everyone shared at first, theory had it, and only later, as populations rose and economies gained sophistication, did true private property emerge. It was a comforting conclusion, for it placed at the apex of property's evolution a world view based on the individualism and progressive thought of nineteenth-century Europe.

By the early twentieth century, further research produced a more nuanced understanding of the institution and how it evolved. In terms of property's beginnings, no instance could be found in any society, including tribes embracing Stone Age economies, in which private ownership was entirely absent.[9] Earlier scholars had inadvertently overlooked private ownership regimes when they studied tribes, largely because the property forms they found differed so considerably from the ones they knew from their homelands. Private rights in tribal groups were crafted and allocated to group members in ways that reflected the members' needs, economies, and values.[10] Rights to land typically took the form of specific use rights—rights to use a given tract for one or more specified purposes—not the vast package of rights that European countries vested in a single owner. Typically, more than one person or family had enforceable rights to use a given piece of land for differing purposes. Moreover, many use rights—to hunt, gather berries and nuts, and the like—were retained by the group as a whole, with all members (but not outsiders) able to exercise them. Rarely could private rights be sold outright; instead, groups reallocated unneeded rights to members in greater need. In the case of tribal groups that migrated, whether seasonally or after longer periods (when planted fields declined in fertility, for instance, or firewood ran short), private rights ended when departure day arrived. By the standards of western Europe and the United States, these rights appeared insubstantial, but they were private rights all the same and suited the people and the land.

Such tribal property arrangements are useful to keep in mind when studying private property today because they illustrate the immense variation in form that property has taken and can take. Landownership as now known in the United States is only one of many possible forms, in terms of the rights that landowners have to use, exclude from use, transfer, and protect their land. Significant variations in private ownership show up not just between widely differing cultures and eras but within particular cultural traditions and over periods of a few generations. Given these variations, we need to approach the past carefully, particularly when probing the roles that private property has played in our own history and making sense of our nation's commitment to respect and protect landowner rights. What did property mean to America's founders of the late eighteenth century, for instance, when they proclaimed private property such an important civil right? What had it meant even earlier, when the first English-speaking colonists arrived on the continent, starting life anew? And how far does the contemporary wise-use image of minimal landowner restraint deviate from inherited understandings of the public's role in land planning?

To American writers of the late eighteenth century—a critical era, given the Constitution's adoption in 1789—property most plainly meant the system of ownership with which they were familiar, shaped by English common law. Although many were unaware of it, that property system was in the midst of change, and it would undergo substantial alteration in the nineteenth century. Change would come not just in the details of what it meant to own land but in the basic ideas about where private property came from and how it fit with the market on one side and with state and local governance on the other. Already, conflicting ideas abounded in American culture. Property was an individual right, people knew, and yet it was also a creature of law. An owner's dominion was vast, and yet so were the regulatory powers of legislatures, save when they ran afoul of specific constitutional limits. Government could threaten property, and yet it was the law and the state's enforcement tools that secured all liberties, property included. Private ownership created a sphere of individual liberty, yet an owner's ability to act was constrained by an obligation to avoid harming neighbors or the common good. To make sense of it all was no easy task.

Before turning to this formative time of the late eighteenth century, however, it is worth considering briefly one further chapter in private property's earlier history: the landed property system of the manorial economy in late feudal England. This episode is far removed from tribal culture but just as far removed from the eighteenth century. To glimpse this distant world, some two centuries after the Norman Conquest, is to see early versions of many ownership ideas that would eventually take hold in America. By looking forward from that era, we can see both the major tensions inherent in private ownership and the ways cultural and economic forces have continuously reshaped it—drawing and redrawing the lines between neighbor and neighbor, individual and community, humans and nature, present and future.

In the autumn of 1066, William the Conqueror declared himself the owner of all English land by fiat. Accompanying William and his invading nobles as they crossed the Channel were important elements of the feudal landholding system that William knew back in Normandy. Once in place, feudalism and the new class of French-speaking nobles rearranged the upper levels of property rights in England, even as they left largely intact the local arrangements that governed day-to-day lives.

To a thirteenth-century peasant who lived and worked on an English manor, the term *private property* would have meant little or nothing. It would be centuries before the word *property* acquired its primary definition as a distinct thing that a person owns. People knew what it meant to own, but the land rights they held in the feudal hierarchy were hardly at all market commodities and were rarely thought about as such. Indeed, a holder of rights in land had no legal power to sell them to another person, though Parliament and the king would soon grant him that right. (Not until the reign of Henry VIII in the sixteenth century would landowners acquire the related power to designate by will who would take their lands upon their death.) Throughout thirteenth-century England, land was integrally linked to status and power in ways that far exceeded any modern equivalent. To control land at any level in the feudal hierarchy was to be enmeshed in a complex arrangement of rights, responsibilities, and loyalties. Entitlements were jealously guarded yet remained vulnerable: an untimely death, an act viewed as disloyal, a feud among noble families, a sudden call from the crown—all could upset even highly prized entitlements. As a whole, the feudal system was constructed to maintain public order and concentrate wealth rather than to protect individual rights or economic freedoms. Historian Karl Polanyi summarized this attitude toward land in his classic study, *The Great Transformation*:

> Land, the pivotal element in the feudal order, was the basis of the military, judicial, administrative, and political system; its status and function were determined by legal and customary rules. Whether its possession was transferable or not, and if so, to whom and under what restrictions; what the rights of property entailed; to what uses some types of land

might be put—all these questions were removed from the organization of buying and selling, and subjected to an entirely different set of institutional regulations.[11]

Within the typical English village of the thirteenth century, populated by 400 to 600 inhabitants, the landscape was divided into three categories of space: *public* places, where anyone could go, including outsiders; *communal* places, where inhabitants of the village but not outsiders held distinct use rights; and *private* places, normally homes and private gardens, where owners expected an element of privacy. To a modern visitor, the communal spaces would stand out most prominently in terms of their vastness and economic importance. The village green, the pound where livestock was kept, village wells and ovens, perhaps a pond, and most of all the open fields—all would be communal property, subject to clear understandings of who could use them, when, and how.[12]

Farming practices followed either a two- or three-field system of crop rotation. Tillers of the soil held their lands as tenants of the lord, with their rights recorded on official manor rolls. Tenants in this "open-field" arrangement held individual rights to specific strips of arable land, scattered among the village's fields and allocated, ideally, in such a way that each tenant family held a mixture of good and not-so-good lands. Decisions about the fields—what to plant, where, and when—were not made by tenants acting individually but by the group as a whole. Work schedules were orchestrated through collective decision-making. In the case of meadows, fallow fields, waste plots, and fields after harvest, common-use patterns prevailed, subject again to long-standing customs and to the collective voice of village members. As one pair of historians has put it, "The open field system was thus not one of free enterprise. Its practitioners were strictly governed in their actions and made to conform to a rigid pattern, agreed upon by the community, acting collectively."[13]

Although nearly all village residents were tenants of the lord and thus owed duties, services, and other obligations in exchange for their use rights, they by no means lacked legal rights in their lands. Their entitlements were governed by custom and were legally enforceable, theoretically at least, even against the lord. Tenants also played a surprisingly strong role in making decisions about fields. Field work was governed by the rules of the manor, which typically took the form of bylaws. According to records remaining from the thirteenth century, bylaw revisions were enacted by "the community," the assembled "tenants," or the "neighbors," rather than by the lord's resident agent.

Variants on this manor system prevailed in England and much of northwestern Europe for centuries. Yet to examine it closely at any time is to see ongoing change. Even as lords urged the king to make land more transferable, feudal tenants were pushing to turn their obligations to the lord into cash rents, which they could satisfy by selling surplus food at emerging markets. Tenants, though, would have had little interest in withdrawing their lands from the feudal scheme altogether. Wandering brigands and feuding lords posed real, familiar threats. Property rights, peasants well knew, existed only within a framework of public order. Subservience to a lord brought with it membership in a system of governance and military protection. Only within such a system could tenants work their lands securely.

Over time, the manor system gave way, yet the principles that infused it would persist in cultural patterns for centuries. Landed rights were held subject to the rights of a higher lord at every level save for the crown itself. Ownership created a personal bond between lord and vassal or tenant that involved not just payments of produce and money but (particularly in earlier centuries) duties of loyalty and protection. Landowner rights, especially rights to use what was owned, were guided by customary rules that people accepted as ancient and timeless, even as they pushed for reform. Landownership, in short, was a status, and to enter into the status was to enjoy the rights and be subject to the responsibilities that pertained to it. With few exceptions, the community had a voice in the ways people used their lands. Beyond that, many land-use rights were held by tenants or village members together and were overtly subject to group control. Finally, there was the fundamental idea that property rights existed within and were made secure by complex arrangements that fused every acre and every person. To own property was to be situated firmly within that order.[14]

Only faint echoes of institutional feudalism remained by the time of America's colonization. Yet, stripped of their feudal trappings, a surprising number of these land-use ideas and practices made their way to North America. There they would gradually merge with other ideas and be reshaped by local conditions to give rise to something quite new: private land ownership, American style.

The English colonization of North America was a diverse, poorly guided affair, lacking anything like the central direction that shaped Spain's colonizing efforts. Several English colonies began life as commercial enterprises run by London-based companies or by individual proprietors. Because of the special rights these proprietors received from the crown, the property regimes they created often took peculiar forms, particularly in the early decades when proprietors drew upon corporate and feudal models of organization to prescribe the types of rights settlers could obtain. In New England, however, settlers were left largely on their own and allowed to arrange matters as they saw fit. Given free rein, settlers there generally duplicated property arrangements they had known at home. Back in England, practices varied from region to region, which meant that widely divergent practices were carried to the New

World. Some immigrated from regions where tenants held extensive individual rights and farmed their fields with considerable independence. Others arrived from areas that continued to employ open-field, communal farming practices roughly similar to those used on thirteenth-century manors. When forming such towns as Sudbury and Andover, Massachusetts, early settlers tended to reenact their old ways. Everywhere, town leaders asserted the community's interest in private land-use decisions, just as communities in England had done since time immemorial. To keep settlements and social orders intact, for example, towns often compelled residents to build their homes in compact villages, prohibiting them from building on individual farm plots farther away. Several towns banned sales of town land to outsiders without the town's permission, as a way of restricting entry by undesirables.[15]

By the time of the American Revolution, open-field farm practices had disappeared almost everywhere. Land had become more of a market commodity. Restrictions on land transfers had also largely ended, save for rules here and there that curtailed speculation by outsiders. The powerful force of individualism, with its rhetoric of rights, encouraged people to think of private property in new ways. Old hierarchies among white males were rapidly fading, propelled by the Revolution's leveling spirit. Meeting particular resistance was the idea that land was held subject to the rights of a lord—or the lord's substitute, the colonial government—rather than by an individual owner outright. Landowners demanded outright ownership—full *allodial* rights, the law termed it—rather than *tenurial* rights subordinate to a higher title. In colonies where powers were still retained by proprietors or other distant lords, tenant obligations had long since given way to modest cash payments known as quitrents. Even when the quitrents were small, colonists resented them bitterly, in part because the colonists got nothing from the lords in return, unlike in the old feudal system. This desire to end quitrents and sever duties to distant lords provided a potent impetus for the colonists' break with England. A related complaint against the crown and Parliament had to do with their practice of making decisions about ownership and land use in America without giving colonists a voice. For colonial lawmakers to control land was entirely appropriate; for a distant royal government to do so was a different and increasingly intolerable matter.[16]

Out of this complex record from the late eighteenth century—the formative era for American rights and institutions—we can isolate four strands of thought dealing with private ownership, as an individual right and as an institution. The first three of them—the right to acquire, property as civic building block, and the preeminence of the right to quiet enjoyment—would fare badly as the nineteenth century wore on, giving way to alternative ideas about ownership that were more consistent with the mood and values of the new era. Only the fourth strand—the government's power to regulate land use in the public interest—would retain its force throughout the century, though even this strand of thought would be talked about in much different ways by century's end.

The Right to Acquire

One vital strand of property thought, easily seen in late-eighteenth-century writing (and largely a product of the postfeudal, Enlightenment era), was the idea that a person's right to property was first and foremost the right to *acquire* land on reasonable terms. This understanding reflected one of the chief reasons settlers had come to the New World. It also drew upon a characteristic of the new nation to which Americans often pointed as evidence of their superiority over repressive, aristocratic Europe. In Europe, land was controlled by wealthy barons at whose mercy ordinary people lived. In America, by contrast, aristocrats were gone and opportunity abounded. In

Europe, the wealthy sat back and lived off the labors of the working classes. In America, according to the rhetoric (if not the reality), everyone labored and enjoyed the fruits of his labors.[17]

Few writers embraced this thinking more fully than Thomas Jefferson.[18] In his various drafts for Virginia's new constitution in 1776, Jefferson made clear that feudal tenures had no place in the new land; landowners, he provided, were to hold their lands "in full and absolute dominion, of no superior whatever."[19] Years in France showed Jefferson the misery produced when the vast landholdings of the few left the many landless. His home state, Jefferson hoped, would take the lead in implementing this right to acquire property. Under his draft state constitution, 50 acres of land would go to "every person of full age" who neither owned nor had owned so much land, to be held "in full and absolute dominion."[20] On this point, John Adams pragmatically agreed: "The only possible way then of preserving the balance of power on the side of equal liberty and public virtues, is to make the acquisition of land easy to every member of society; to make a division of land into small quantities, so that the multitude may be possessed of land estates."[21] When the Bill of Rights was under debate, its chief author, James Madison, proposed that a preamble be added to the Constitution that granted express recognition of the right "of acquiring and using property."[22]

The problem in honoring this right of acquisition, of course, was that it became harder to satisfy as more and more land passed into private hands. Land became expensive long before all of it was gone. One means of addressing the problem was to restrict the practice of land hoarding by banning it or making it economically infeasible. In 1732, Cadwallader Colden, lieutenant governor of New York, proposed a sizable quitrent on each 100 acres a person owned in the colony. The tax was affordable by those who actively used their lands but harsh on those who left land unused. Colden "admitted that this would not redistribute the land as needed," historian William Scott concludes, but "at least the quitrent would make estates larger than twenty thousand acres unprofitable. The owners would be forced either to sell their land or to surrender their grants."[23] Virginia adopted a variant of this idea when it imposed a twice-yearly tax on tracts larger than 1400 acres. North Carolina dealt with the problem more directly by prohibiting a person from purchasing tracts over 640 acres and banning the purchase of two tracts less than 2 miles apart. Both to encourage land use and to free up unused parcels, several colonies adopted laws declaring forfeitures of land that their owners left unused for specified periods, sometimes as short as 2 years. Forfeited land reverted to the government for resale. Supplementing such laws were ones such as James Madison's bill, introduced in Virginia, that specifically allowed members of the public to hunt on unenclosed private land. In the legislature, then, as well as in popular thought, the acquisition and active use of land enjoyed a higher degree of legal protection than did mere passive or speculative ownership.[24]

This view of unused land as less worthy of protection by no means originated with colonial and early state lawmakers. The inhabitants of Thomas More's *Utopia* (1516) were said "to consider it a most just cause of war when a people which does not use its soil but keeps it idle nevertheless forbids the use and possession of it to others who by the rule of nature ought to be maintained by it."[25] In the opinion of Thomas Aquinas, centuries earlier: "Whatever a man has in superabundance is owed, of nature right, to the poor for their sustenance."[26] Aquinas's assertion reflected a widely held (though much violated) medieval moral view that people could not rightly own more land than they could use. Natural-rights theorists later drew upon similar reasoning to assert a "need and use" limit on the amount of land a person could own. Boston minister Joseph Morgan heartily endorsed the standard in a 1722 pamphlet, *The Original Rights of Mankind*. Morgan condemned land shortages brought on by the hoarding of unused tracts and called for taxes on them, set high enough so that none would remain and so that all citizens might "be supplied with farms, according to the donation of God freely, without price or purchase for it is their birthright as they are men."[27] In 1746, a New Jersey newspaper writer declared more radically that all land not cultivated should be "as free and as common for all to settle upon as the waters of the rivers are to all to drink."[28]

Property and Civic Stability

A closely related strand of property thought during America's founding era was an updated variant on feudal ideas linking property ownership and sound public order.[29] In the Revolutionary era, land-ownership was directly connected to a person's ability to act virtuously. Economic independence was a prerequisite for virtue, and those who lacked land were inevitably (so it was believed) subservient to the wills of others. When backed by sufficient private land, a person could meet his own needs directly, without having to manipulate government or bow to others. Thus positioned, he could rise above self-interest and act for the good of the whole. Englishman James Harrington used this reasoning to support proposals to broaden land distribution during the English civil war. He argued that private land, when widespread and made subordinate to the common good, fostered the public order and good governance.[30] Revolutionaries in America agreed, as historian Drew McCoy explains:

> The personal independence that resulted from the ownership of land permitted a citizen to participate responsibly in the political process, for it allowed him to pursue spontaneously the common or public good, rather than the narrow interest of the men—or the government—on whom he depended for his support. Thus the Revolutionaries did not intend to provide men with property so that they might flee from public responsibility into selfish privatism: property was rather the necessary basis for a committed republican citizenry.[31]

The purpose of government was to promote the public good, and the sacrifice of individual interests to that public good was one of the Revolution's most idealistic goals. The public good was not merely "the sum or consensus of the particular interests that made up the community." According to historian Gregory Alexander, it was something more real and more independent than that:

> Society was thought of as a homogeneous body whose members were organically linked together. The common good, then, was not merely what the consensus of society's individuals wished but a substantive conception of the moral good that transcended individual interests.... The central dilemma of American politics was not thought to be the protection of individual freedoms against collective encroachment, but rather, the protection of the public rights of the people against aristocratic privileges and power.[32]

Eighteenth-century writers who embraced this "civic republican" perspective were of two minds about the wisdom of making land more freely transferable. On one side, transferability enhanced opportunity and hence helped liberate people from their servile dependence; by broadening landownership, it enhanced overall virtue. On the other side, a free right to sell land enhanced the oppor-tunities for wealthy owners to acquire even more land. If they pursued those opportunities vigorously, republicans feared, "individuals would be subjects of the market, and the common welfare would be subordinated to the limitless pursuit of self-interest."[33]

The Importance of Quiet Enjoyment

A third strand of private property thought emanating from eighteenth-century writing endorsed the practical reality that ownership meant little unless its possession was secure. The essence of property was the right to remain undisturbed in one's use of it. Local and colonywide governments might limit how one could use land, and rights of use were always constrained by the equal rights of other owners, but security was not abridged by such legitimate, ordinary limits. Security entailed protection from having one's lawful land use physically disrupted or, even worse, having land physically seized by a private party or government official.[34]

By the time the U.S. Constitution was drafted in the late 1780s, this concern for security was often expressed as a fear that unpropertied masses might press for state laws that undercut existing property arrangements, to the detriment of trade and sound public order. Jefferson's response to this distinct fear was to make property ownership widespread while retaining requirements that only men who owned land could vote. These measures, Jefferson asserted, would keep irresponsible interests small and politically powerless. Madison and Hamilton, in contrast, proposed a different response. They sought to arrange the powers of government in such a way that no element of society acting alone could damage private rights. The masses might gain control of the popular assembly, the two admitted, but they could enact new laws only with the approval of a senate or other higher legislative body. That higher body would not be popularly elected, and it would remain composed of major landowners who could be counted upon to protect existing rights.

In retrospect, it is hard to know how much and what types of security the Founding Fathers deemed essential. Even as the eighteenth century wound down, many people still believed that private owners held their property at the sufferance of the state. This line of thought showed up in public policies affecting unoccupied lands. Colonies and early states seized private land to construct roadways. Although they usually compensated landowners; compensation was viewed as a matter of legislative discretion. The rationale was that the land came from the state, and while it remained vacant the state could take it back when needed. In addition, various laws directed landowners to make productive use of their lands. Sometimes a statute even specified a use (such as mining, operating a mill dam, or draining a wet meadow) and provided that the land be forfeited to the state if it was not so used. Such laws did not seem to disrupt the security of private lands in the minds of leading writers. A particularly revealing statute in Virginia allowed any person accompanied by a justice of the peace to prospect for iron or other ores on unimproved private land, without the owner's consent. If a valuable ore was found, the prospector became its owner with full rights to mine, subject only to a duty to compensate the landowner for damage. Such statutes typically applied only to private lands that were undeveloped, but similar rules did sometimes apply to developed land as well. Another Virginia statute, for instance, declared that a landowner who deserted a plantation could forfeit it, even if the plantation had been adequately improved and "seated."[35]

On the issue of security, it seems, an unresolved tension resided in the late eighteenth-century mind. Vermont jurist Nathaniel Chipman identified that tension in a much-read 1793 essay and proposed his own resolution of it. The right to property that all people possessed equally, Chipman asserted, contained two key elements: the right to acquire property, and the right to hold it for use. Between these two, the right to acquire was the more important. Accordingly, when conflicts arose, a person's right to hold property might require sacrifice to honor the right of another person to acquire land, particularly when monopolies and special privileges left ordinary people landless.[36]

Liberty and Government Regulation

Landowner security was closely linked to the fourth and final strand of property thought that pervaded America's formative era: an owner's right to use land and the corresponding power of government to control that use. To a degree that even historians tend to understate, America's colonial era was a time of extensive land-use regulation, by colonies, counties, and towns. England's unwritten constitution gave Parliament virtually unlimited power to resolve conflicts between private right and public need. That same understanding of power governed in the colonies. America's vehement objection to Parliament's rule did not have to do with legislative power generally but with the exercise of that power in America by a distant legislative body that excluded Americans and that seemed oblivious to their needs. Speaking at Gettysburg "four score and seven years" after the Revolution, Abraham Lincoln would portray it as a struggle over liberty in America, as indeed it was. But Lincoln's influential summary glossed over the fact that for the drafters of the Declaration of Independence, it was *collective* liberty that was the primary issue of the day: It was the power of the colonists as a people to govern themselves without interference, not the rights of individuals as such to resist constraint. Of the many complaints lodged against George III in the Declaration of Independence, nearly all addressed perceived violations of the colonists' collective rights. Even Thomas Jefferson's complaint against the king on the volatile issue of slavery, which was deleted from his draft during congressional debates, addressed not the rights of slaveholders (much less of slaves) but those of the people through their assembled representatives to ban slave trading if they chose, without being overridden by the king.[37]

For America's revolutionaries, liberties were rights that people possessed by participating in society. They were secure when people were able to govern themselves free of outside interference. Benjamin Franklin affirmed the point when describing what he understood as the state's broad powers to control property not essential for subsistence. All property beyond this minimum was "the property of the public," Franklin declared, "who by their laws, have created it, and who may therefore by other laws dispose of it, whenever the welfare of the public shall demand such disposition. He that does not like civil society on these terms, let him retire and live among savages."[38] (Franklin, we might presume, knew little about property arrangements among "savages.") When the eighteenth century ended, as historian William Novak tells us, "civil liberty consisted only in those freedoms consistent with the laws of the land. Such liberty was never absolute, it always had to conform to the superior power of self-governing communities to legislate and regulate in the public interest."[39]

Throughout the eighteenth century, these ideas were translated into a vigorous tradition of regulating land uses in the public interest. Many laws constrained harmful activities, such as lighting fires under dangerous conditions or allowing noxious weeds to spread. Other laws contained detailed building codes aimed at promoting health, safety, and the "uniformity and gracefulness" of communities, as a New York City law expressed it. Laws in many places regulated building construction to reduce fire hazards (wooden buildings were commonly banned) and to deter development that was considered either too dense or not dense enough. Other laws required owners to put their lands to good use. Laws common in rural areas required owners to fence their lands or to work with neighbors in area-wide drainage operations. Owners of attractive sites for water mills could have their lands seized if they failed to use them in the public interest. Mining sites were subject to similar burdens. Owners of town homes sometimes were compelled to keep them well maintained.[40]

One common topic of regulation was forestry, an issue that would arise again much later in Progressive-era Maine and elsewhere. Even before the Puritans arrived in Boston in 1630, the Pilgrims of nearby Plymouth had begun restricting the right of timber owners to export their products without the approval of governor and council. Forest laws all along the colonial coast repeatedly prohibited the unlawful cutting of trees on commons and banned "timber trespass" on private lands. Equally common were laws that limited the entitlement of landowners to set fires in their woods during specified seasons. Before the first Pennsylvania colonists arrived, William Penn had prescribed that at least one acre of standing timber out of every five would be left uncut. Several New Hampshire towns restricted the right of town residents to cut wood near the town center. In New Hampshire and elsewhere, large trees suitable for ship masts were claimed as public property, even when located on private land. Noteworthy because it required affirmative acts rather than merely restraint was an early Philadelphia ordinance that required town dwellers to plant trees along public sidewalks to provide shade for passing pedestrians. Perhaps the first law specifically limiting the cutting of small-diameter trees came in 1772 when New York passed an act forbidding anyone from bringing into Albany any firewood less than 4 inches in diameter (6 inches in the case of pine).[41]

At times, colonial and early federal-era statutes went so far as to force landowners to halt or change existing land uses that were ordinary and generally beneficial. A particularly onerous law in several New England colonies required landowners to destroy barberry bushes to prevent the spread of wheat blight. Barberry, a deliberate import from England, was useful in preparing food and medicine and harmful only to nearby wheat farmers. A colonial Connecticut statute, echoing New England's early engagement with open-field farming practices, allowed farmers to reassemble their lands into a single unit that they could manage collectively. So long as the owners of five-sixths of the land consented, the unit could include lands held by dissenting owners. The statute was later reenacted, with the necessary majority reduced to two-thirds. Similar shared-management provisions would be included in the federal law governing the Northwest Territory and in the specific statute creating the Indiana Territory.[42]

As many of these colonial and early federal-era laws illustrate, land-use regulations went well beyond the avoidance of harm to impose affirmative duties on private owners to help achieve social aims. Later generations would resist the imposition of such duties, portraying them as unprecedented, but the generation that led America's formation seems to have had little trouble with them. Indeed, historian John Hart concludes that the legal record they left behind "reveals no sign of the later-imagined right of landowners to be let alone as long as they do not harm others."[43] That idea would gain currency only toward the end of the nineteenth century, after lawmakers had fundamentally reworked laws to support America's insatiable desires to develop the continent, expand markets, widen choices, and multiply the nation's wealth.

As the eighteenth century came to a close, then, private property displayed elements of the old as well as the new. The Revolution's leveling individualism and the rhetoric about rights were making their mark. People spoke of private property more often in self-centered, individualistic terms and insisted that property rights be defined in ways that aided commerce and facilitated economic enterprise. Earlier views of society that knitted people together were still strong, however, including ideas that bore the heritage of feudal hierarchies and the subordination of private claims to the collective good. As for the republican claim that ample land made an owner virtuous, the dying off of the old planter-patricians and New England aristocrats made the idea seem less and less plausible. Replacing these Revolutionary-era leaders, who were so interested in issues of virtue, were more aggressive, market-oriented thinkers who judged land by its sale value rather than by its suitability as a self-contained family seat. In the age ahead, landowner independence would come from tangible wealth, employees, and income flows, not from a family's ability to live on its land without having to rely on markets and imported goods. Already, entrepreneurs were at work, hatching increasingly ambitious plans to use land for private gain.

In American culture if not yet in the law, the ways of the boomers and the migrants were gaining the upper hand.

CHAPTER THREE

INDUSTRIALISM

and the

RIGHT TO USE

Hardly had the nineteenth century begun when a dispute between two competing sawmills on the Hudson River gave notice that the new century would bring vast changes in the ownership of nature. Industrialism was coming, and by the time it had fully made its mark late in the century, landowners would hold a bundle of rights far different from the one they held when the century began. Yet government's powers to control damaging land uses would remain strong— if often unexercised—throughout the era, and industrial land uses would face increasing constraints as the twentieth century progressed. By century's end, powerful forces would be pushing property law in conflicting directions. Industrial and land-development interests would be working to retain and strengthen understandings about landowner rights that prevailed when industrial values were at their peak. Diverse conservation and community interests would fight back with demands for a far different understanding of land-ownership, one that protected sensitive land uses, natural ecosystems, established neighborhoods, and communal land-governing processes.

New York, 1805

While New York was still a British colony, one Palmer erected a sawmill on land that he owned along the Hudson River in Saratoga County, north of Albany.[1] Because the river was a public highway, Palmer could not block it entirely. As an owner of shoreland, however, he could construct a dam that extended well into (but did not completely cross) the river. Once in place, his dam raised a head of water to supply power for his new mill. It also provided a convenient way to collect and store logs being floated to the mill.

Years later, a competitor constructed a similar dam and mill a mere 200 yards upstream. The new mill, Palmer complained in the lawsuit he soon filed, injured his business and thereby interfered with his property rights. His principal injury was the greater expense he incurred in paying laborers to navigate logs carefully around the new upstream dam to reach his mill. The work took time; fewer logs could be handled at once; and hundreds of logs were washed down the river during the maneuver.

Palmer no doubt went to court with a high degree of confidence, for the law was clearly on his side. As a riparian landowner, he possessed the right to make use of any waterway that flowed alongside his land. The upstream landowner had the same right, but the water-use right that the law protected in this circumstance—the "natural flow" rule—was sharply limited. "Every man has a right to have the advantage of a flow of water, in his own land, without diminution or alteration," one of the justices explained. In other words, landowners had the right to use water only in ways that left downstream owners unaffected. Except for household and subsistence uses, a riparian landowner could not alter the quantity, quality, or timing of a water flow to the detriment of others. In this instance, the upstream landowner was disrupting the Hudson's natural flow in ways that cost Palmer money.

Nevertheless, when the drama ended, Palmer had lost his case. In time historians would view the contentious 3–2 ruling as a sign that property rights in America were on the move.[2] Writing in support of the upstream defendant, Justice Brockholst Livingston admitted that the "no harm" rule was "a familiar maxim" of property law. *Sic utere tuo ut alienum laedas*, courts had long phrased it: "Use your own so as to cause no harm." The natural-flow rule was merely a specific application of this protective doctrine. Applied rigorously, *sic utere tuo* meant that no use of land should cause harm to other landowners or to the public at large, even if it was otherwise reasonable. Livingston acknowledged the rule's wisdom, but its application to the facts of Palmer's dispute seemed to him neither wise nor fair. Mills and dams such as the defendant's benefited the public, Livingston observed. The law should encourage such structures, not suppress them. The upstream landowner, moreover, had the same property right to use the river as Palmer did. To hold him liable—or even worse, to insist that he remove his dam—would deprive him of his own right to use what he owned. To side with the plaintiff would simply grant Palmer a local monopoly:

> He who could first build a dam or mill on any public or navigable river, would acquire an exclusive right, at least for some distance, whether he owned the contiguous banks or not; for it would not be easy to build a second dam or mound in the same river on the same side, unless at a considerable distance, without producing some mischief or detriment to the owner of the first.[3]

Packed into Livingston's assessment of public policy was a line of reasoning that was surprising, given how the law had long protected a landowner's right to remain undisturbed when using his land. It was vital in resolving the dispute, Livingston asserted, to consider "the public, whose advantage is always to be regarded." In the past, the public interest had been equated with protecting landowners such as Palmer from being disturbed. No longer so, Livingston announced, or at least the protection of quiet enjoyment no longer overrode all competing considerations. The public good was also served by "competition and rivalry" among landowners. Hence, the right of individuals to "the free and undisturbed enjoyment of their property"—the right that Palmer was asserting—had to be weighed against "the public benefits which must frequently redound" from new land uses that incidentally harmed others.

To reconcile these competing policies, Livingston proposed a significant shift in the law of waterway use and, by extension, in private property rights generally. The upstream defendant should be allowed to continue using his dam, despite the *sic utere tuo* and natural-flow rules that banned all harm, so long as the damage done to Palmer was not "manifest and serious." If the harm was less serious than that, Livingston ruled, Palmer simply had to put up with it.

Livingston's opinion in *Palmer v. Mulligan* (1805) at once uncovered and tried to resolve a little-noted problem with the familiar property-as-dominion idea. William Blackstone, an English treatise writer widely read in America, had waxed eloquent decades earlier about the "sole and despotic dominion" that landowners enjoyed under the common law—that is, under the body of judge-made law (as opposed to statutes or ordinances) that had accumulated over time through the accretion of judicial rulings. For Blackstone, however, dominion meant the right to quiet enjoyment, which meant the right to halt any appreciable interference by a neighbor: "for it is incumbent on a neighboring owner," Blackstone proclaimed, "to find some other place to do that act, where it will be less offensive."[4] So long as low levels of economic activity made land-use conflicts rare, property-as-dominion worked well enough as a guiding idea. But as land uses intensified, the contradictions within the idea became manifest. One landowner's quiet enjoyment could effectively curtail a neighbor's right to use his land productively. In *Palmer*, the conflict was

68

particularly stark because the competing land uses were identical. The natural-flow rule favored Palmer because he was downstream and first established.

Cases such as *Palmer* illustrate how the law of property, carried over from the eighteenth century, protected settled, agrarian land uses. When two land uses conflicted, it was the earlier land use, often an agrarian one, that took precedence over the later, disruptive one. The constraining effect of that legal approach showed up early in the new century, largely in disputes over the harnessing of eastern waterways to power the nation's first factories. The natural-flow rule posed a serious hurdle for the new industries, for it barred a land-owner from blocking a waterway if the blockage harmed another riparian owner. A further complication was that because riparian rights included the right to take fish, any blockage that halted fish migrations was likely to violate the quiet enjoyment of some land-owner, upstream or downstream.

Something had to change, or so the new industrialists believed. The law that protected the stickers (as Wallace Stegner would call them), the law that protected the America of the settlement (in Lewis Mumford's words), needed to make room for the surging boomers and the industrial migrants whose work and capital would dominate the century that lay ahead.

Embedded in the *sic utere tuo ut alienum non laedas* rule, the foundational element of land use, was the principle of "strict lia-bility." Under it, landowners who caused harm were responsible for that harm, even if they acted as carefully as possible and even if their harms were largely unavoidable. It was a potent rule, and it was the rule that Blackstone and others had in mind when they cele-brated the landowner's "sole dominion" under the common law. But as *Palmer* and other cases revealed, full protection of quiet enjoy-ment translated into tight limits on the land-use options of others. And as industrialism began to unfold, landowners increasingly had intensive uses in mind. Those who did, unsurprisingly, favored a frontier or industrial property regime that defined landowner rights and responsibilities in ways that allowed harm-causing activities to take place.

A measure of the full change in property law over the ensuing decades was offered by the Supreme Court of Pennsylvania in a ruling handed down in 1886. It was the height of Mark Twain's Gilded Age, the era of the Great Barbecue (as historian Richard Hofstadter described it), characterized by ostentatious displays of wealth and the manipulation of government by moneyed interests. As in *Palmer*, the dispute that led to this ruling involved a waterway. This time, though, the litigants were far from evenly matched, and the plaintiff was using her land not to run a sawmill or other business enterprise but as her private home. The court's ruling in the case could hardly have deviated further from the property regime that America's revolutionaries had fought to secure.

Pennsylvania, 1886

In 1868, Mrs. Sanderson purchased land in the city of Scranton, Pennsylvania, near where Meadow Brook emptied into the Lackawanna River.[5] As a court later explained, "the existence of the stream, the purity of its water, and its utility for domestic and other purposes ... was a leading inducement to the purchase." By 1870, Mrs. Sanderson had erected a house and built a dam across the stream to supply herself with fresh water, fish, and ice. Upstream on Meadow Brook stood a 1,600-acre mining operation owned by the Pennsylvania Coal Company. Beginning about the time that Mrs. Sanderson bought her land, the coal company opened coal seams and sank mining shafts and tunnels. To keep the shafts dry, the company installed powerful pumps to bring the water to the surface, where it flowed into Meadow Brook through an artificial watercourse. The pumping not only materially increased the water flow in the stream, it also degraded the brook's water quality by introducing natural impurities contained in the mine water. Within a few years, the ill effects of the pumping had become manifest. The water in Mrs. Sanderson's pond had become "totally unfit for domestic use," the fish in the pond were dead, and pipes in the house were corroded. The hydraulic system that conveyed water into the house had been "rendered totally worthless," and in 1875 it was abandoned. Mrs. Sanderson filed suit against the coal company, seeking to recover monetary damages in the amount of her injuries.

In its portrayal of the case's background, the Pennsylvania Supreme Court took pains to describe the value of the mining company's operations, which were conducted, the court argued, in the normal manner of coal mines of the day and without negligence or malice. The excess mine water and its contaminants were all natural products of the land. Coal mining, moreover, was the natural and perhaps only possible use of the company's land, given its physical features. As for the water flowing into Mrs. Sanderson's pond, gravity was the agent that took it there, without purposeful diversion by the mining company. Given these facts, the court asked rhetorically, why should the mining company be liable for the pollution?

Several facts weighed heavily upon the court as it pondered the dispute. Foremost was the importance of coal mining to Pennsylvania's economy. Mrs. Sanderson, to be sure, was only one person, and the coal company could easily have covered her out-of-pocket losses. But if she could obtain damages as a riparian landowner for the harm done her, so too could all other landowners who were injured. With enough landowners lined up, hat in hand, the coal company's liability could mount up. Furthermore, it was "impossible to foresee what other modes of enjoyment" existing riparian owners or their successors might undertake in the future "or to estimate the extent of damages to which the continued pollution of the stream might proceed."

What principally worried the court, though, was not the mine's monetary liability for actual harm but the possibility that riparian landowners such as Mrs. Sanderson would ask the court for punitive damages or for an injunction to halt all mining operations.[6]

As the court saw the matter, an interpretation of nuisance law that allowed Mrs. Sanderson to recover money spelled doom for the state's coal industry. And if the coal industry failed, the public in turn would suffer greatly. The court was not inclined to let that happen. In any event, Mrs. Sanderson's injuries were not all that severe, or so the court callously asserted; they were a matter of "mere personal inconvenience," nothing more. "To encourage the development of the great natural resources of a country trifling inconveniences to particular persons must sometimes give way to the necessities of a great community."

The court turned next to the property rights that the coal company itself held:

> It may be stated, as a general proposition, that every man has the right to the natural use and enjoyment of his own property; and if, while lawfully in such use and enjoyment, without negligence or malice on his part, an unavoidable loss occurs to his neighbor, it is *damnum absque injuria* [injury for which there is no legal remedy]; for the rightful use of one's own land may cause damage to another, without any legal wrong. Mining in the ordinary form is the natural user of coal lands. They are, for the most part, unfit for any other use.[7]

This, then, was the crux: the coal company itself had property rights, and on the facts of the case it was merely exercising those rights: "Every man is entitled to the ordinary and natural use and enjoyment of his property." So long as a landowner avoided negligence and malice, a land use was permissible, even when it severely disrupted neighbors.

With *Sanderson,* the pendulum had completed its swing, at least in the coalfields of Pennsylvania. From an agrarian property system that protected quiet enjoyment and enforced *sic utere tuo* firmly, ownership law had swung completely to the industrial property side, freely permitting intensive land uses with only modest concern about resulting harms—just the point of view reflected in the Iowa statute in *Bormann* that authorized mega hog farms. Property law was no longer about the right to remain undisturbed in one's lawful use; it was now chiefly about the right to use land for maximum gain. The mentality of the migrants and boomers had triumphed.

Looking at the *Sanderson* ruling today, we can see that the court had more options than it realized, and its inability to see those options helped to bring about its harsh ruling. The court could have compensated Mrs. Sanderson and others similarly harmed for their actual injuries without halting the mining or imposing punitive damage liability on the miners. Had the court done that, mining might have continued while the company paid for the resulting losses. Yet even taking into account the court's myopia, the ruling marked the logical end of an extraordinary redefinition of what it meant to own land. Coal mining had become important to the state, and the old agrarian property system was being pushed aside to make room for it. And in pushing it aside, the court was prepared to let innocent victims subsidize the state's aggressive enterprises. Industrial activities of the day inevitably imposed costs. Mrs. Sanderson and landowners like her, not the Pennsylvania Coal Company, would be the ones to bear those costs.

The path that property law in the new nation followed from the Revolutionary era to *Sanderson* was complex and erratic, and not all states shifted as far as Pennsylvania. In general outline, though, the movement is easy to chart. In ways both overt and subtle, courts revised the judge-made common law of property so as to allow owners to engage in more intensive land uses. In doing so, they altered the "absolute dominion" that Blackstone and others had so proudly proclaimed as property's core. In drainage law, for instance, many states at the beginning of the nineteenth century allowed landowners to alter the land's natural drainage only when the change harmed no one else. By midcentury, states had revised drainage law to permit landowners to engage in more intensive, "reasonable" drainage practices, even when their practices did cause harm. As for which practices were deemed "reasonable" under this new regime, that too would change with the growing social acceptance of widespread land alteration. Nuisance law, which landowners had long used to enforce the *sic utere tuo* limit on neighbors, was similarly revised to make it harder for landowners to protect themselves. A landowner now committed a nuisance only if the harm he caused was both substantial and unreasonably imposed. Even substantial harm was now allowed—as Mrs. Sanderson's plight illustrated—when it predictably flowed from an economically important enterprise. Related to these changes in the substantive law of property were changes in the procedures that courts employed to resolve land-use disputes. Courts in many states diminished the role of juries in resolving disputes, thereby reducing the chance that a sympathetic jury of peers might upset the court's view of public policy and side with the Mrs. Sandersons of the day.[8]

In 1873, the New York Supreme Court frankly summarized the shift that had taken place in the common law of property:

> The general rules that I may have the exclusive and undisturbed use and possession of my real estate, and that I must so use my real estate as not to injure my neighbor, are much modified by the exigencies of the social state. We must have factories, machinery, dams, canals and railroads. They are demanded by the manifold wants of mankind, and lay at the basis of all our civilization.[9]

An earlier opinion from Kentucky matter-of-factly defended the change as legitimate, citing shifting public values and wants as the justification:

> The onward spirit of the age must, to a reasonable extent, have its way. The law is made for the times, and will be made or modified by them. The expanded and still expanding genius of the *common law* should adapt it here, as elsewhere, to the improved and improving conditions of our country and our countrymen.[10]

While courts were infusing the common law with a spirit of free enterprise, legislatures were doing their part to use statutory law and public funds to promote economic growth. Many legislatures approved tax exemptions and subsidies for canals and railroads. Corporations, once chartered reluctantly and with limited powers, became easier to create and no longer required specific authorization from legislatures. Corporate powers became almost unlimited, paving the way for the Supreme Court late in the century to proclaim that corporations were "persons" within the meaning of the Constitution's protections for individual human rights. States removed limits on the transferability of land and on the ability of creditors to seize a debtor's land in payment of a debt; in doing so, they increasingly made land into a market commodity.[11]

Legislatures also promoted enterprise by helping entrepreneurs acquire the land they felt was needed to expand their operations. Water-powered businesses were the first to ask for aid. Grain mills and other water-powered industries often required reservoirs, which flooded upstream private lands. Their owners were willing to buy land that their reservoirs inundated, but they wanted the right to flood the upstream land even when upstream owners refused to sell—as those owners had the right to do under existing law. Similarly, mining companies soon wanted the right to transport water from rivers to their distant mining sites, crossing private lands along the way. So long as any landowner en route could block a canal by refusing to sell access rights, the mining project could fail. In the West, irrigators who wanted to construct ditches across private lands faced similar problems. So too did Midwestern farmers, whose desire was for ditches to drain water from their fields, particularly the spring rains that delayed planting. Railroads, canal companies, early telegraph operations—all wanted to make use of lands owned by others, without giving those property owners the chance to say no.

Such requests pushed hard against older notions of what it meant to own land. An owner's quiet enjoyment was never more visibly disrupted than when someone seized her land or invaded it physically. Yet for state lawmakers, economic growth was often an irresistible lure. Early statutes responded to the needs of mill owners by enabling them to get lands for their reservoirs indirectly: They allowed upstream landowners to sue only for the value of their lands that were flooded, with no right to obtain an injunction halting the project. With the right to an injunction taken away, landowner consent was no longer needed. Later statutes helped industries more directly, by expressly granting them the power to condemn private land. Statutes allowed private railroads and canal companies to take land to construct their routes; they were required to pay the owners of the land taken but were not required to ask consent. Mining companies, irrigators, and farmers in many states acquired the same condemnation rights. Constitutional provisions did bar the condemnation of land except when it was done for a "public use," but most courts had little trouble finding this requirement satisfied. They routinely concluded that railroads and canals served the public directly. Mining, irrigating, and farming enterprises served the public indirectly, by stimulating economic growth. Their land uses were not "public" in the sense that government would own the land condemned, nor would the public have physical access to it as they did to railroads and canals; they were public because the land would be used in ways that were felt to promote the public good.

Historians have characterized this remarkable shift in property law in varying ways. J. Willard Hurst described it as a forceful "release of energy," brought about as changes in the law enabled people to exploit nature more fully. The old property regime honoring stability had yielded to a system that gave greater protection to a landowner's desire to change, intensify, and take risks. It was a shift, Hurst believed, that reflected well the tenor of the times:

> People in the nineteenth-century United States had already sighted the promise of a steeply rising curve of material productivity as the dynamic of a new kind of society. Some saw this dynamic mainly as a means to create new power and positions of leadership. . . . Some visioned an enlarged, more self respecting and creative life for greater numbers of people. . . . All had in common a deep faith in the social benefits to flow from a rapid increase in productivity; all shared an impatience to get on with the job by whatever means seemed functionally adapted to it, including the law.[12]

Historian Morton Horwitz would draw attention to the internal dynamics of this overall process and to the people who lost out when the law changed. Though Hurst's "release of energy" was good for some, it was distinctly bad for others and distinctly harmful to nature itself. The winners, Horwitz noted, were often the newly emerging corporations; the successful entrepreneurs; the owners of railroads, steam engines, and coal mines. Forced to bear significant costs with little or no recourse were people like Mrs. Sanderson, the fishermen whose catches were devastated by pollution, and the farmers whose wheat fields were burned by stray railroad sparks. Then there were the sensitive souls like Henry David Thoreau who would mourn the loss of nature itself.[13]

Paradoxically, as courts amended the common law of property to facilitate industrialization, they were at the same time articulating more clearly than ever the powers that government possessed to enact new laws protecting the common good. The community-based regulatory tradition that was so evident in the eighteenth century showed few signs of abatement as the nineteenth century gained steam. Even during the Jacksonian democracy of the 1830s and 1840s, which so openly espoused liberty and opportunity, the regulation of land and economic activities remained widespread. Regulation made sense because personal liberty was still shaped and protected by the laws of the land. For Jacksonians, liberty was not the same as unbridled license, William Novak concluded in his study of nineteenth-century America. Liberty

> always had to conform to the superior power of self-governing communities to legislate and regulate in the public interest. From time immemorial, as the common law saying went, this liberty was subject to local bylaws for the promotion and maintenance of community order, comfort, safety, health, and well-being.... Freedom and regulation in this tradition were not viewed as antithetical but as complementary and mutually enforcing.[14]

Lemuel Shaw of the Supreme Judicial Court of Massachusetts expressed this view in an 1851 decision upholding a ban on waterfront structures that exceeded a prescribed wharf line in Boston harbor:

> We think it is a settled principle, growing out of the nature of well ordered civil society, that every holder of property ... holds it under the implied liability that his use of it may be so regulated, that it shall not be injurious to the equal enjoyment of others having an equal right to the enjoyment of their property, nor injurious to the rights of the community. All prop-

erty in this commonwealth ... is derived directly or indirectly from the government, and held subject to those general regulations, which are necessary to the common good and general welfare.[15]

A New York court in 1827 expressed the same point:

The sovereign power in a community, therefore, may and ought to prescribe the manner of exercising the individual rights over property.... The powers rest on the implied right and duty of the supreme power to protect all by statutory regulations, so that, on the whole, the benefit of all is promoted.... Such a power is incident to every well regulated society.[16]

The guiding image, repeated by courts again and again, was not one of minimal government but of the "well-regulated society." Individual rights were respected, yet they were understood to be social in origin and to exist relative to the rights of others. Two common law principles gave shape to this well-regulated society: the limiting do-no-harm rule of *sic utere tuo* and the more overarching moral principle of *salus populi suprema lex est*—the welfare of the people is the supreme law. "From these two seemingly unassuming common law principles," Novak has remarked, "flowed a multitude of governmental restrictions on property, contract, morality, and a host of other aspects of social life."[17] Vermont jurist Nathaniel Chipman explained the situation plainly: "The rights of man are relative to his social nature, and the rights of the individual exist, in a coincidence only with the rights of the whole, in a well-ordered state of society and civil government."[18]

As the Civil War came and went, however, American courts tended to speak less and less about the rights of the community, and they drew less often on the maxim *salus populi*. The rights of the individual as such had gained rhetorical strength, aided not only by developers and speculators but by the antislavery campaign, which exalted individual liberty as the highest human value. Contributing to the declining respect for community rights was the growing disgust that many people had with the corruption then overtaking state legislatures. Private commercial interests clashed so openly and crudely in legislative arenas that legal commentators seemed doubtful that society would ever achieve a "well-regulated state." Yet even as their language shifted, less often elevating the community's rights over those of the individual, the courts continued to uphold the power of legislatures to regulate in the public interest when specific laws were challenged. Courts increasingly referred to that regulatory power as Lemuel Shaw had done: as the police power, the inherent power held by government to act to promote the public health, safety, welfare, and morals.[19]

By late century, evolving legal thought had come to portray American life as separated into two spheres: a *private* sphere and a *public*, governmental sphere. Private property was placed in the private category, along with the various individual rights created by the Constitution. Regulation, by contrast, was a public, governmental act. This conceptual separation led to an awkward division of the various laws that combined to prescribe what landowners could and could not do. On one side, the common law of property appeared to set forth the private rights that individuals possessed in the private realm of life. Statutes and police-power regulations, on the other side, were viewed as expressions of public power and designed to promote the welfare of the people collectively. Few doubted that the government's police power was expansive or that it could limit private rights whenever necessary to promote the public welfare. But the mere fact that legal rhetoric divided the private and public realms represented a critical shift in reasoning, a shift that would have far-ranging implications up to our day. Law and government would be set apart from ordinary people and given a new, more hostile image. The mutual reliance of individual and community would decline, and liberty would be seen more as immunity from governmental interference and less as freedom to engage with other community members in collective self-governance.

The new public-private divide particularly influenced the ways people thought about private property and how police-power laws affected it. Private property became an entitlement that people held in their private lives. It was something they exercised not as a springboard to virtue and public service as in the eighteenth century or as part of a larger community, but to protect their privacy and promote their personal economic welfare. Particularly for conservative legal writers, property rights now seemed to exist in the abstract, as a natural right in full form. Property was no longer thought of as a product of law, nor were civil liberties creations of the law. Indeed, the law in this view was no longer even the protector of property, or not chiefly that. More often it was perceived as a tool that government used to invade private rights. As an intellectual concept, private property had largely been freed from communal obligations in a way that both reflected and fueled the breakdown of community-centered sentiment.

In important ways, these three developments in nineteenth-century property law—the relaxation of the common law *sic utere tuo* doctrine; the rise of the regulatory police power; and the growing conceptual divide between private and public—contained an inner logic. When courts relaxed common law limits on intensive land uses, allowing owners to harm their neighbors, they kept the law in line with the entrepreneurial spirit of the age. The judge-made common law, courts implicitly announced, would no longer provide a serious barrier to the continent's economic development. At the same time, legislatures and local governments would possess broad police powers to combat the resulting harms that the more aggressive land uses produced. In institutional terms, the legal positions fit together. Courts wielding judge-made common law would no longer be the ones to decide whether a landowner could engage in an intensive land use. The legislature would do so. Legislatures were better able to undertake studies and investigations, to hold hearings on complex social issues, and to craft laws in great detail—just the kind of work needed to deal with the complex and powerful market. This division of power, in turn, both reflected and strengthened the public-private split—the third of the property-law developments. The common law that courts tended would specify the property rights that existed in the private realm; legislatures and local governing bodies, working in their separate realm, would constrain those rights as they looked after the public interest.

Private property, in short, had become the product of two bodies of law, increasingly viewed as distinct: the common law of property, reworked by courts to facilitate enterprise, and the many statutes and land-use ordinances that taken collectively implemented the legal maxims of *sic utere tuo* and *salus populi*. The division set the stage for large-scale conflict. Probusiness critics of government began to argue that it was the common law alone that defined a landowner's rights—the common law that was now so slanted in favor of industry. Statutes and regulations were part of a different body of law entirely, a body of public law that was seen to threaten private rights. And, like all threats, public law needed to be contained if private rights were to survive. To gauge how far a particular regulation interfered with a landowner's rights, critics said, one should properly look at the economic effect the regulation had on the value of the land. To do that, one started with the assumption that an owner could use his land as he saw fit, almost without limit. It was present-day common law alone, critics argued, that should provide the baseline for making such economic measurements, given that the common law alone defined the rights that inhabited the private realm. When judged from this perspective, many police-power regulations became constitutionally suspect, for many of them did reduce the market values that lands would have if owners were free to do as they pleased.

Defenders of regulations, to be sure, continued to press for them and to argue for their legitimacy. More often than not they won. But even as defenders urged courts to uphold regulations, they allowed the imagery of private rights and public good to shift in a way that conceded the new individualistic view of private property, in which landowners had few duties to neighbors and little or no obligation to keep their activities consistent with the community's well-being. Defenders worked to uphold statutes only by arguing that they were necessary to protect the public health, safety, and welfare. The statutes were legitimate, that is, even though they cut deeply into private rights.

These various changes would have startled and displeased many eighteenth-century legal thinkers, including a number who thought of themselves as defenders of private rights. To them, the limits on ownership summed up in *sic utere tuo* and *salus populi* were internal limits on an individual's private rights. A person's right to property extended only up to the point where it ran into the *sic utere tuo* restriction on causing harm or when private desires conflicted with the welfare of society. In this view, laws banning harm, as well as laws protecting the public interest, did not reduce private rights in any way; they merely described more clearly the limits on ownership that already existed. Far from conferring the right to do as one pleased, property law gave owners only the right to act in ways that harmed no one else.

Thus, by the end of the nineteenth century, a new understanding of private property had largely taken hold. Private ownership, set by the common law, gave vast powers to act as one saw fit. Existing apart from the common law were public statutes that curtailed private rights when necessary to foster the public good. One piece of *sic utere tuo* remained as an internal limit, showing up in the common law of private nuisance. But otherwise, internal limits had been removed, allowing the rights of ownership to expand greatly to encompass all manner of intensive, destructive actions. Removed from the inside, the old limits now appeared as restraints imposed from the outside. They became tools that government used to sacrifice individual private rights in furtherance of the public good. It was a corrosive line of thought, particularly when merged with ideologies that equated the public good with the market's unbridled operation or with the maximum liberty of individuals to act free of restraint. Cut loose from property's history, the reasoning would undergird the ardent antigovernment sentiment of a century later, fueling passionate claims for the community to compensate landowners whenever it asked them to halt community-harming activities.

Supreme Court, 1922

Few major decisions displayed this new individualistic reasoning more visibly than a 1922 ruling of the U.S. Supreme Court in another dispute involving the Pennsylvania Coal Company. This time it was the coal company that was on the defensive, alarmed by a statute that limited its power to mine subsurface coal if it undercut and ruined the overlying land. Justice Oliver Wendell Holmes, Jr., penned the Court's ruling striking down the statute on the ground that it took the company's property rights in the coal without compensation. The government held broad police powers to curtail private rights, Holmes acknowledged. But when a statute went "too far" in its curtailment of those rights, it amounted to a taking of that property and the landowner deserved compensation.[20]

Readers of the *Pennsylvania Coal Co. v. Mahon* opinion would wonder what the court meant by going too far, and scholars would question where the Supreme Court came up with the legal rule it employed. Prior to *Mahon*, the constitutional rule requiring compensation for takings had applied only to physical confiscations of private lands, not to regulations. But few would pause to ponder the assumptions and imagery that Justice Holmes employed. Few would stop to question why, in measuring the statute's effect, one started with the assumption that the coal company as landowner had the right to do as it pleased.

Four years after its ruling in *Mahon,* setting forth the frustratingly vague "goes too far" limit on government's police power, the Supreme Court came forward with another ground-breaking ruling on land-use regulation, *Euclid v. Ambler Realty.*[21] This one would not just uphold the government's power to control property, it would do so with language nothing short of shocking. In an important way, *Euclid* completed the Supreme Court's embrace of the public-private distinction and of the new, individualistic view of private property linked to it. *Mahon* assumed that landowners possessed vast powers to alter their lands as they saw fit unless constrained by statute. *Euclid,* focused on the public side of the divide, would recognize the equally vast powers of government to control the ensuing harms. With potent forces on both sides and with powerful interests groups divided between them, the Court's two decisions made future clashes inevitable.

The industrialism and energetic growth of the American nineteenth century had not come without costs. So visible were they that even die-hard boomers and industrial migrants could not help but pause and reflect. Deforestation, soil erosion, declining wildlife populations, disease-ridden rivers, smoky urban skies—all contributed to a rising public resistance to unbridled market forces. But public resistance did not always or even usually translate into legal change, given the vast political power wielded by the forces of the market. So powerful were these forces even then, and so vast the scale on which they operated, that local and even state governments were often too weak to deal with them. Still, public protest did sometimes translate into new laws, particularly laws that protected residential areas from annoying disruptions.

On the eve of World War I, New York became the first American city to adopt a comprehensive zoning plan. Other cities soon followed suit, despite uncertainties about the constitutionality of such plans. Initial ordinances divided cities into zones according to the types of land uses allowed, specifying for each zone the maximum height, size, and density of buildings along with such matters as setbacks from streets and permissible signs. At the forefront of the zoning campaign was the U.S. Department of Commerce, which drafted model zoning statutes and ordinances for states and cities to consider for adoption.[22]

Supreme Court, 1926

Of the many pending cases challenging urban zoning, the one that would make history emerged out of Euclid, Ohio, a suburb of Cleveland. Euclid's zoning plan differed little from plans widely used elsewhere, yet so prominent did this suburb's case become that the initial generation of zoning plans would thereafter be known as "Euclidean zoning."

The lengthy opinion that the Supreme Court handed down in 1926, upholding Euclid's zoning ordinance, showed a surprising lack of awareness of the history of land-use regulation in American cities. So far as the Court knew, zoning laws dated back a mere 25 years; before then, it asserted, "urban life was comparatively simple." The Court seemed unaware of the extensive ordinances that governed life in colonial cities. Indeed, it had forgotten the common law vision of the well-regulated society, and it made no mention of the once-influential "greatest welfare" principle, *salus populi*. Even without this history, however, the Court would rule strongly in the city's favor.

The challenger to Euclid's zoning plan, Ambler Realty, owned a vacant, 68-acre tract of land along a busy street, adjacent to railroad lines. The land's market value was said to be $10,000 per acre if available for industrial use. Restricted to residences by the ordinance, the land's market value, it was said, had slipped to $2,500 per acre. Where those figures came from the justices did not say and apparently did not ask, nor did they wonder whether the $10,000 per acre figure might be premised on an exaggerated understanding of what landowners could do in the absence of any zoning ordinance. Desirous of preserving its land's higher value, Ambler Realty challenged Euclid's zoning ordinance as an unconstitutional infringement of its property rights.

As the Court considered the zoning ordinance, it had no trouble with the provisions limiting building heights, imposing setback requirements, and segregating residences from polluting industries. The Court paused only over the provisions that distinguished among types of residences—allowing single-family homes but not apartments in some zones—and over the rules that kept businesses and retail shops out of residential areas. The city defended the ordinance by pointing to various health and safety considerations that made it appropriate to segregate uses. What did not get mentioned was the probable desire of Euclid's affluent, white homeowners to keep undesired populations away from their homes: the racial and ethnic groups who inhabited apartments and who often ran small shops or other businesses out of their homes in order to survive.[23]

When the Court's ruling was handed down, legal readers wanted to know not just whether the Court upheld the ordinance but what legal standard it applied to judge the validity of such ordinances. It was on this point that the Court's ruling raised eyebrows across the land, pleasing urban planners and disheartening industrial and development interests. The key language, set apart by Justice Sutherland in a separate paragraph for emphasis, was breathtaking:

> If these reasons [in support of the zoning ordinance], thus summarized, do not demonstrate the wisdom or sound policy in all respects of those restrictions which we have indicated as pertinent to the inquiry, at least, the reasons are sufficiently cogent to preclude us from saying, as it must be said before the ordinance can be declared unconstitutional, that such provisions are clearly arbitrary and unreasonable, having no substantial relation to the public health, safety, morals, or general welfare.[24]

The language was hardly lilting, and no doubt every reader had to reread the 73-word sentence. But when fully parsed, its meaning was clear. No sentence in the history of land-use law would take on more importance. The Court was not going to second-guess zoning laws. It made no difference that the law was debatable in policy terms. It made no difference, even, that the Court might think it unwise or might suspect the motives of the lawmakers who enacted it. A court's job in reviewing such laws was merely to provide a crude screen to keep out the most misguided ordinances. To get caught in the screen and be declared unconstitutional, an ordinance had to be "clearly arbitrary and unreasonable." It had to have, the Court said, "no substantial relation to the public health, safety, morals, or general welfare." The effect of all this was to give regulators vast powers to control land uses, should they choose to exercise them, even when their regulations greatly diminished land values. Land-use planners could not have been more satisfied.

Although the Supreme Court's opinion in *Euclid* went far in encouraging the new land-planning profession, it did little to assist them in their work. It said nothing about how zoning and private property fit together. It was silent about how regulators might best assess the effects of what they did on private property as an institution. By all appearances, the divide between the public and private realms remained alive and intact in the law of private land.

Planners may have liked what they read, but those who thought seriously about private property were worried about the implications of this new clash of potent forces: expansive private property on one side and expansive public power on the other. For either force to overwhelm the other seemed unwise, yet who would be in charge of charting a sensible middle course? If government was pushed into the public realm and told to look after only the good of the community as such, might it not trample on private rights? Yet if private property was solely a matter of promoting the owner's self-interest, would not advocates for landowners shortchange their once-strong duties to act in the public interest?

Among those disturbed about *Mahon, Euclid,* and the state of contemporary property thought was philosopher Morris Cohen of the College of the City of New York. The year after the ruling, Cohen was invited to deliver a lecture at Cornell University's law school. His talk, later published, would become a classic of property law scholarship, widely read by legal scholars even as it had little immediate effect on courts and lawmakers. Cohen used the occasion to reflect on what were now viewed as two distinct forms of power: private property and the sovereign, public powers of government. These two forms of power, Cohen recognized as he began his talk, were viewed as emanating from entirely different realms of law and life. Private property abided in the private realm, government's sovereign powers in the public realm. The private-public divide had become dogma, despite its short, dubious heritage.

Step by step, Cohen would challenge this divide and push for a revitalization of older ideas about ownership that overtly linked individual rights and social responsibilities, bringing public and private back together. Under feudalism and in medieval England, Cohen noted, land ownership and political power had been fused.

The king's powers over the realm as proprietor and sovereign were joined. A similar blending of functions and powers existed all the way down the landholding hierarchy. What the English had long known, he asserted, and Americans seemed to have forgotten, was that land ownership inevitably brought power over the people whose lives depended on the land. "In a regime where land is the principal source of obtaining a livelihood, he who has legal right over the land receives homage and service from those who wish to live on it."[25] Private property, in short, was a form of governing power, backed by the legal engines of the state. Even in the modern age, with feudalism long gone and forgotten, property and governmental power were still joined. To recognize property as a form of sovereignty, Cohen noted, was not an argument against private property. But sovereign power needed to be justified, and not all forms of it were equally valid. "The issue before thoughtful people," he observed,

> is therefore not the maintenance or abolition of private property, but the determination of the precise lines along which private enterprise must be given free scope and where it must be restricted in the interests of the common good.[26]

Cohen concluded that the rights of private ownership needed to be matched with affirmative obligations to the public: "If the large property owner is viewed, as he ought to be, as a wielder of power over the lives of his fellow citizens, the law should not hesitate to develop a doctrine as to his positive duties in the public interest."[27] Cohen's proposal would languish—there would be no legal doctrine of "positive duties" that landowners owed, at least not soon—but the ideas he presented would nonetheless linger, awaiting their day.

Urban land planning increased in scope in the wake of *Euclid,* aided by rulings from the Supreme Court in the 1930s in which the Court reduced its role in reviewing laws that restricted economic activities. The wisdom and fairness of such laws, property laws included, were left for legislatures to gauge. State courts retreated in the same manner, although some were more willing than others to second-guess local zoning actions. At the national level, debates over private ownership gave way to more pressing concerns as the crisis of the Depression continued and then World War II began. Yet if private property was not talked about expressly, the forces that shaped it continued to evolve. Industry was losing some of its luster, as people became concerned about the mounting costs of expansion. Ecological degradation, once accepted as the price of progress, was increasingly called into question. Particularly at the local level, the citizenry was more willing to restrict intensive land uses because of the resulting harms. In terms of public opinion, the pendulum was slowly swinging away from the boomers and the industrial migrants and back toward the stickers and settlers.

A decision of the Pennsylvania Supreme Court in 1954, at the dawn of the environmental age, would illustrate this ongoing shift in public opinion and give warning of the kinds of conflicts that lay ahead as the rising sticker ethos began to challenge industrial understandings of private rights.

Pennsylvania, 1954

Joseph and Agnes Waschak, brother and sister, owned a "modest home" in Taylor, Pennsylvania. The region was dominated by coal companies, whose methods of mining generated large amounts of mineral waste. That waste was deposited into large piles, sometimes of "mountainous proportions," known as culm banks. These banks often caught fire after wastes had accumulated for long periods. Some of them leaked hydrogen sulfide, carbon monoxide, and sulfur dioxide gases.[28]

Upon buying the home in 1948, the Waschaks painted it white. "Some time later," one of the justices recounted,

> the paint began to turn to a light colored brown, then it changed to a grayish tint, once it burst into a silvery sheen, and then, as if this were its last dying gasp, the house suddenly assumed a blackish cast, the blackness deepened and intensified until now it is a "scorched black."[29]

The cause of the blackening was the hydrogen sulfide gas coming from the nearby culm banks owned by the mining defendants, all located in residential districts. The hydrogen sulfide not only blackened the white house, it "snip[ed] at the silverware, bath tub fixtures and the bronze handles of the doors, forcing them, respectively, into black, yellowish-brown and 'tarnished-looking tints.'" Along with this damage to the Waschaks' home, the record in the case contained evidence that "the poisonous hydrogen sulfide was of such intensity that the inhabitants compelled to breathe it suffered from headaches, throat irritation, inability to sleep, coughing, lightheadedness, nausea and stomach ailments."

The Waschaks filed suit to collect money damages for the harm to their home. They were not alone; as their case was considered, 25 similar suits were also pending against the mining companies. A jury decided that the culm banks were a nuisance and ruled for the plaintiffs. On appeal, however, the Pennsylvania Supreme Court disagreed. A nuisance only arose, the court held, when a landowner's actions were either intentional or negligent. Here, the coal company did not intend the harm, nor did it foresee the harm when it began to deposit the mining wastes in the piles. As for negligence, there was nothing the coal company could do to eliminate the gases except move the wastes. Their operations followed standard practices in the mining industry, and people living in the area all knew about the piles. Indeed, the piles were present when the Waschaks arrived. In resolving the suit, the court took note of the *sic utere tuo* rule but also noted the corresponding rights of the mining company to make "the normal and customary use of their land." So long as the company did that, it would be immune from liability for resulting harms. "One's bread is more important than landscape or clear skies," the court proclaimed, quoting an earlier ruling and echoing the sentiment in its *Sanderson* decision from the 1880s. "Without smoke, Pittsburgh would have remained a very pretty *village*." The Waschaks' quiet enjoyment, like Mrs. Sanderson's, was of lesser consequence.

Waschak was nevertheless a transitional case; what made it so were the passionate dissents in it, for the majority's view did not go unchallenged. Justice Musmanno was the most outraged. The law had fallen behind the times, he said. Whatever sense the ruling might have made a generation or two earlier, it made none now:

> For decades Pittsburgh was known as the "Smoky City" and without that smoke in its early days Pittsburgh would have remained a "pretty village." But with scientific progress in the development of smoke-consuming devices, added to the use of smokeless fuel, Pittsburgh's skies have cleared, its progress has been phenomenal and the bread of its workers is whiter, cleaner, and sweeter.

The majority's claim that the culm piles were reasonable was nonsense:

> I do not think there can be any doubt that the constant smell of rotten eggs constitutes a nuisance. If such a condition is not recognized by the law, then the law is the only body that does not so recognize it.[30]

Increasingly, as this nation confronted its environmental degradation, Justice Musmanno's view would gain ground. Courts handling suits under common law began to sympathize more with landowners whose quiet enjoyment was disrupted and to find ways to compensate them, even when they allowed the harms to continue. Pollution-control laws began to curb many of the worst abuses. Although styled as environmental laws, such laws nonetheless directly reshaped the rights and responsibilities of private ownership. Landowners faced restrictions on their rights to engage in intensive, polluting land uses, while they gained new rights to seek relief when they were harmed by the pollution of others. By means of many small steps and with little regard for how the pieces all fit together, the law was moving toward a modern, ecologically informed variant of the agrarian property regime of the late eighteenth century.

Where these many small changes were heading, in terms of property rights, was not at all clear, and many observers were worried about it. If new statutes could restrict one activity by a landowner, might they gradually take away all use rights, leaving private property nearly worthless? Adherents of the old industrial-property perspective were troubled, and no judicial ruling would alarm them more than the 1972 opinion of the Wisconsin Supreme Court in *Just v. Marinette County*. In it, the court upheld a zoning ordinance that prohibited landowners from placing fill material on wetlands in preparation for development. Other courts would hear similar disputes, and most would reach similar conclusions. But no court would speak as provocatively as Wisconsin's about what it ought to mean to own private land in the emerging environmental age.[31]

Wisconsin, 1972

In 1961, Ronald and Kathryn Just purchased 36.4 acres of land along the south shore of Lake Noquebay in Marinette County.[32] Over the next half-dozen years, they sold off approximately three-quarters of the tract in parcels. In 1967, the county enacted a shoreland protection ordinance that banned the deposit of fill material into designated wetlands without a permit. Six months later, Ronald Just hauled in 1,040 cubic yards of sand and filled 12,000 square feet of wetland without a permit. When Marinette County objected, the Justs filed suit, asking the court to declare the shoreland protection law unconstitutional because it took their property rights in violation of the just-compensation clause.

In the court's view, the dispute posed "a conflict between the public interest in stopping the despoliation of natural resources, which our citizens until recently have taken as inevitable and for granted, and an owner's asserted right to use his property as he wishes."[33] The effect of the county ordinance, the court observed, was not "to secure a benefit for the public" by compelling the Justs to leave their property unaltered; instead, it was "to prevent a harm from the change in the natural character" of the Justs' property. To gauge how severely the law curtailed the Justs' property rights, one first had to decide what property rights they possessed in their wetland. If the Justs had no right to fill it in, then the law took nothing from them. "Is the ownership of a parcel of land so absolute that man can change its nature to suit any of his purposes?" the court asked rhetorically. Assuredly not, it responded, at least not when public officials view the change as harmful to the public good:

> An owner of land has no absolute and unlimited right to change the essential natural character of his land so as to use it for a purpose for which it was unsuited in its natural state and which injures the rights of others. The exercise of the police power in zoning must be reasonable and we think it is not an unreasonable exercise of that power to prevent harm to public rights by limiting the use of private property to its natural uses.[34]

Landowners possessed the right to use their lands "for natural and indigenous uses," much as earlier courts had declared. But such uses had to be "consistent with the nature of the land," which meant, in the case of wetlands, uses that were consistent with their continued retention as wetlands, not uses that required filling or draining.

Because the county ordinance merely limited the Justs to uses consistent with the land's natural character, it took no vested property rights from them.

In ruling as it did, the Wisconsin Supreme Court directly challenged the industrial understanding of property. The right of landowners to use their lands was now limited to ecologically sound activities. The baseline in terms of landowner entitlements was nature itself, at least when a landowner challenged a public regulation. The do-no-harm *sic utere tuo* principle had returned in something like its eighteenth-century form, and so had the idea that communities and the public, not just individuals, held rights.

The ruling in *Just* drew widespread comment; it was the herald, environmentalists hoped, of a new legal era that warmly embraced laws protecting the land.[35] Few other courts, however, were willing to go so far in proposing a new understanding of ownership, even when they upheld the validity of similar environmental statutes. As many judges saw matters during the twentieth century's closing decades, environmental problems were best dealt with by legislatures rather than courts; it was the legislature that should keep the law of property up to date, not judges through their rulings. Few judges, though, seemed to consider the implications of this deferential stance seriously. The common law in many states still reflected the proindustry slant of the nineteenth century. To leave it there was to foster problems when legislatures lacked the will or the time to alter its outdated norms. Even when legislators did act, the courts' deference came at a cost. Opponents of land-use rules would point to the outdated common law as the base of their vested rights and from that base would ardently oppose statutes that cut deeply into those alleged rights.

Whether courts should revive their old practice of keeping the common law up to date was openly discussed by justices of the Wisconsin Supreme Court a decade after *Just* in a case involving a new, green technology: solar panels. For centuries, property law in England had included a doctrine known as "ancient lights," which enabled the owner of a building who made extensive use of sunlight to object if a neighbor, by building on his land, later blocked that light. Predictably, American courts in the nineteenth century abolished the doctrine because it inhibited tall buildings and other urban land uses.[36] But the late nineteenth century had not known about solar panels, nor did it share the environmental concerns that would carry such weight a century later. Should these new developments lead to changes in the common law of property, just as the common law in the previous century had taken new industrial technology into account? Was it still true, as the Kentucky Supreme Court had said in 1839, that "the law is made for the times"?

Wisconsin, 1982

At the end of the 1970s, one Prah built a residence on his land, with solar collectors installed on the roof. Defendant Maretti proceeded to buy the lot next door and to construct a residence of his own. When Maretti began construction, Prah immediately pointed out that the new residence would partially block his solar collectors. He asked Maretti to build the new home a few feet farther away from the lot line. Maretti refused. Prah turned to the courts, complaining that the blockage of light interfered unreasonably with his use and enjoyment of his land, thus amounting to a common law nuisance. The trial court sided with Maretti, but the Wisconsin Supreme Court reversed that decision. It did so not by deciding that a nuisance had in fact occurred but by concluding simply that Prah should have the chance in court to prove the unreasonableness of Maretti's conduct.[37]

In its ruling, the Wisconsin court went beyond answering the specific legal question to speak to the need for the common law of property to keep up with the times. In the nineteenth and early twentieth centuries, the court observed, courts had been reluctant to protect an owner's access to sunlight. This reluctance was supported on three grounds: a general desire to safeguard an owner's right to use land as he saw fit; the fact that sunlight was used only for illumination, not for heat and hot water; and society's interest in promoting land development. "These three policies," the court announced, "are no longer fully accepted or applicable. They reflect factual circumstances and social priorities that are now obsolete." Land-use regulation had become increasingly common. In addition, access to sunlight had taken on new significance, given energy shortages and pollution concerns. Finally and most generally, "the policy of favoring unhindered private development in an expanding economy is no longer in harmony with the realities of our society." Legal change was in order, and for a court to refuse to act was wrong:

> Courts should not implement obsolete policies that have lost their vigor over the course of the years. The law of private nuisance is better suited to resolve landowners' disputes about property development in the 1980's than is a rigid rule which does not recognize a landowner's interest in access to sunlight.[38]

In dissent, Justice Callow would have none of this. The common law should not restrict development, he contended, particularly when the beneficiary was simply another private landowner. If a policy decision had to be made and the law brought up to date, it was not the court's job to do it. The issue in the dispute was fundamentally a question of policy in an area "best left for the legislature."

By the end of the twentieth century, Callow's position on judicial versus legislative change would retain many adherents. Numerous probusiness advocates and think tanks labored to keep property law back in the nineteenth century. Critics of government pointed to the common law as the one true source for the meaning of ownership, as if decades of statutes and ordinances had not really changed what it meant to own land. In doing so, they voiced continued support for a public-private distinction that was drawing fire from adherents to Morris Cohen's view. The rulings in *Just* and *Prah*, in short, represented only one of many late-century strands of thought. What people were increasingly recognizing, however, was that private property is a flexible institution. The rights and responsibilities of property ownership could change again, just as they had in the past. Drawing particular attention was the matter of development rights and development values. When scarcity made nature's parts more valuable, when should private rights give way to community needs?

CHAPTER FOUR

JUSTIFYING

the

LANDOWNER'S POWER

Imagine a frontier region named Aridia, beyond human settlement and heretofore lacking any inhabitants. Over the mountains comes the first settler, who upon arriving finds himself in a land that receives little rain but is well watered by a single river. The settler, Boone we might call him, approaches the river and, standing high on its banks, proclaims aloud (with no one to listen) that he owns the river and everything in it. To confirm his ownership, Boone posts signs with his name on it up and down the river.

Other settlers soon arrive to take up lands in the region. To meet their water needs, they buy from Boone—as they must, having no choice—and divert water from the river at their own expense. Immigration continues and settlements spread throughout Aridia, all using water from Boone's river. In time Boone dies, and his water rights are divided among his children. Years go by, the region's wealth continues to grow, and the younger Boones charge increasing prices for their water. With rates rising, many citizens have trouble buying water to meet their needs. Some better-off residents respond with compassion by establishing a charity fund for them. Occasionally, a citizen tries to steal water and is punished harshly. Because of their considerable wealth, the Boones wield vast political influence and government officials know them well.

The day eventually comes when more powerful pumping equipment is invented, and the current Boones announce plans to install it. With it, they can extract almost the entire flow of the river. Newly formed conservation groups raise a ruckus and ask the Boones to leave a minimum flow in the river to sustain the river's fish and other aquatic life. "But if we must do that," the Boones respond, "we would be forced to use our private property to confer a benefit on the public. If the public wants our water used in this manner, it should buy the water from us. We will be happy sell water to any conservation group that cares to buy it and then leave the water in the river to support aquatic life and recreational activities. That way, market forces will set the precise amount of water that remains in the stream. If any conservation group wants the water, it simply needs to outbid other users of it; if they don't, then it shows that conservation is less valuable than alternative uses of the water. No regulatory measures will be needed to promote conservation, nor will taxpayers be forced to contribute against their will. As Aridian citizens step forward to buy water for conservation, we Boones will have an economic incentive to apply our water in that way. The more they buy, the more water we'll leave in the river."

"This scheme," the Boones conclude, "is perfect in all regards, in that it limits no one's liberty, it fully protects private property rights, it keeps government off people's backs, and it harnesses market mechanisms to promote better and better conservation outcomes." Having presented their own proposal, the Boones agree that they are good citizens, far wiser than those who mutter about government action and who lack faith in the market's ability to apply resources to their optimal uses.

While the controversy brews, George, a new citizen, arrives in Aridia from a distant land. He carries a pack and looks remarkably like the old Boone when he came to Aridia long ago. He begins at once to raise questions.

"Why do the Boones get to own all the water?" he asks. "There is no reason for it. After all, old man Boone did not create the river or the water in it. Indeed, I have done exactly what old Boone did. Like him I walked over the mountains and up to the river. Why should he get all the water and I get none when we did the same thing?"

As George continues, more citizens gather to listen: "Furthermore, the Boones have sat back while their water has gone up and up in value, carrying their incomes to great levels. Why should the water's rising value go to them, when they've done nothing to create it? When old Boone got here and lived alone, why, the water was worth virtually nothing. And now look at it, selling for exorbitant prices."

No sooner does George finish than word arrives that a new water source has been discovered in Aridia, beneath land on the edge of settlement. It is a confined aquifer, located entirely under the land of a single owner. Instantly, the value of the land rises sharply. When he hears about it, George erupts.

"I say the water should go to the people as a whole. Why should it go to the owner of the land surface? The economic gain would simply be a windfall for the owner. What did he do to deserve it?"

A quiet man in the back steps forward, and in a barely audible voice says, "Well, the law inherited from our ancestors provides that the owner of a land surface owns the water beneath the surface, so it seems that the issue is settled."

"Settled, nonsense," George exclaims. "Isn't this a democracy? Who makes the laws around here anyway, and whom are they supposed to serve?"

District of Columbia, 1999

In 1961, an investment partnership purchased Cathedral Mansions South, an apartment building on Connecticut Avenue across from the National Zoo in Washington, D.C. The area was fully developed, and other fine structures surrounded the apartment building and its spacious lawn. In 1987, the partnership decided to split the parcel, severing much of the lawn from the apartment building and then dividing the severed land into eight small building lots. The subdivision was performed, and the partnership applied for permits to build townhouses on the lots.

Because the apartment building was near the National Zoo, the owners were required by a 1930s law to submit their townhouse proposal to the Commission on Fine Arts, which would decide whether the townhouses would impair the "public values belonging to" the zoo or to other important parks or buildings in the area. After hearings, the commission decided that the townhouses would indeed harm the public values, and it recommended that the application be denied. Meanwhile, in March 1989, after several years of organizing, a neighborhood group formally petitioned to have the apartment and its lawn designated a historic landmark. The petition was soon granted, which meant that now the city's Historic Preservation Review Board was also required to pass judgment on the proposed construction. Like the Commission on Fine Arts, it recommended the permit be denied. When the partnership ran out of administrative avenues for appeal, it filed suit in federal court, claiming that the government's action amounted to an unlawful taking of its newly divided lots.

The law that governed the partnership's case was the body of judicial precedent that had built up around the Supreme Court's foundational decision back in 1922, in *Pennsylvania Coal Co. v. Mahon,* in which it first ruled that a land-use regulation could go "too far" in curtailing private rights. In the intervening years, Supreme Court rulings had clarified when a regulation went too far and thus triggered the government's obligation to compensate the private landowner. One strand of its decisions required compensation for any permanent physical occupation of an owner's land. A second strand required compensation when a regulation deprived a land parcel of essentially all land value, unless the regulation merely implemented a long-standing principle of property law, such as the *sic utere tuo* doctrine. A more complex, multifactor test was employed to resolve the many cases of alleged takings that did not fit within either of these two narrow categories. This test gave governments substantial power to regulate private land without having to pay compensation. Rarely did a regulation amount to an unlawful taking, in the Court's opinion, even when the regulation drastically reduced a parcel's market value.[1]

In court, the partnership attacked the construction permit denial by claiming that the land parcels at issue—the eight small lots—had lost all value as a result of the permit denial. If the lots could be developed, they possessed high market value, particularly because few vacant home sites remained in the area. The partnership's suit made its way to the U.S. Court of Appeals for the District of Columbia Circuit, which ruled in 1999 that no taking had occurred.[2] As the court saw things, the critical first step in applying Supreme Court precedents was to select the proper land parcel to examine when measuring whether the parcel's value had declined to nothing. Was it, in this case, the entire original parcel including the apartment building or merely the severed portion of the lawn? Predictably, the partnership argued that it was the severed portion alone. The court, however, ruled that the eight lots formed part of the larger single parcel that included the apartment building. Because the building retained value, so did the parcel as a whole.

Filing a separate opinion in the case was conservative judge

Stephen Williams, who complained that the court's ruling was unfair to the landowner. Elementary economics revealed what was going on, Williams claimed. When the lots were maintained as a manicured lawn, they provided positive aesthetic benefits to adjacent landowners and to the surrounding community. These positive benefits might be worth preserving, he acknowledged, but the landowner who generated them should be paid for doing so, either by taxpayers or by owners of the nearby lands who benefited the most. To force the partnership to provide the benefits without payment was tantamount to confiscating the development value of its lots, which was unfair.

These two tales—one fanciful, the other not—shed useful light on private property as a source of power, political as well as economic, and on the fairness of allowing (or not allowing) landowners to lay claim to increases in land values that are caused not by the landowner but by external factors.

Property law today vests landowners with considerable power, particularly in the case of vital resources such as water and land for housing. To own such resources is to wield power over other people whose lives and activities depend upon them. In the case of land, a law that vests an owner with control over a parcel necessarily imposes duties on everyone else to leave the land alone. Only when nonowners accept these duties as legitimate does private ownership begin; until then, a claim of ownership means little. Thus, the original Boone did not gain ownership of Aridia's river when he took possession of it and posted his signs. He became its owner only later, when other settlers arrived and expressed their willingness to be bound by his property claim. The Boone family's ability to wield state power is easy to see: just look at the Aridian citizens imprisoned for water theft or at Aridians who can only watch idly as the river flows by unless they pay for the right to use it.

Because private property is a form of state-sanctioned power, it is legitimate and worthy of respect only when it is adequately justified. When it is not justified, the power becomes suspect if not intolerable. Moreover, it is not just private property generally but every element of ownership that requires justification. A rationale that justifies a farmer's planting and harvesting of crops may or may not also justify a right later on to pave his farm field or to build apartments on it. A rationale that sustains a forest owner's right to manage his land as a mixed-species, mixed-age timber lot may or may not also justify a plan to convert the forest to an even-aged, single-species plantation.

In Western culture, a need to justify private ownership has been recognized since the time of ancient Greece. Justifications have commonly taken two competing forms. One views property as a natural right that arises independently of any governmental or social action; the other presents property as a distinctly human creation, dependent on law and subject to substantial alteration by those who make the laws. For centuries, the medieval church espoused the view that property arose out of nature, which meant that private owners (including the church itself) possessed rights that were superior to those of the state. It was a convenient theory for the church because it meant that secular kings had no power to seize their vast landholdings. When, in the sixteenth century, Henry VIII of England decided to do just that—to abolish monasteries and confiscate church lands—he needed to counter the church's reasoning. He did so by embracing the opposing view, which enjoyed an equally long intellectual lineage. Property was a human convention, Henry argued. As secular ruler and lawmaker, he therefore possessed the power to rewrite ownership rules and to reclaim private lands as needed. Henry's nobles (churchmen aside) admired his wonderful logic on this issue. Many of them had benefited personally from Henry's seizures by gaining ownership of former church lands, and they were anxious to quell doubts about the validity of their own land titles.

Within a century, however, the winds of English politics had changed. The Stuart kings aggressively claimed to have full, divine powers over all property. To resist such arguments, Parliament once again needed to justify private property as a natural right that arose independently of the king and that was hence immune from royal interference.[3]

If the precise issues of the seventeenth century have faded, the underlying question nonetheless remains, as important as ever. Is private property an individual right that the law merely protects, or is it instead a creation of law that lasts only so long as the law recognizes it? In practice, philosophy has often taken a backseat to raw power, as it did in early modern England. Guns and steel have provided their own arguments, as have the germs that rid many lands of their previous owners. By virtue of their power, those who can seize land and defend it hold de facto property rights. Yet when power becomes subject to legal control and lawmakers take justice to heart, the issue becomes paramount. Where do the rights of the individual end and the powers of the community begin?

In recent generations, justifications of private ownership have rested on four lines of reasoning: one insignificant (first-in-time), two that carry weight in limited settings (the labor and personality theories), and one that carries far greater power (overall social utility). The Boones of Aridia, the owners of Cathedral Mansion South—indeed, landowners everywhere—necessarily defend their powers by means of one or more of these justifications.

First-in-Time

The first, insubstantial line of reasoning deserves mention largely so that we might dispense with it. It is the claim that private ownership is justified whenever a person seizes an unowned thing and becomes its first possessor. Ownership of a thing is deserved, according to this simple theory, whenever a person is the first to take an unowned thing into possession. This was the type of claim that old Boone made when he set himself up as owner of Aridia's river. It is the hallmark of invaders and conquerors at all times.

Only a bit of thinking is needed to see that this claim lacks any real moral force. For a justification to work, it must explain why the ownership claims of one person should be honored by others, to the point of submitting to punishment for failure to do so. Private ownership almost always benefits the owner; to show that means little. To justify property, another, tougher question needs answering: What is in it for the nonowners? Why should they respect an owner's claim? First-in-time as a justification provides no response. The first people who settle an area might all favor a first-in-time rule for allocating resources so long as enough property exists to meet everyone's needs. But those who arrive later, after everything is taken, have no reason to go along. Mere happenstance, fortuity, or swiftness of foot can account for a person's being first, yet none carries moral weight. The first to arrive has done nothing that is morally worthy of a reward, nor (despite frequent claims to the contrary) does first-in-time fit with any other theory of individual rights, natural or divine. It fails as a justification, as philosophers have concluded for generations.

Despite its failure to justify ownership, priority-in-time has practical value as a method of allocating resources when their ownership is justified in some other ways. Societies often hand out resources by making them available to the first person to take them. This is particularly common in the case of low-valued resources that people hold temporarily, such as the right to use a park bench or picnic table. First-in-time can also prove useful when property rights are offered as rewards to stimulate socially valuable behavior. The first to build a needed railroad, for instance, might be offered land along the route as a reward for construction and as a stimulus to act quickly. The discoverer of a rare mineral deposit that society needs might similarly receive mining rights as a stimulus and reward for the discovery. In such settings, however, it is not actually priority-in-time that justifies the property rights being handed out, nor indeed is it even the chief reason a person receives the property. Society allocates the resource because of the socially valuable labor performed by the recipient—because of the newly built railroad or the successful mineral prospecting.

The Labor Theory

Of the three more substantial justifications for private property, the first is based on the idea that a person who creates a valuable thing with his labor ought to own the thing created. This labor theory was known and widely accepted in medieval Europe and in colonial America. English philosopher John Locke, writing in the seventeenth century, presented the theory in what became its authoritative form, and his name has been associated with it ever since.[4]

Locke's thoughts about private property dated from early in his career, and they began in America. In 1660, Charles II reclaimed the English throne from parliamentary rebels, thereby ending the Civil War and Interregnum and paving the way for renewed colonial settlement. To stimulate further colonization, Charles granted friendly nobles a patent to establish a colony that would carry his name, Carolina, and the proprietors in turn hired Locke to write the colony's constitution. Locke proposed that the wealthy proprietors create a feudal hierarchy of land ownership. The equivalents of earls and barons, carrying new names that Locke coined, would rule over a colonial peasantry and grow rich off its labors on their plantations. To no one's surprise, few English settlers were willing to head to Carolina on these terms, given the better options available in other colonies. Locke's plan was shelved.

Two decades later, Locke returned to the issue of property ownership, this time with different clients and aims. James II, a Catholic, had ascended the English throne upon his brother's death in 1685, and he promptly set out to revive the expansive claims of royal power that had caused such strife for his father and grandfather. To craft arguments supporting these broad claims, the Stuart clan years earlier enlisted Sir Robert Filmer. In his defense of the Stuarts, Filmer asserted that the king owned all land in England in his capacity as successor in title to Noah's sons, to whom God had given the earth as recorded in Genesis. Noah's sons and their successors later divided the earth and appointed owners for each part. In England, Noah's successor in interest was the reigning king, which meant that James II held divine power over all English land.

To help his friends in Parliament respond to this bold assertion, Locke reinterpreted the Genesis narrative. The gift recorded there, Locke argued, was not a gift to the sons of Noah personally, as Filmer had alleged, but to humankind collectively. God gave the earth to all people, to hold and use in common.

Locke's interpretation was not a new one; many others read Genesis the same way. Only at the next step did Locke's originality as theorist begin. If Locke's interpretation of Genesis undercut the king's claim of absolute power over land, it did not succeed in getting land from the common pool into the hands of private individuals, which was where Locke wanted it. To do that, a harder step had to be taken. Common property was well known to readers of Locke's day; the town commons and the common pathways were staples of English life. A person who improperly took things from the common fund was considered a thief. Why then should a community stand back and let an individual seize a valuable part of the common heritage?

One way to justify this crucial step was to posit that people long ago had gathered in a single place and unanimously agreed to divide up the land. For various reasons—not just because it was historically ridiculous—Locke disliked this explanation. Instead, he decided to make use of the long-standing labor theory of value.

Individual ownership arose, Locke asserted, when a person took an item from the common fund and, by mixing his labor with it, created something of value. The laborer, Locke reasoned, owned himself and his labor. Because of that ownership, he also owned the fruits of his labor. When a person mixed his labor with a physical thing, it was only proper to allow him to own the thing as well as the value added, for only in that way could he retain his creation. Indeed, it would be morally wrong to let anyone else use the valuable thing without the laborer's consent, given the laborer's right to the fruits of his labor.

This was Locke's argument, and it worked to get property into private hands. Yet even as Locke developed it, he recognized that it had limits. Other citizens would allow a laborer to seize a thing from the common fund only if they could do the same themselves—if they too could labor in the same way with the same expectation of becoming owners. Locke addressed the problem by attaching to his theory his now-famous "proviso": a laborer owns the thing with which he mixes labor *provided that* there remains "enough and as good" of the same thing for others to seize and use in the same way. Only when a resource is essentially inexhaustible in supply, that is, does the labor theory apply. Locke relied upon this key limit when explaining why his theory was fair to community members. A thing that was abundant possessed no value in its natural state because anyone who wanted the thing could simply take it for free. When a person took such a valueless thing and by laboring produced something of value, the value was due entirely to the labor itself—or at least 99 percent of it was, Locke said. To give such a thing to the laborer, then, was, in value terms, merely to allow the laborer to retain the value he created.[5]

A second limit on Locke's theory of property arose out of moral law. Moral thought had long questioned whether a person could rightly own more of a resource than he could put to good use. It was morally wrong, theorists concluded, to own so much of a commodity that it spoiled. Locke viewed moral law as binding, and he therefore included this limit in his scheme: No person could legitimately acquire more of a thing than he could use without spoilage; any property claim to the surplus was therefore void.

Having reached this point, Locke felt that he had succeeded at his assigned task. He had undercut the king's claimed ownership of all land, and he had sketched a way for individual property rights to arise in nature without the approval of government or of an assembly of all humankind. Property that arose in this manner did not depend on the king's consent and was therefore immune from royal claims of power.

As for Parliament and the regulatory power it claimed, Locke had no particular worries. He was content to give Parliament vast authority over private land, and he did so as he carried his narrative forward. As time passed, Locke argued, people who gained property by means of their labor came together to set up governments that would protect their property. Later still, gold was discovered and money was invented. With money, people could amass more wealth than they needed without running afoul of the no-spoilage rule, and with money they could hire servants to labor on their behalf. With the establishment of governments and monetary systems, private property ceased to be a natural right and became instead a conventional right. As such, it became fully subject to laws passed by the legislature. There matters stood, Locke believed, during his day. It was Parliament, not the king, that possessed power to govern private land.

Locke's labor theory proved understandably popular with parliamentary advocates. It was also popular in America, where it was used not just to resist the king but also to resist Parliament, on the ground that Parliament lacked power in America so long as Americans had no actual representation in it.

Before many generations had gone by, however, critics began pointing out weaknesses in Locke's logic. It was also not long before social reformers recognized the theory's great potential to promote aims far different from Locke's: not to defend private property but to question the legitimacy of massive private landholdings and the extensive powers wielded by factory owners. Because of these much different arguments based on Locke's labor theory, defenders of industry, the market, and large landholdings soon stopped relying on it to justify broad private powers. Instead, reformers who spoke on behalf of factory workers, small farmers, the landless, urban poor, and even slaves picked up the theory. Conspicuous among them was Karl Marx, who (with help from others) transformed the labor theory from a capitalist shield into a battleaxe.

One big problem with Locke's theory was that few natural resources were so plentiful as to lack all value. Vacant land certainly had value, and so did almost all other useful parts of nature. Indeed, it was hard to think of any part of nature—aside from the acorn that Locke used as an example—that literally met the proviso's strict requirement of overabundance. When a resource was scarce, a laborer might still claim to own the value that he added to the resource, but he could no longer claim the resource itself, because it possessed an independent, scarcity-induced value.

A related problem with the Lockean justification of property rights had to do with land and the difficulty people would have in finding available land to till. When land was scarce, why should one person get to mix labor with a tract of land when other people seeking the same opportunity were denied the chance to work? Why should those left out agree to stand back quietly and watch? This seemed unfair, even when the working laborer gained no rights to the land itself.

In time, critics who probed Locke's theory found even further limitations to it. For instance, when a person mixed labor with a natural resource in a way that degraded or consumed the resource, the common property fund was made worse off. Because the laborer did not own the resource being degraded or consumed—only the value added to it—it seemed that the laborer in fairness ought to have to compensate the common fund for that degradation or consumption; otherwise, everyone else would be worse off.

Particularly forceful use of labor-theory reasoning was made in colonial America to challenge property claims.[6] Under the labor theory, no one in a state of nature owned unused land because no one had yet mixed any labor with it. By English standards, many Indian lands appeared unused, so lightly did Indians live on them. Unused to the English colonists meant unowned, and unowned meant they could be taken freely, all because of the labor theory. From the early seventeenth century on, labor-theory reasoning was also used to question private rights in vacant land, particularly the rights of owners to exclude public hunters and foragers. Later, in the nineteenth century, social reformers used similar reasoning to challenge absentee land ownership as well as the huge incomes of factory owners. If laborers had a natural right to the value they created, why then did tenant farmers have to share their crops? As for factory workers, their wages were often much less than the value of the things they produced. Why did they not earn more? Then there was the nagging issue of slavery and the value added by slave labor, an issue that few were willing to touch.

Personality Theory

Enjoying popularity in the nineteenth century, particularly in Europe, was a third justification for private property centered on the ways that private property enhanced the essential personal development of its owner. For a person to exercise his will fully, nurturing his personality as richly as possible, he often needed to have exclusive control over certain physical things. Deprived of all property, people were often stunted in their psychological development; with the right property, they had better chances to flourish. To become a pianist, one needed a piano; to become a master craftsman, one needed the tools of the trade. Private property was justified, accordingly, whenever a person mixed his personality with a thing to such a degree that it became an extension of who he was.[7]

This personality theory, as it would be called, built upon earlier thought recognizing people's needs for sufficient resources to live. Thomas Aquinas used such reasoning to explain why a person could legitimately steal if necessary to survive (though he viewed begging as more honorable). John Locke echoed this idea in the seventeenth century: One of the virtues of his labor theory, he said, was that it explained why in a world of abundance a person could legitimately occupy vacant land to live on. Benjamin Franklin expressed similar views a century later when he claimed that although property generally was a creature of the state and subject to recall, the state could not seize the minimum things a person needed to survive. For Thomas Jefferson, the hoarding of empty land by the rich violated the basic rights of the unemployed poor to have land to till.

Personality theory appeared in the nineteenth century in various guises, sometimes alone, sometimes (as with Marx) in tandem with labor-theory rationales. In the United States, the theory also enjoyed a renaissance in the late twentieth century, when academics used it to support welfare initiatives to provide the poor with sufficient resources to live, as well as statutes giving residential tenants greater legal rights against their landlords.

The personality theory is at its strongest when it offers protection for the rights of individuals to have some way to make a living. People cannot live without sustenance, and they cannot develop fully without reasonable sustenance. Yet what property rights arise from these practical realities? Do they give rise to an individual entitlement to food, clothing, and shelter, for instance, whether or not a person can pay for them? If so, who has the corresponding duty to provide these resources? Do they mean, less powerfully, only that society is obligated to support a market system in which people can purchase these essentials when they have the money to do so?

Whatever clarity exists in the personality theory of property dissipates as soon as one moves beyond the basics of life. Many people are able to flourish better when endowed with adequate property. But a given individual's personality can be invested in all manner of objects, big and small, from diaries and modest homes to fancy cars, gambling casinos, and million-acre ranches. Where does one draw the line in recognizing property claims based on the way property fosters character and development? Can the Donald Trumps of the land rely on the personality theory to defend their rights in skyscrapers? In the land-use arena, the personality theory faces particular problems. One landowner's personality-driven acts can easily clash with a neighbor's. A mega hog farmer's personal development can clash with that of the neighbor who seeks the quiet life; a landlord's personal control of an apartment building can clash with the needs and claims of the tenants.

In practice, the personality theory offers little help in resolving land-related disputes and in judging the legitimacy of landowner claims. Its chief effect is to encourage extra respect in any property rights system for the basic resources that people need to live. A person's long-inhabited home ought to enjoy special consideration, given the owner's psychological attachment to it. Subsistence land uses ought to receive special weight when they clash with industrial land uses. When advocates of the personality theory seek to make more forceful use of it, they typically do so by arguing that society as a whole is better off when individuals are allowed to develop themselves fully and have the private resources to do so. Arguments of this type, however, are no longer about individual rights in isolation; they are about the good of society as a whole. As such, they are best taken into account as part of an "all things considered" assessment of how a private property regime might best promote the overall social good.

The possibility that such an overall assessment could justify private property philosophically became the subject of discussion late in the eighteenth century. Out of that discussion would emerge the fourth, and most important, justification for private rights in land.

Aggregate Social Utility

Writers about private ownership have long considered the overall effects that private property has on people and their communities, for good and ill. Even earlier, tribal groups routinely tailored private rights to promote the needs of the tribe as a whole. Indeed, it seems safe to guess that lawmakers everywhere have instinctively shaped the rights of private owners in ways intended to promote the good of the group as they perceived it.

This commonsense perspective gained a theoretical grounding with the rise of utilitarian thought during the decades spanning the eighteenth and nineteenth centuries. The underlying idea was plain enough: private property exists and is legitimate because of the overall utility it generates for society as a whole. With reasonably secure rights, a person can plant in the spring confident that she can harvest in the fall; as she plants and harvests, she adds to the overall stock of food. Homes will be built, farms cleared, canals dug, factories built, all because secure rights encourage owners to make long-term investments. As they invest, society as a whole gains. Landed property rights also protect personal and family privacy, and widespread ownership helps stabilize social arrangements of all sizes, from families and neighborhoods to the state as a whole. In short, private property in this view stimulates resource-use patterns that aid the community at large.[8]

Well before the nineteenth century reached its midpoint, American defenders of extensive property rights dropped their labor theory and turned instead to this new, utilitarian justification of rights. Property was good, not intrinsically and not because it was an individual natural right, but because of its overall utility for society. To citizens of the day, this practical justification rang true. Particularly quick to embrace it were owners of large land parcels, as well as people engaged in land uses that ran afoul of the old *sic utere tuo* limit. Utilitarian thought contained no built-in limits on owning vacant land or on owning more than one needed and could use. Nor did it necessarily prefer the settled, less intensive land use over the noisy, polluting newcomer. So long as rapid development was the dominant social goal, utilitarian reasoning justified expansive development rights.

Utilitarian thought of this type is, without question, the main way private property is justified today. And it is a powerful justification, at least potentially. It can justify any manner of extensive property rights so long as their recognition is felt to produce the greatest good. But the provision "so long as" is an important limitation, one that needs as much probing as did Locke's great proviso.

First, the phrase "greatest aggregate good" necessarily refers to the good of the people collectively, owners and nonowners alike. By no means can it refer merely to the good of a single owner or even of all owners collectively. Second, the good of the people is always contested and hard to discern. Market mechanisms provide crude measures of overall good in those spheres of life having to do with goods and services that individuals buy and sell. But many elements of overall good are not governed by markets, and market measures are greatly skewed by inequalities in wealth. Many public goals are best formulated through group discussion and processes of civil governance. Third, there is the practical reality that public values, desires, and circumstances inevitably shift over time. An assessment of greatest good that is accurate at one time can become highly inaccurate later on; as, for example, when there is a change in public attitudes about the worth of such things as historic buildings, older residential areas, and wild wolves. A property system that is well geared to generate the greatest good at one time can become poorly suited to do so later.

Countless questions could be raised about the common good and how private property might best serve it. Looming above them all, however, are two overlapping issues. To identify them clearly—even if they cannot be resolved fully—is to shed essential light on the various land-use conflicts now taking place in the United States.

First, what should be done about resource-use practices that now seem to harm the common good? This question includes both existing practices (for instance, using scarce water for socially trivial purposes such as growing surplus cotton in the desert) and proposed practices (such as converting rare wildlife habitat into a shopping mall that could easily be placed elsewhere). Such actions harm the common good and thus lack legitimacy, at least under the utilitarian justification for private ownership.

Second, when is it appropriate to change property-ownership rules midstream? A new calculation of the overall common good could easily lead to a new mix of landowner rights and responsibilities. Changing the rules incurs costs, however. For a community to ban a land use the moment it deems the use annoying might be best in terms of protecting the landscape. But it could curtail further long-term investments because of the uncertainty that legal change creates among investors.

Two observations supply a useful place to begin considering these questions. First, laws defining the rights and responsibilities of landownership in America have been changing ever since private property was introduced. The historical record on this point is beyond dispute. To argue that change is always wrong, therefore, is to call into question both the history of the institution and the legal mechanisms that have kept landowner rights in line with shifting values and circumstances for centuries. Inevitably, changes in landowner rights benefit some people and injure others—particularly landowners who pay little attention to where society is heading and who are taken by surprise when laws change. Second, in assessing the ill effects of revising property laws midstream, there is a big difference between a change that halts an *existing* land use, which can be quite disruptive, and one that merely keeps an owner from engaging in some *future* land use. One of property's main contributions to the common good is that it provides an inducement for private enterprise. In good Lockean fashion, people can mix their labors with the land, aiding themselves and their communities. For this inducement to work, landowners need security in their property rights, including security against new laws that render their prior labors useless. This need for security, however, can collide with the equally legitimate need of communities to have landowners avoid disturbing the common good. An existing land use that is reasonable when begun can become harmful later on because of changes in social values, circumstances, and surrounding land uses. Conflict can also arise over anticipated future uses: An established owner might harbor plans to build vacation homes on his hillside pasture—only to find, when the time comes to begin construction, that the community views the proposed use as harmful.

If protecting the landscape were its only policy goal, a community could simply ban all unwanted land-use practices; after all, why should a community allow them if they mar the common landscape? But communities also have other goals, and the picture becomes at once murkier and more realistic when these other goals are considered. The protection of lands and communities is a goal that inevitably needs balancing against the benefits that the community gets when landowners are reasonably secure in their entitlements.

Locke's labor theory and the history of property rights provide particular help in thinking about this trade-off. What Locke deemed worthy of legal protection was the value that a person added to land through his labors. Natural law secured the value that came from labor—not the value of nature alone, and not value that arose from other sources. Homes, barns, fences, stores, mills, even the value of clearing land—these were the things that the law of nature protected.

America's founders, so influenced by Locke, apparently embraced similar ideas, although they formulated them less crisply. Vacant land was less respected than land that was enclosed and put to use. *Sic utere tuo*, as applied during the era, protected existing land uses when they conflicted with newer ones. By giving new uses less protection, the law told owners that they initiated new uses at their peril. It also told owners of vacant land that their hopes to engage in future land uses were legally uncertain. In the practices of eighteenth-century America, then, just as in Locke's theory, there was a distinct divide: existing land uses enjoyed considerable protection, whereas far less protection was offered to new uses and to plans for the future.

The wisdom underlying this divide is not hard to discern. To encourage a landowner to plant crops in the spring, the fall harvest must be secure. But to encourage spring planting, the landowner need not possess a secure right years later to convert a farm field into a residential subdivision, nor even the right to flatten uneven farm fields with bulldozers so that huge combines might ignore the natural terrain. What owners need most is security in the improvements already made to their land, not in the improvement they might make in the future.

During the nineteenth century, lawmakers deliberately weakened legal protections for existing land uses when they revised the meaning of the *sic utere tuo* doctrine. It was more important, lawmakers decided, to make room in the landscape for more intensive, higher-valued land uses, even when such new uses undercut the settled expectations of existing owners. Was this shift really in the best interests of the people as a whole, or did it represent (as some historians have suspected) a successful effort by the moneyed, commercial class to manipulate the law in ways that benefited it at the expense of farmers, fishers, and residential dwellers? Did the law accurately mirror prevailing social values, or had powerful development interests captured it and used it to their advantage? These questions are still debated.

Lurking within these various land-use issues is the volatile matter of the landowner's "right to develop." What is it, and does a ban on particular types of land use violate it? Revolutionary-era lawmakers understood that statutes could ban all construction on private land. In 1580, for instance, Queen Elizabeth had imposed a ban on all new construction within 3 miles of the city of London, a ban that Parliament approved soon thereafter.[9] Early New England towns often banned landowners from building on their private farms away from the town center. Such development bans, though rarely needed given the vast open spaces in early America, were not viewed, so far as we can tell, as inconsistent with private rights in vacant land.[10]

As a strictly legal matter, landowners possess only such rights to develop as property law allows at any given time. Property law, like other law, evolves to keep in line with shifting communal needs. Future development rights, therefore, are inherently speculative, and they need to stay that way if property law is to remain a living institution. Thus, a landowner's right to develop 5 years in the future would need to be merely the right to develop under laws in effect 5 years hence. Of the various justifications for private property, only the utilitarian one provides any real protection for future development rights. And what it counsels is a slow, deliberate approach: respecting development options when it is in the community's best interest to do so but ignoring them otherwise.

In light of these justifications of private property, what might we learn from the travails of Aridia and the saga of the town homes at Cathedral Mansion South?

Boone's initial seizure of Aridia's river could have been, and should have been, ignored by the settlers who arrived later. His priority-in-time was unimportant in terms of natural justice. For the settlement to grow, part of the water needed to be turned over to private owners, individually or through some collective arrangement. But the rights that owners received and the methods of handing them out were matters for the assembled settlers as a whole to decide, not Boone alone. Inevitably, of course, many settlers would arrive too late to get in on the initial decision-making about the water, but sound decision-making would have anticipated their arrival and taken their needs into account fairly. Once later immigrants arrive, they become community members and their needs necessarily enter into the overall calculation of common good. A system that serves them poorly is, to that extent, flawed and illegitimate.

Even after Aridian law accepted Boone's bold claim to own the entire river, the leaders of Aridia could still have altered his rights, given that the rights served the common good so poorly. As it revised Boone's rights, Aridian lawmakers might wisely have protected his investments in diversion equipment and pumps—that is, in the labor he had invested. Less deserving of protection was the value of the water itself, given that neither Boone nor anyone else created the water. And least deserving would be the desire of the younger Boones to take yet more water from the river with their new pumping equipment. A law that ignored that desire would not disrupt any existing use, nor would it confiscate any value that the Boones created with their labors.

The Aridian landowner who found the confined aquifer under his property presents a similar case. The jump in his land's value was caused by discovery of the water, which the owner did not create. That being so, the community could fairly claim control of it by adopting a new groundwater law—or it could, that is, except for the fact that labor was (presumably) involved in finding the water. Aridians might want to offer landowners an inducement to find more water (which could, but need not, mean giving the water to the landowner or the discoverer).

In the real-world case of Cathedral Mansion South, Locke's labor theory gives the apartment owners no protection because their land remains unworked. Eighteenth-century property law, based on *sic utere tuo*, would also have been hostile, if the construction would in fact (as two commissions determined) harm the local status quo. In utilitarian terms, a ban on construction would not devalue any improvements made to the land. Once these matters are put aside, the partnership's claim to build is reduced to a less weighty policy assertion: the claim (dubious on the facts) that unless development rights are protected in such an instance, other owners will be encouraged to build on their lands prematurely to avoid the danger that their development rights might be taken away.

To complete a picture of the property rights in these two disputes, one final issue needs addressing: the matter of rising market values for the land and the water. There is immigrant George's testy allegation that the Boones are benefiting unfairly by reaping high income from water they did not create. There is Judge Williams's claim that, in economic terms, the neighbors around Cathedral Mansion

South have effectively forced the apartment owners to confer an economic benefit on them by keeping the apartments' manicured lawn undeveloped.

To make sense of this final matter, it may help to transform Mr. George from the fictional realm to the historical and consider more of his real-world critique of land values and landowner rights.

He was known in his day as the "prophet of San Francisco." His unlikely bestseller on land ownership, political economy, and the causes of wealth would go through more than 100 editions. By 1906, perhaps 6 million people had read it. As historian Willard Hurst recorded:

> Peddled in railway coaches and by candy "butchers" along with the paperback joke books and thrillers of the day, Henry George's *Progress and Poverty* (1879) evidently responded to some pervasive, deep-felt need to probe and grasp for more understanding of cause and effect in social relations.[11]

Among those captivated by Henry George's thinking was Hamlin Garland, who wrote of his awakening in his autobiography:

> Up to this moment I had never read any book or essay in which our land system had been questioned. I had been raised in the belief that this was the best of all nations in the best of all possible worlds, in the happiest of all ages. I believed (of course) that the wisdom of those who formulated our constitution was but little less than that of archangels, and that all contingencies of our progress in government had been provided for or anticipated in that inspired and deathless instrument.
>
> Now as I read this book, my mind following step by step the author's advance upon the citadel of privilege, I was forced to admit that his main thesis was right. Unrestricted individual ownership of the earth I acknowledged to be wrong and I caught some of the radiant plenty of George's ideal Commonwealth.[12]

From his home in California, George journeyed east to New York City in 1869. Not yet 30 years of age, he was, as his son later wrote, "small of stature and slight of build"; "poor, unheralded, unknown"; his *alma mater* "the forecastle and the printing-office."[13] George had come east to set up a telegraphic news bureau so that papers such as his own in California could circumvent the monopoly on news created by powerful presses and telegraph companies. His effort to do so failed, but in New York he would gain a headful of ideas as he walked the city's streets and pondered the juxtaposition of vast wealth and extreme poverty.

Out of George's ruminations came a 48-page essay, published as a small book under the title *Our Land and Land Policy.* One thousand copies sold quickly. Thus encouraged, and realizing how the land issue was linked to larger economic questions, he returned to his desk. Writing the longer book would drain George and his family; the intense effort, his son later reported, "frequently forced the author to pawn his personal effects."

In *Progress and Poverty,* George considered why the United States and its growing wealth seemed to produce both great fortunes and abject poverty. What statistics showed, he decided, was that the nation's growing wealth paradoxically brought increased poverty along with it. Poverty in George's day was excused by many observers, who based their opinions on the population theories of conservative economist Thomas Malthus. In Malthus's view, poverty was a natural, inevitable product of rising populations—so inevitable that nothing should be done about it. George ardently disagreed. Poverty had nothing to do with population growth, he announced. It arose because the country's valuable lands and resources were all in private hands, and the poor had no choice but to work for them. As populations rose and competition for resources increased, more and more of the nation's wealth went to owners of property. Something was wrong, not in nature but in human institutions. Those who constructed buildings deserved a return on them; that was not the issue. It was the return on nature itself that bothered George, the return on vacant land; farmland; and land beneath tenement houses, factories, and stores.

George's lengthy analysis was complex and detailed, yet at its center stood a simple idea. Land values escalated as cities and economies expanded. Part of that rise in value came from improvements landowners made, but raw nature itself was also increasing in value. Landowners were getting rich for doing nothing. When a person lived alone in isolation, land had no value. Value came only later, when other people showed up, when populations became denser, regions prospered, and cities arose. All the while, the original landowners watched their lands gain value. As for where that value came from, it arose from the city itself: from the people who settled there, from their labors on surrounding lands, and from the land scarcity they induced. As prices rose, rents increased. As rents rose, the landless paid greater portions of their incomes to live, and they took home in wages a falling percentage of what their labors created. Much of the rent paid by tenants, in fact, was rent paid on the land itself, on nature, which no owner created. The producer's right to the fruits of his labor, so lucidly endorsed by Locke, was being frustrated by the landowning class.

George questioned the fairness of the entire idea that people could own nature individually. Nature was a gift to humankind in common, George asserted. Locke was right in acknowledging the ownership claims that people had in their improvements. But the land itself, in the real world of scarcity (as opposed to Locke's hypothetical world of unlimited supply) remained the common property of all people. The laborer-owner merely had the right to use land. Rents attributable to the land itself still belonged to the public.

George was pragmatic enough to recognize that truly common

ownership of land was impractical in a complex world. Individuals had to have the right to control land and make decisions about it. What would work, he believed, and what would fairly protect the public's interest, was for the public to claim all income attributable to land itself. Rent from an office building would be divided between return on the building and return on the land, with the land portion going to the common fund. The same rule would apply to all lands, urban and rural. No one's labor would be disrupted or upset. No one would be discouraged from investing more labor. So considerable would this revenue be, George estimated, that all other taxes could be eliminated. Government would live off a single tax.

So powerful did George's logic seem that adherents lined up by the thousands to carry his message. Single Tax clubs arose; Single Tax political rallies were held. Support for the idea swelled, despite the predictable resistance of landowners.[14]

George's book remained popular for decades, particularly in Europe. It influenced public policies toward land, land-use regulation, and real estate taxation. Because of practical problems and widespread opposition, George's single-tax scheme never came to fruition, but his reasoning remained alive, awaiting application in ways that could work.

Henry George's analysis is useful today in many ways. One service it performs is that it helps to update Locke's labor theory for a world of scarcity. The value of land today results not just from labors expended on it. Value also comes from what other people have done to surrounding lands; from the neighborhoods, communities, and vast cities that have arisen over time. Value comes to a parcel from its proximity to these surrounding improvements, as well as from local scarcities of land generally. Value also comes from nature itself—a point that neither Locke nor George took into account. Fertile soil and nature's ecological processes account for part of the variation in land values, and collectively (as contemporary ecological economists have shown) bring huge benefits for human communities. A land parcel's value, then, stems from three sources: nature itself; the surrounding human community; and the improvements, if any, made by the owner. Only the final element of value is protected by Locke's natural-rights reasoning.

Informed by George, we can return for a concluding glance at the two cases we have considered, one fanciful, one not.

The Boones of Aridia have become rich not from their labors but because the flourishing community has made their water more valuable. What the community creates, the community might properly enjoy. The law could insist that the Boones earn a return only on their improvements and services, not on nature's bounty. The same can be said for the just-discovered aquifer in Aridia, though here one must take care to note the labor involved in discovering it—labor of a type that the original Boone did not perform.

As for the dispute at Cathedral Mansion South, Judge Williams, it would seem, had his elementary economics reversed. It was not the neighborhood that was trying to reap value from the open lawn, it was the owner of the lawn who by raising more housing structures wanted to capture the value created by the surrounding community. To see this, we might compare the value of the partnership's eight small lots with the value of similar lots hundreds of miles away, in a rural place with no development pressure. The two lands in natural terms could be identical, and the owners of each would have performed identical, minimal labor. The lots across from the National Zoo could fetch hundreds of thousands of dollars if offered for sale as building lots; the lots many miles away might bring merely hundreds of dollars. Only one fact accounts for the difference: the presence of the community.

Judge Williams implicitly based his economic reasoning on the assumption that the partnership already possessed the right to build town homes and hence had already captured the economic value created by the local community. Because the partnership already possessed that value, the denial of its permit application took it away. But to embrace such reasoning is to miscast what the government agencies were doing and to slant the analysis strongly in favor of the landowner. As a legal matter, the partnership's development rights were only those rights recognized by local law, including the law in effect since the 1930s that protected the National Zoo and other public buildings. Under local law, the owner's right to develop was highly uncertain. It was the job of local lawmakers, when they received the partnership's building application, to decide whether the right would exist. Should the property rights of the partnership include the right to develop? This was a policy matter, properly resolved in utilitarian fashion by considering how development would affect the aggregate good. Only if construction promoted the aggregate good would the property right be justified. Only then would the landowner gain the legal right to develop.

Resolving this dispute by drawing upon utilitarian reasoning is proper because the utilitarian justification is the only one that applies on the facts of the case. The partnership had mixed no labor with its land and created no value. It therefore lost nothing in the way of improvements when its permit was denied. It did lose its hope to make money—its expectation of profit. But that hope was based on a gamble, on a poor guess, as it turned out, about what government would do. According to the record in the case, nearly every property up and down Connecticut Avenue, from M Street to a full mile north of the apartment building, was subject to similar limits on new construction. The partnership's gamble was a long one.

Once we clearly understand the justifications for private property—along with the origins of land values—it becomes hard to see why government should protect the monetary hopes of landowners or land buyers who want to develop. Land values are based on estimates of future earnings, and future earnings are dependent on many uncertainties, the law among them. The law does not protect land investors against market forces, which can wipe out land value overnight. Similarly, the law does not protect stock market investors against the risk that changes in law will radically reduce the value of companies in which they invest. Why should it protect holders of land—in Henry George's sense—against the risk of law changes, thereby encouraging them to take even greater risks?

The neighbors around Cathedral Mansion who pushed for its designation as a historic structure were part of a larger movement in American culture working for the conservation of landscapes and the good elements in them. The urge to conserve has been with Americans since the first years of settlement, yet it has routinely been the minority voice: the voice of the stickers, the settlers, the defenders of community. In all eras, conservation has clashed with boomer and migrant views of private property. On the current scene, conservation appears in many forms, some focused on the built environment, others on the natural; some on established social communities and ways of life, others on the achievement of social justice in resource allocations.

In many of its forms, conservation has challenged the rights of owners to change or use intensively the lands and resources they own. Historic preservation efforts directly challenge the rights of landowners to alter culturally valued structures. Related conservation efforts, seeking to preserve neighborhoods and downtown areas against fringe development, have posed similar legal challenges. Many interest groups have worked to reverse trends in food production that have undercut small-scale farms, narrowed the genetic variation of crop species, proliferated antibiotics and toxic chemicals, and diminished the taste and nutritional value of human foods.

These efforts, and similar ones dealing with industrial forestry and fishing practices, have routinely questioned landowner powers.

Of these various strands of conservation, the ones dealing with the natural landscape have been most at the center of property debates. Among those, most have addressed the health and productivity of landscapes where people live and work, rather than wild areas and wild creatures. It is hard to overstate the importance of such controversies in shaping not just the substance of current debates but the ways that people instinctively think and talk about private rights and government powers.

In the view of fair-minded observers, particularly those familiar with easily overlooked signs of ecological degradation, many occupied American lands continue to decline in quality. Natural ecological functions, particularly fertility and hydrologic cycles, are severely disrupted. Biological communities continue to unravel as many species decline for every one on the rise. Farms, forests, grazing lands, and other working lands are typically used in ways that cannot be sustained ecologically; their high productivity is made possible only by high-tech methods that conceal declines in natural productivity and that have significant adverse side effects—known, suspected, and probably also unsuspected. Private land uses have produced, and routinely continue to produce, landscapes that people find less appealing, in terms of congestion, aesthetics, and the trials of daily living.

For this reason, any discussion of private property today needs to attend seriously to the conservation impulse. It must see how conservation has pressed against older, industrial ideas of ownership and how private property might be reshaped to accommodate conservation needs. Land conservation is a diffuse movement, varied in aims and values. But it does have an intellectual and ethical core, and over the past century it has had a leading intellectual figure—Aldo

Leopold (1887–1948)—although his name is known only dimly by most Americans. Leopold's writings—and those of his most prominent successor, Wendell Berry—reflect serious thought about conservation, particularly its claims about private ownership and about the need for a new, ecologically guided understanding of owning nature. They provide the logical next installment in an inquiry into private property and the common good.

CHAPTER FIVE

The

OWNER

and the

LAND COMMUNITY

In December 1935, in a hotel room in Nazi-governed Berlin, Aldo Leopold sat down at a desk and pulled out a sheet of hotel stationery. Turning the paper over, he scratched the word *Wilderness* across the top and then proceeded to write 10 sentences in his tight cursive hand. Thoughts had come to him that day, and he wanted to get them on paper. The ideas were not new ones, at least not for him, but the phrasings that evening seemed more precise.

Leopold's aim in writing was to explain in the simplest language the conservation predicament of his time. How did human life fit into the planetary whole? And what cultural shifts were needed before people would stop abusing the land and align themselves with nature's order?

In his first three sentences, Leopold considered the planet's living and nonliving parts:

The two great cultural advances of the past century were the Darwinian theory and the development of geology. The one explained how, and the other where, we live. Compared with such ideas, the whole gamut of mechanical and chemical invention pales into a mere matter of current ways and means.[1]

Darwin showed how life evolved and how humans were related to other life-forms. Geology explained the rest of the story: how the Alps rose, how the Nile River set its course, how Illinois got its rich soil.

In his next three sentences, Leopold turned to the connections between and among these living and nonliving parts:

> Just as important as the origin of plants, animals, and soil is the question of how they operate as a community. Darwin lacked time to unravel any more than the beginnings of an answer. That task has fallen to the new science of ecology, which is daily uncovering a web of interdependencies so intricate as to amaze—were he here—even Darwin himself, who, of all men, should have the least cause to tremble before the veil.

Nature was not a collection of distinct pieces, randomly located and operating independently. It was an interrelated community of life— the land community, as he termed it, or simply "the land." So complex and mysterious was this organic whole that Leopold needed metaphors to describe it: the land was akin to a living organism; it was like a complex machine. These metaphors were not fully apt, Leopold knew, but they were useful rhetorically when talking to people who knew about healthy and diseased plants and who grasped the wisdom of saving parts when tinkering with tractors. Nature's constituent elements interacted in unique, dynamic, and perplexing ways.

The land community that Leopold assessed in his Berlin note was a community that emphatically included humans. People arose from Darwinian evolution in the same manner as other life-forms. They drew minerals from the same rocks, drank the same water, and breathed the same air. It made sense, then, to understand humans as community members, just like other organisms. It made sense, when studying life and talking about right and wrong living, to direct one's attention to the entirety of this diverse, pulsing, complex natural whole. And yet, as sensible as this orientation was, humans routinely saw the world in more fragmentary terms:

> One of the anomalies of modern ecology is that it is the creation of two groups, each of which seems barely aware of the existence of the other. The one studies the human community almost as if it were a separate entity, and calls its findings sociology, economics, and history. The other studies the plant and animal community, [and] uniformly relegates the hodge-podge of politics to "the liberal arts."

At this point, Leopold had reached the root of the matter. People saw themselves as separate from the rest of nature, when in truth they were not. Humans did not form a distinct entity, one that could be studied and understood alone. They were embedded in nature as much as any living thing.

The overriding trouble, as Leopold knew, was that humankind was overstepping its bounds. It had shifted from using the land to abusing it. The signs of land sickness were all around: in the decline of good soils, in the disruption of hydrologic cycles, in the radical reorganization of biological communities, and in the shortening and deterioration of nutrient flows. Step by step, the land was losing its ability to sustain life.

What was the treatment for this sickness? What would it take for humans to recognize that they too were part of this community and that they too depended on its healthy functioning? The answer, Leopold decided that December evening in Berlin, lay in a merger of perspectives on the human condition into one overarching, holistic perspective. Leopold expressed that goal and his cautious optimism as to its achievement in the last of his 10 sentences:

> The inevitable fusion of these two lines of thought will, perhaps, constitute the outstanding advance of the present century.

Leopold did not underline the word *perhaps,* but no doubt he emphasized it in his mind. He knew what kind of toil and social learning lay along the path to fusion. People needed to take seriously their connections to all other life. But the bigger challenge was to confront the deep-seated arrogance that pervaded Western culture—what biologist David Ehrenfeld would later term the arrogance of humanism.[2] Westerners believed that they stood apart from and above all other species, divided from the rest by their superior reason, knowledge, and tools. Among all life-forms, they alone possessed moral value, or so they believed. This was an arrogance rooted less in scientific knowledge than in emotion and myth.

The harm wrought by this arrogant approach, Leopold believed, could be seen everywhere. One needed to look no further than the typical farm field or working forest. Before visiting Berlin, he wrote:

> We of the machine age admire ourselves for our mechanical ingenuity; we harness cars to the solar energy impounded in carboniferous forests; we fly in mechanical birds; we make the ether carry our words or even our pictures. But are these not in one sense mere parlor tricks compared with our utter ineptitude in keeping land fit to live upon? Our engineering has attained the pearly gates of a near-millennium, but our applied biology still lives in nomad's tents of the stone age.[3]

Land-use practices were backward, and chiefly because social norms and values, particularly private property, did not yet reflect the proper human role. "Land, to the average citizen," Leopold would write, "is still something to be tamed, rather than something to be understood, loved, and lived with. Resources are still regarded as separate entities, indeed, as commodities, rather than as our cohabitants in the land-community."[4]

A new concept of land was needed, one shaped by ecology, grounded in an inclusive community, and given force by senses of wonder, beauty, and love. The creation and embrace of such a new concept, Leopold believed, was the central challenge of the day. No issue would occupy his own attention more fully in the years leading up to his death in April 1948.

Inevitably, Leopold's thoughts about private lands led him to probe the underlying institution of private property itself and to question the extensive rights that landowners possessed. They led him also to craft a far different understanding of private ownership, one in which landowners owed distinct responsibilities to sustain not just their social communities but their natural communities as well. Leopold's new understanding would include no legal details, nor would he resolve all the issues. But he would speak clearly about the broad contours. The common good, he insisted, was best served by nurturing the land's ecological health. Landowners, accordingly, needed to shoulder duties to use their lands in ways consistent with that overriding health. Unfortunately, the economics of individual land use worked against sound, conservative land use. That reality made it all the more important for the community to act affirmatively to protect its legitimate interests in the ways private lands were used.

No writing by Leopold has exerted as much influence on conservation thought as his essay "The Land Ethic," which concluded his widely admired work, *A Sand County Almanac and Sketches Here and There*, published in the year after his death. In the essay, Leopold called for the expansion of human moral sensibilities to encompass all life-forms, viewed collectively as the land. Humans should no longer perceive land simply as an economic commodity, Leopold argued; as something to use and discard at will. They should understand it as a community of life, a community that surrounded them and included them. Land-use decisions ought to rest not on economics alone but on ethics and aesthetics as well. As members of the community, landowners owed duties to support the well-being of

139

the landscapes they helped form. "A thing is right," Leopold sum-marized in the sentence of his "Land Ethic" that has become best known, "when it tends to preserve the integrity, stability, and beauty of the biotic community."[5] If landowners everywhere would embrace this community-focused ethic, if humans could see beauty and prosperity in a healthy land, they would have gone far in address-ing the conservation problem.

Leopold began his professional forestry career guided by the principles of sustained-yield forestry, which used scientific expertise to manage forests so that they produced a continuous timber flow in perpetuity. He was guided too by the idea that a single public forest could be used in multiple ways: to protect water flows and wildlife habitat, provide recreational opportunities, and supply wood prod-ucts. Before long, Leopold recognized that these sustained-yield, multiple-use principles applied equally to private lands. When man-aged scientifically, they too could produce multiple benefits, includ-ing conservation benefits, in perpetuity. Yet as Leopold learned more about nature's complexity, he recognized how difficult it was to use land wisely. Trained experts who knew only their narrow disci-plines might succeed in their researches, but a land manager needed to know everything. The year before his Berlin trip, he would write:

> The plain lesson is that to be a practitioner of conservation on a piece of land takes more brains, and a wider range of sympathy, forethought, and experience, than to be a specialized forester, game manager, range man-ager, or erosion expert in a college or a conservation bureau. Integration is easy on paper, but a lot more important and more difficult in the field than any of us foresaw.[6]

Good land use required not just the integration of scientific disci-plines but a healthy respect for human limits. Nature was highly com-plex, and even leading scientists could not predict its interactions or decipher the functions of all its parts. Only an attentive, caring landowner stood much chance of drawing sustenance from land with-out degrading it. Science, to be sure, was learning more and more about land as a biological mechanism, but it was also producing ever more powerful tools to disrupt and reshape nature in unheralded ways. In his somber moments—moments that came more often as he aged—Leopold despaired that humans would ever gain the knowledge and ethical grounding required to live within nature's bounds. In a 1938 talk on the subject at the University of Wisconsin College of Engineering, Leopold extended both a condemnation and a challenge:

> We end, I think, at what might be called the standard paradox of the twentieth century: our tools are better than we are, and grow better faster than we do. They suffice to crack the atom, to command the tides. But they do not suffice for the oldest task in human history: to live on a piece of land without spoiling it.[7]

By the time Leopold reached this point, he could see clearly that it was not the land that needed managing so much as the land-owners themselves. And as he pondered the enigma of land-use motives, he saw that the chief impediments to better landowner behavior were the cultural values and ethics that then prevailed, along with the institutions that reflected them—particularly private property. In his extraordinary essay from 1947, "The Ecological Conscience," Leopold used case studies to explain society's painfully slow progress. What studies showed, he announced, was "the futility of trying to improve the face of the land without improving our-selves."[8] A cultural transformation was needed, one that reoriented the fundamental ways people perceived the world and their role in it. A particular need, he wrote in 1933, was for "a rebirth of that social dignity which ought to inhere in land-ownership." He observed,

> Granted a community in which the combined beauty and utility of land determines the social status of its owner, and we will see a speedy

dissolution of the economic obstacles which now beset conservation. Economic laws may be permanent, but their impact reflects what people want, which in turn reflects what they know and what they are.[9]

Leopold was not content merely to offer encouragement to landowners. Each community, he believed, ought to act forcefully to protect its interests and translate its ecological needs, fairly but firmly, into duties imposed on landowning members. In "The Ecological Conscience," he lamented that conservation work "on the actual landscape of the back forty" was "still slipping two steps backward for each forward stride." He continued,

> The usual answer is more conservation education. My answer is yes by all means, but are we sure that only the *volume* of educational effort needs stepping up? Is something lacking in its *content* as well? I think there is, and I here attempt to define it.
>
> The basic defect is this: we have not asked the citizen to assume any real responsibility. We have told him that if he will vote right, obey the law, join some organizations, and practice what conservation is profitable on his own land, that everything will be lovely; the government will do the rest.
>
> This formula is too easy to accomplish anything worthwhile. It calls for no effort or sacrifice; no change in our philosophy of values. . . .
>
> No important change in human conduct is ever accomplished without an internal change in our intellectual emphases, our loyalties, our affections, and our convictions.[10]

It is possible to tease four strands of thought from Leopold's written legacy that have particular bearing on private property as a cultural and legal institution and on how it might better promote the good of the whole.

The Land as a Community

Preeminent in Leopold's thought late in his life was the idea that land was an integrated community, not a collection of distinct parts or resources. "We abuse land because we regard it as a commodity belonging to us," he would write in his brief *Almanac* foreword. "When we see land as a community to which we belong, we may begin to use it with love and respect."[11] In promoting this ecological understanding of land, Leopold knew that he faced a daunting challenge. He would downplay that challenge in published writings, but he left behind plentiful evidence that he held no illusions:

> The concept of land as a community, of which we are only members, is limited to a few ecologists. Ninety nine percent of the world's brains and votes have never heard of it. The mass mind is devoid of any notion that the integrity of the land community may depend on its wholeness, that this wholeness is needlessly destroyed by present modes of land-use, or that the land-sciences have not yet examined the possibilities of preserving more of it.[12]

To conceive of land as a community, and of individual parcels and individual owners as parts of it, was to pose a direct challenge to the individualism of American culture. When land parcels were discrete, their separate management by owners made sense; when they were parts of something larger, separate management alone became more problematic. By seeing land as he did, Leopold expanded and updated the vision of the "well-regulated society" that had guided Lemuel Shaw and other nineteenth-century jurists. In Leopold's land community, as in the nineteenth-century vision of the well-regulated society, the private rights of individual owners were appropriately constrained by the good of the whole.

The Goal of Land Health

A recurring complaint of Leopold's had to do with the fragmentation that characterized conservation in his day. There were many workers for conservation, but they pushed in different directions. Conservation was a "house divided,"[13] Leopold protested; it lacked a philosophy and would not get far without one.[14] The result often was that conservationists worked at cross-purposes and without coordination, sometimes with unfortunate results. "The divided counsels of conservationists," moreover, gave governments "ample alibi for doing little."[15]

Leopold's worries about conflicts within conservation would soon merge with his ideas about land as community. To coordinate its efforts, conservation needed an overall goal. Given that land worked as an integrated system, the logical goal was one that promoted the system's ability to function well over time. For Leopold, there was "only one soil, one flora, one fauna, and one people," which was to say "only one conservation problem."[16] A single problem called for a single solution, however diverse the implementing means. As a community, Leopold concluded, the land could be more or less healthy in the ways that it functioned. The health of that community, then—land heath—was the logical goal of conservation. And as a vital component of the common good, Leopold believed, land health should be a major consideration when society calibrated the rights of private owners.

"Land health," Leopold would write in 1944, "is the capacity for self-renewal in the soils, waters, plants, and animals that collectively comprise the land."[17] "Health expresses the cooperation of the interdependent parts: soil, water, plants, animals, and people. It implies collective self-renewal and collective self-maintenance."[18] Health, of course, was a characteristic commonly associated with a single organism. Leopold applied the term to land in the much same way and with the same good connotations, but without asserting that land operated as tightly and coherently as an organism. Central to the land's health was its ability to retain its font of fertility—its soil. Land was healthy "when its food chains are so organized as to be able to circulate the same food an indefinite number of times."[19] Only when this happened would the soil—"the repository of food between its successive trips through the chains"—retain its fertility and produce abundant, nutritious yields.[20]

Like human health for physicians today, land health for Leopold the land-doctor was easiest to explain by identifying symptoms of disease. A concise list appeared at the beginning of one of his most important essays on the subject, "The Land-Health Concept and Conservation":

> The symptoms of disorganization, or land sickness, are well known. They include abnormal erosion, abnormal intensity of floods, decline of yields in crops and forests, decline of carrying capacity in pastures and ranges, outbreak of some species as pests and the disappearance of others without visible cause, a general tendency toward the shortening of species lists and of food chains, and a world-wide dominance of plant and animal weeds. With hardly a single exception, these phenomena of disorganization are only superficially understood.[21]

As he thought about land health, Leopold was perplexed most by the roles of native species and of species preservation in sustaining land health. Species played vital roles in keeping food webs intact and returning nutrients to the soil. The land's functioning, therefore, was threatened by the shortening and simplification of food webs. Species were also important in the community's functioning in general, and yet humans had only vague understandings of how that functioning occurred. Ignorance was vast, and humility was the proper response. "As far as we know," he observed cautiously in 1942, "the state of health depends on the retention in each part of the full gamut of species and materials comprising its evolutionary equipment."[22]

As he brought together his ideas about land sickness and health, Leopold would return repeatedly to the challenges posed by nature's built-in dynamism; by the fact that nature itself continuously shifted, even without human interference. Pondering the matter, he found himself unwilling to commit to any particular model of ecological functioning. He saw merit in various views, yet what impressed him most was how little any ecologist really understood. Nature was dynamic and flexible, Leopold knew. But change occurred at differing rates and on differing scales, and lands varied greatly in their abilities to withstand change. Human-induced changes caused as much damage as they did not because they disrupted static balances but because they altered conditions too swiftly, radically, and extensively. "The combined evidence of history and ecology," wrote Leopold in 1939, "seems to support one general deduction: the less violent the man-made changes, the greater the probability of successful readjustment in the [biotic] pyramid."[23]

Once formulated, the idea of land health brought vast changes to Leopold's thinking about conservation generally and about private ownership in particular. For the land to become healthy, all lands needed to be well used; the conservation challenge, as he put it, was "coextensive with the map of the United States."[24] In one way or another, accordingly, society had to push private owners to use their lands in ways consistent with the land's health. In one way or another, private ownership had to include an obligation—cultural if not legal—to use one's land only in ways that sustained the whole. Leopold would formulate such an obligation when he composed his now-famous land ethic. His ethic urged owners to use land in ways consistent with its beauty, its integrity (that is, retention of its biological parts), and its *stability*—a term that Leopold used, peculiarly, as a shorthand synonym for his complex notion of land health. For Leopold, it was the land ethic that transformed land health from an overall social goal into an individual landowner duty.

Conservation Economics

A third element of Leopold's conservation thought that bears directly on private property had to do with the economic realities of conserving land.[25] How private owners used land materially affected the surrounding land community. Because of that, and because communities endured far beyond any owner's life-span, the public should take a strong interest in how landowners behaved.

As Leopold assessed the economics of sound land use, he was quick to see that conservation paid dividends, but the dividends were largely ones that landowners acting alone could not capture. Benefits spread to the entire community, of which the landowner was only a part. When all landowners conserved, each might gain, just as a landowner who failed to conserve could drag others down with him. But full conservation by an isolated owner rarely made economic sense. Existing institutions simply did not attend to this public interest:

> The present legal and economic structure, having been evolved on a more resistant terrain (Europe) and before the machine age, contains no suitable ready-made mechanisms for protecting the public interest in private land. It evolved at a time when the public had no interest in land except to help tame it.[26]

In the face of this challenge, Leopold's initial inclination was to turn to the self-interest option as the centerpiece of a private-lands policy. To influence a landowner who viewed the land as an economic asset, conservation needed to improve the financial bottom line. Public funds could reward landowners who set land aside for wildlife. Tax abatements could reduce a landowner's need to drain wetlands. Hunting fees could go to owners who tore down their no-hunting signs. As he put it in his 1930 "Report to the Game Conference": "Compensation to the landowner in some form or other is the only workable system for producing game on expensive private farm land."

For a few years, this economic-inducement approach was the one Leopold favored. But trial results were soon in, based largely on federal soil-erosion programs, and they were not impressive. Leopold had known all along that incentive programs could do little to help migratory game; its future "was black," he said in 1933, "because motives of self-interest do not apply to the private cropping of birds so mobile that they 'belong' to everybody, and hence to nobody." But he was soon disappointed even in programs focused on resources that did not move around. "For a full generation," he would lament several years later, "the American conservation movement has been substituting the profit motive for the fear motive, yet it has failed to motivate."[27] Incentive programs induced good behavior so long as the money flowed, but when the money stopped, old habits returned. Conservation measures were implemented when governments paid for them, but incentives did not bring about new ways of viewing the land. Indeed, in one respect incentives were counterproductive, for they gave landowners the sense that they bore no duty to promote land health. The baseline of acceptable land use was set low, with landowners entitled to compensation whenever they voluntarily rose above it.

By the end of the 1930s, Leopold's assessment of incentive programs, standing alone, was quite sober:

> I no longer believe that a little "bait" for the farmer, either in cash, service, or protection, is going to move him to active custodianship of wildlife. If the wildlife cropping tradition is not in his bones, then no

external force, either of my kind or any other kind, is going to put it there. It must grow from the inside, and slowly.[28]

In an unpublished manuscript from around 1937, he went further:

> The current doctrine of private-profit and public-subsidy is defective in these respects: It expects subsidies to do more—and the private owner to do less—for the community than they are capable of doing. We rationalize these defects as individualism, but they imply no real respect for the landowner as an individual. They merely condone the ecological ignorance which contrasts so strongly with his precocity in mechanical things.[29]

Economic incentives, education, legal restraints, boycotts, social ostracism, community-based conservation measures—Leopold would consider them all, only to find in time that none would do the trick, not alone and not in any combination that seemed feasible.

Images of Ownership

For Leopold, the leading conservation challenge of his day was starkly posed by the individual landowner, living on and using a single tract of land. For the land to become healthy, this owner had to act well. Achieving this outcome was a challenge because economic factors were so unfavorable. Adding to the challenge was private property itself and the way property rights were commonly understood. So long as ownership gave a person the right to ignore the common good, legally and culturally, conservation was doomed.

Leopold was no legal scholar, and he knew little about the history of private property. Had he known more, particularly about the many forms private ownership has taken in different times and places, he might have called even more loudly for institutional change. Even so, Leopold could see clearly that private ownership as commonly understood was itself a conservation problem. Ownership gave landowners too much freedom to drag down the landscape. Worse, landowners who did so were viewed as perfectly good citizens, so long as they paid taxes and obeyed the law.

In the fall of 1946, Leopold would accentuate the need for new thoughts about ownership in a conservation platform that he prepared at the request of a fledgling (and ill-fated) political party launched to promote progressive change. In his brief statement, Leopold made no mention of the specific challenges about which he knew so much: wildlife, forestry, and soil conservation. To avoid diluting his central points, he limited his platform to two elements. Land health as conservation's overall goal appeared as the second element. What came first was Leopold's critique of American individualism and of the institution of private ownership that crystallized it:

> The average citizen, especially the landowner, has an obligation to manage his land in the interest of the community, as well as in his own interest. The fallacious doctrine that the government must subsidize all conservation not immediately profitable for the private landowner will ultimately bankrupt either the treasury, or the land, or both. The nation needs and has a right to expect the private landowner to use his land with foresight, skill, and regard for the future.[30]

With this platform element, Leopold would bring together the major strands of his thinking about private land: the land as a community of life, land health as the proper social goal, and the need for the community to counteract conservation's unfavorable economics. His critique was far more than merely a complaint against land degradation. He had rethought, from the ground up, how humans related to nature, how they related to one another, and how their well-being was ecologically linked to the well-being of the larger natural order. The legal community was not listening at the time; indeed, even Leopold's fellow conservationists had trouble making sense of his conclusions. But Leopold's ideas would remain alive, awaiting future readers.

In retrospect, Aldo Leopold's death in 1948 proved particularly costly. No one like him stepped forward to carry on his conservation work. No one could match his breadth of experience, vision, and ethical sensibilities. As the nation entered the 1950s, prosperity and the further industrialization of the landscape brought changes that would have disheartened Leopold greatly. The scientific fields that Leopold unified became the domain of narrow specialists. Few voices endeavored to link science, ethics, and aesthetics. So vigorous was the postwar exploitation of federally owned lands that national conservation groups had little choice but to put their limited resources into protecting them. As they did so, they had to turn their backs on the afflictions of private lands and on the issue of landowner rights and responsibilities. Yet the private-lands issue did not disappear for long. The environmental era of the 1960s would bring it back, leading to new laws restricting landowner powers. And out of that era would come such judicial rulings as the Wisconsin Supreme Court's 1972 opinion in *Just v. Marinette County*, with its proclamation of ecological interconnection and its proposal that private actions be limited to the land's natural uses.

Of the voices for conservation that have arisen since Leopold's death, perhaps the most wide ranging and penetrating has been that of Kentucky farmer and writer Wendell Berry. From his hilly farm along the Kentucky River, Berry has dispatched sharp critiques of the ways of the world. He has brought more of the social community into the conservation picture and has linked that community, more strongly than Leopold had, to past and future generations. He has expanded Leopold's critique of economic factors affecting land-use decision-making, while adding force to Leopold's call for a new

vision of private property. And, like Leopold, Berry has put the community and its long-term health at the top of the conservation
agenda. These various factors have led Berry, too, to call for a new
understanding of private property, for a new mix of landowner rights
and responsibilities.

Wendell Berry grew up in the 1930s and 1940s under circumstances rare for Americans at any time. He entered the world not just
in the rural neighborhood where his parents were born, but where
all his grandparents were born and where his great-grandparents
had lived. Drawn to his grandfather's farm at an early age, Berry
learned to work fields with draft horses and to manage a diverse family homestead. His sensibilities were deeply agrarian before he even
heard the word. Like Leopold, Berry developed a fascination with
and love of the soil; it sustained all terrestrial life and hence undergirded long-term fertility. Berry would differ from Leopold only in
that he would speak of soil in overtly religious terms. It was the great
connector of life and death, the mysterious medium through which
old life might lie down and rise up, resurrected. To work the fields
was a form of worship.

Berry's observations about land and land use would build upon
the years he spent conversing with respected farmers and nourishing
the soil. Land use was good only when it sustained the health of the
community, including its human members. Land health, Berry concluded, was "the one value," the one "absolute good" that upheld the
entire web of life.[31] When speaking on the subject, Berry has often
quoted English reformer Sir Albert Howard, who urged readers to
understand "the whole problem of health in soil, plant, and animal,
and man as one great subject."[32] For Berry, a community is the small-
est unit that might properly be called healthy. "To speak of the health
of an isolated individual," given the individual's dependence on the
whole, "is a contradiction in terms."[33] As Leopold did, Berry defines
this community broadly:

If we speak of a *healthy* community, we cannot be speaking of a community that is merely human. We are talking about a neighborhood of humans in a place, plus the place itself: its soil, its water, its air, and all the families and tribes of the nonhuman creatures that belong to it. If the place is well preserved, if its entire membership, natural and human, is present in it, and if the human economy is in practical harmony with the nature of the place, then the community is healthy.[34]

Even more than Leopold, Berry has regularly spoken of land use as an ethical issue—indeed, a religious one. To abuse land is immoral as well as unwise. At the same time, Berry understands the complexity of good land use and how difficult it is for anyone to use a tract well. Good land use is an art, and locally adapted skills take time to develop. In settled agrarian cultures, practical ways of using land accumulate slowly and are handed down, generation to generation. An individual's success depends upon the presence of a flourishing land-based culture.

Predictably—given his own part-time farming operations—Berry has turned his mind to the challenge of farm economics, particularly to the market forces that have debased rural communities such as his own. So competitive is farming that few farmers earn more than modest incomes, especially on marginal lands. Free trade is an important cause of the problem—particularly global trade, which forces owners to cut costs ruthlessly and to operate on ever bigger scales. Bigger scales, though, mean fewer farmers, which means fewer people to patronize community stores and fewer children in local schools. As stores and schools close, towns no longer serve as community hubs. Farmers wonder whether they themselves can survive on the land, much less whether their children can do so. With neighbors few and far between, the sense of community weakens and shared memories fade:

As local community decays along with local economy, a vast amnesia settles over the countryside. As the exposed and disregarded soil departs with the rains, so local knowledge and local memory move away to the cities or are forgotten under the influence of homogenized salestalk, entertainment, and education.[35]

The plight of farmers has powerfully shaped Berry's thoughts about private property. As a true agrarian, Berry shares Thomas Jefferson's vision of a countryside populated by farmers who attend first to their own needs and only then produce commodities for the market. Also like Jefferson, Berry draws upon important elements of natural-rights reasoning dealing with the limits on private rights. "I am an uneasy believer in the right of private property," Berry records, "because I know that this right can be understood as the right to destroy property, which is to say the natural or the given world. I do not believe that such a right exists, even though its presumed existence has covered the destruction of a lot of land."[36]

In Berry's view, the public has a rightful interest in all land, public and private. Private owners hold their titles to land under "an obligation to use it in such a way as to not impair or diminish" that public interest.[37] The entire institution, accordingly, is properly infused with ethical considerations:

> Property belongs to a family of words that, if we can free them from the denigrations that shallow politics and social fashion have imposed on them, are the words, the ideas, that govern our connections with the world and with one another: property, proper, appropriate, propriety.[38]

The connection between property and propriety is best fulfilled when land is well tended, in person, by an owner whose landholdings do not exceed the "need and use" limit set by natural law:

> The word property then, if we use it in its full sense (that is, with a proper respect for the pattern of meanings that surrounds it) always implies the intimate involvement of a proprietary mind—not the mind of ownership, as the term is necessarily defined by the industrial economy, but a

mind possessed of the knowledge, affection, and skill appropriate to the keeping and use of its property.[39]

Like Leopold, Berry has been reluctant to use the law in a heavy-handed way, pushing landowners to use their lands properly—that is, in ways that sustain the "one value," the health of the whole. Yet Berry understands private property as a cultural institution as well as a legal one, and it is entirely appropriate, he believes, for society to put social pressure on landowners to act responsibly. For Berry as for Leopold, land use is sound only when it pays attention to the land's natural features and accepts nature as an equal partner in decision-making processes. Taken seriously and together, these ideas yield a far different view of property from the now-dominant image of ownership as an abstract bundle of rights defined with little regard for the land's natural features.

It hardly needs to be said that Aldo Leopold, Wendell Berry, and others like them stand firmly in the tradition of America's stickers; they reside in the America of the settlement. The core of their message is simple and direct: the time has come for America to put the pioneer urge behind, to craft ways of living that allow life to flourish in every neighborhood, consistent with the health of the whole. One hesitates to reduce their considerable contributions to a short list, but doing so helps us to identify the elements of their thought most useful in reconceiving private rights in nature.

Preeminently, Leopold and Berry recognize that humans are embedded in social and natural communities and that their long-term well-being is linked to the well-being of these communities. Land health was Leopold's shorthand formulation of the goal he proposed to guide right living on the land. Berry has spoken more generally about the land community's health as the "one value" that humans most need to respect. A property-rights system that is justified by its ability to promote the greatest aggregate good would necessarily place great emphasis on these ideas. It would view as harmful, and thus legally suspect, land-use activities that threaten or undercut this preeminent value.

Leopold and Berry also have useful insights into conservation economics, particularly the economics of individual land use. As a result of their acute awareness of the social and ecological ties that bind parcels together, they have seen what so many others have trouble seeing: that one landowner's actions inevitably affect other owners, often in invisible ways. An owner who acts selfishly, ignoring ripple effects that spread across land and time, is almost sure to drag down the whole. When all owners act well, the community can thrive; when owners are given rein to act largely as they see fit, culturally as well as legally, socially responsible behavior becomes a challenge. Many benefits of good land use go to the community and future generations, not to the landowner. For a property-rights regime to promote conservation, it must come to terms with this stubborn reality.

Finally, both Leopold and Berry have recognized that good land use simply must become an obligation of land ownership. So important was the idea for Leopold that he placed it first in his proposed political platform, ahead even of land health. Berry in turn would emphasize the point again and again. Yet how could this idea take root in a country that gives individual liberty such a place of honor? If more people could see the ecological harms—including the wounds visible only to the trained eye—the situation might improve. But more than attentive vision was called for. Ideas of ownership, like ideas about the domination of nature, grew out of deep-rooted cultural values and practices. For lands to regain and sustain their health, cultural change needed to reach just as deep.

CHAPTER SIX

The

LURE

of

PRIVATIZATION

The challenge of using land well without degrading it—the oldest task in human history, Leopold termed it—has not proved easy for Americans. Some landowners have succeeded, but many have not, and there have been failings too in the handling of waterways, aquifers, fisheries, and wildlife populations. Some private land uses are damaging in and of themselves because of such consequences as soil erosion or contamination. Others are harmful in combination, producing landscapes that diminish human life: sprawling urban areas with congested traffic, long commutes, ugly vistas, frayed nerves, and lives detached from nature.

Why do some resources get used decently while others are abused? And what adjustments might be made to redirect landowner activities so that decent land use becomes the norm? Confident in their ways, Americans have avoided answers to questions that challenge major strands of modern culture, particularly individual liberty and free markets. Instead, they have sought narrower explanations that call merely for technical solutions or institutional tinkering.

In 1968—a time of plummeting wildlife populations and visibly polluted waterways and urban skies—biologist Garrett Hardin stepped forward with a study of resource misuse that provided just such an explanation. In a few pages of writing, centered on a single hypothetical story, Hardin seemed to capture the essence of the nation's environmental predicament. It was reassuring for matters to be so simple, particularly when one of the solutions he had to offer was so consistent with America's dominant cultural trajectory.

The essay that propelled Hardin into the public eye was a piece titled "The Tragedy of the Commons."[1] In it, Hardin considered why people who used a shared natural resource tended to overuse it, and ultimately degrade it, when their activities were unrestrained. Hardin employed the example of an unregulated pasture to illustrate his argument, which went something like this. When an individual grazier is free to add more livestock to the communal pasture, he will do so. He will add the livestock because the benefit of doing so—the extra forage eaten by the animals—is pure gain for the grazier. But the extra animals are by no means costless: adding an animal means less forage available for animals already in the pasture, and the pasture's overall productivity declines when too many animals are put on it (that is, once its biological carrying capacity is exceeded). These various costs do not fall just on the individual grazier who added the animals; they are spread among all users of the commons. The grazier who adds the animals enjoys all the gain while bearing only a portion of the total cost. Even when the total cost vastly exceeds the grazier's gain, the grazier has an incentive to keep adding animals. What is true for one grazier is also true for others: each has an incentive to drag down the pasture as a whole.

Hardin was not the first to comment on unrestrained common ownership as a cause of land degradation. Writings on the subject go back at least as far as Aristotle.[2] Sir Thomas Smith, a leading critic of land enclosures in England, noted the problem in his important 1549 work, *A Discourse on the Common Weal:* "That which is possessed of many in common is neglected of all," he wrote. "Tenants in common be not so good husbands as when every man has his part in severality."[3] Hardin added to this old wisdom the catchy phrase of his essay's title, and his phrase quickly caught on. The unregulated commons gave rise to a tragedy, he asserted, a tragedy not just in the sense of a bad outcome but in the sense that ancient Greek dramatists and Shakespeare used the term: a bad outcome caused by the inexorable working of forces that dragged people down, that flowed from a human character trait and was the predictable consequence of that trait. In the tragedy of the commons, the human trait was the penchant of people to promote their separate interests over the good of the whole. And what allowed this to happen was their individual freedom. "Ruin is the destination toward which all men rush," Hardin asserted, "each pursuing his own best interest in a society that believes in the freedom of the commons."

Modern air and water pollution, Hardin asserted, presented analogous natural tragedies. The individual who could pollute freely stood to gain by avoiding the economic costs of pollution control. The pollution itself caused harm, of course, but other people—the people downstream or downwind—largely bore that harm. Once again, benefits and costs were out of alignment. A polluter might rationally go ahead and pollute even when, for society, the costs of the harm caused by the pollution vastly exceeded the costs of halting it.

At this point, Hardin could have turned his narrative into a simple morality tale. The root of his tragedy was the selfish human nature displayed by the grazier and the polluter, their tendencies not just to favor themselves over others but to do so even when their conduct harmed others more than it benefited themselves. This was a destructive form of egotism, which Hardin might have condemned under any well-grounded ethical scheme.

Rather than take that route, though, Hardin looked for institutional arrangements that could channel or contain this resource tragedy. As he saw it, two arrangements offered promise. One approach was for group members to get together and impose restraints on themselves: "mutual coercion, mutually agreed upon," as Hardin would phrase it. If users of the commons limited one another in what each could do, they could reduce the tragedy. If they used good science and sound virtue when doing so, they might even so moderate use of the commons that it would remain healthy in perpetuity.

The second approach to avoid the tragedy was to divide the commons into private shares and assign an individual owner for each. When that was done, he argued, costs and benefits would come into better alignment. The individual grazier would now have complete control of a single parcel. The grazier would still be free to add another animal and get the gain from it, but this time the costs would all be borne by that grazier—or so Hardin assumed. Human selfishness would then no longer lead to tragedy, Hardin theorized; it would normally lead to an economically sound decision on animal-stocking levels.

Hardin's analysis met pointed criticism when it appeared, largely because of its title. Other scholars had spent lifetimes studying common-property regimes, including common grazing lands, and they knew full well that common-property arrangements sometimes worked just fine, with nothing like the tragedy Hardin predicted. What Hardin had described was essentially an open-access commons, one in which outsiders could show up at any time and start using it or in which existing users could increase their use at will. In truth, scholars have pointed out, long-term grazing arrangements do not work this way. They are highly controlled affairs in which usage is carefully restricted by one form or another of Hardin's mutual coercion, mutually agreed upon.[4]

Many readers thought that Hardin's analysis, at least once properly limited to open-access types of commons, offered great insights, both into the fundamental nature of America's environmental predicament and into how a nation devoted to individualism and private enterprise might best deal with it. If resource-use problems were caused by the tragedy of the commons and if privatization was a solution, then the best environmental policy was one that put resources into private hands. If a resource could be divided, it should be. Only resources that could not be divided, such as flowing air or migratory birds, needed to remain commonly owned and required some form of mutual coercion.

"The Tragedy of the Commons" encouraged many American readers to conclude that government regulation was not needed to promote the conservative use of private land, at least beyond the work of defining private rights and ensuring their transferability. For many readers already disdainful of government, it was just the message they wanted to hear. It also appealed to advocates of free markets and to defenders of strong private property rights. America's environmental problem was not a result of its love affair with private property, Hardin seemed to suggest: it was caused by its failure to take that love far enough, its failure to put every resource, whenever possible, into private hands.

No doubt the ideological appeal of Hardin's analysis has been one reason why so many readers have seized upon his conclusion without pausing to check how well it fits with observable facts. Hardin reached his conclusion solely by means of logical reasoning, but the claim he made was factual at root, testable with empirical data. If private owners did take care of what they owned, evidence from the field should sustain the theory.

One challenge in testing Hardin's factual claim is that it requires some means of measuring whether particular lands are being well tended. What does it mean to take care? One approach to take on this point—an approach that simplifies matters significantly—is to treat Hardin's conclusion as essentially a tautology, an argument akin to the claim that consumers spending money in the market act rationally. If rational consumer behavior is defined as essentially anything a consumer does—that is, if we assume that consumers know what they want and act consistently on the basis of what they know—then supporting facts are unneeded. To say that a consumer acts rationally is simply to say that a consumer does whatever he or she chooses to do. In the context of land use, Hardin's assertion could be treated in much the same way: Owners do whatever they want, and what they want qualifies as taking care.

Such a tautology is meaningless, of course; it explains nothing and holds out no reassurance for people who care about lands and their degradation. A more plausible approach links the landowner to the market and to market signals about how land is best used. An owner with secure, full rights in land can put it to economically valuable uses or else sell it to someone else. The human desire to promote self-interest, then, will prompt an owner to devote land to the use that, in the owner's view, generates the most value. In this view, land is properly used—its owner takes care—when its use maximizes its owner's economic return. Although it is the owner who decides highest value, the outside market provides an external, objective measure of the dollar value of land-use options.

This line of reasoning does avoid the tautology pitfall, but with a bit of probing it reveals weaknesses of its own, even if we accept its questionable assumption that one cares for land by applying it to the use that yields the most cash for the owner. Market forces work well only if owners have full information about options and about the full costs associated with them, which they may or may not have. Many landowners who produce commodities face strong external pressures to compete with other land users, and out of necessity they embrace land-use practices that bring short-term gains but sap the land's long-term productivity. Landowners can vary greatly in the ways they discount the future, yet even with a relatively low discount rate, the long-term future—a century ahead, for instance—can diminish into insignificance. Some landowners may care little about what happens after they are gone and may sap the land in short order, even when it is more rational to sell the land to another user. In addition, there are the many parts of the land community—plants, animals, rocks, waterways—that simply have no direct market value and that provide owners no incentive to care for them. Finally, landowner decisions are skewed when they can generate harms and impose them on others (by polluting air and water, for instance, or by altering natural drainage in ways that worsen flooding and droughts).

When economists address this issue, they typically start with the market and with principles of landowner behavior, reaching conclusions through logical steps. Another way of thinking about land use is to attend to the land itself in all its natural complexity, studying how land functions, how plants grow, how and why animals flourish, and how the well-being of one part of nature is linked to the well-being of other parts. For generations, natural scientists have explored the land's mechanisms of production, and it is to them that we might usefully turn for insights into long-term land use.

How humans ought to use nature's integrated order to sustain its health has not been easy to discern, even for attentive land students. Nature's ways are confusing, and human needs shift over time. Added to the mix are ethical questions, which for many people carry great weight. If humans are morally bound to preserve other species, as most people believe, then land is well tended only when other species survive. Similarly, duties to future generations of humans can affect what it means to care for land well. We may feel duty-bound (as many people do) to keep the land fertile for future generations and to preserve for future generations the same range of land-use options that we have had; if so, taking care includes fulfilling these duties.[5]

Many writers on land policy have come to embrace the overall goal of *sustainable development* as the guiding standard for taking care.[6] Land is properly used, they assert, when its use is consistent with the long-term achievement of this goal. Other observers, fearing that the development prong of the goal will overwhelm the sustainable prong, would shorten the goal to *sustainability,* a term usually defined as upholding the ability of the land as a whole to generate desired products, domesticated and wild, in perpetuity.[7] Still other observers argue that conservation policy should center on maintaining biodiversity, especially on preserving those life-forms that would inhabit a landscape but for human alteration.

One team of scholars has brought coherence to the many views on this issue of taking care by dividing current thought into two overlapping categories.[8] In one category are observers who propose that land-use practices should seek to maintain particular ecosystem functions, such as fertility cycles, hydrologic flows, and fire regimes. These are the so-called functionalists. Competing with them are observers who believe that land planning should focus instead on maintaining the land's many living parts, the plants and animals that compose (or ought to compose) a given community. These are the compositionalists, and they are at the forefront in protecting threatened and endangered species and restoring native species to their original ranges. Bridging these categories—though more inclined to the functionalist side—is the foundational work of Aldo Leopold and his writings on land health and land ethics. And, with less concern about the particulars, there is also Wendell Berry's writing about the health of the community as a whole; the "one value" as he terms it; the one absolute good that should guide human dealings with the rest of the natural world.

However phrased, such standards provide essential measures and benchmarks to use in deciding whether landowners do or do not take care of what they own. If landowners in fact fail to take care based on such standards, Hardin's privatization solution must somehow be flawed.

~~

Had Hardin penned "The Tragedy of the Commons" a decade or two earlier, its reception might well have been less favorable. More readers in the 1940s and 1950s would have grown up on the land and would have known about the problems that plagued privately owned landscapes. More of them would have retained vivid memories of the Dust Bowl decade of the 1930s, when the disasters brought on by bad landowner practices made headline news. Dust clouds rising in western Oklahoma and Kansas darkened skies in the East, filtering into congressional chambers in Washington and floating far into the Atlantic. Market pressures had something to do with Dust Bowl abuses, but a key problem—as government reports quickly recorded —was that owners were simply not giving nature due respect. They were employing land-use practices in dry places that were designed for humid climates, trying to get rich on lands ill-suited for their dreams.[9]

The Dust Bowl provided unforgettable evidence of land misuse, and under circumstances remarkably close to Hardin's common-pasture story. Former grazing lands, once used as a commons, had been divided into securely owned private tracts, with results that half the continent could see. Land-use practices, people recognized, would have to change. Careful observers of the 1930s, though, needed no such glaring evidence to know that private lands were often poorly tended, for contrary evidence was present in nearly every landscape. Congress responded to one of the most obvious problems—soil degradation—by creating the Soil Erosion Service, later renamed the Soil Conservation Service, later still the Natural

Resources Conservation Service.[10] Over the ensuing decades, the agency would spend billions of tax dollars waging battle against widespread ills on private lands—ills that, if Hardin's privatization claim were right—would not be taking place. In arid places today, irrigated agriculture on private land slowly ruins the land by crusting soil with salts. Present tree-farming methods are slowly degrading forest soils while disrupting forests as complex living ecosystems. As for the compositionalist side of land conservation, habitat degradation is the key cause of species decline, and no habitat is more on the decline than rare habitats on privately owned lands. Billions of tax dollars are annually devoted to a Conservation Reserve Program, which pays cash to private landowners to induce them to curtail damaging practices. On the not-for-profit side, one can highlight the growing land-trust movement, which pools money from concerned citizens to protect tracts of land that their owners might otherwise devote to undesired uses. Private property helps make good land use possible, but as these ongoing programs and efforts make clear, it is by no means adequate to ensure it.

What evidence from the field shows is that good land use is problematic everywhere, on private lands as well as public, largely because the challenges of achieving it are substantial. In the farmlands of the Midwest, widespread drainage efforts and polluted runoff from farm fields have seriously degraded waterways, so much so that numerous aquatic species have disappeared.[11] The Nature Conservancy has worked with landowners in a few such watersheds to improve land-use practices.[12] But their efforts largely run aground once studies are done and demonstration projects are constructed. Landowners, in truth, are pressed hard financially. Yes, they can see the degradation, particularly when it is brought to their attention. And yes, for the most part, they would like to see shifts in land practices. But the economics of farming are often such that farmers feel they have no choice but to continue acting as they do. The market is a harsh master, demanding that landowners lower costs. And lowering costs often means losing topsoil, degrading rivers, and destroying wildlife habitat.

A powerful irony arises when one investigates such watersheds and then returns to Hardin's popular narrative. In Hardin's story, private landownership creates an incentive to care for the land; it is a solution to land degradation. But in countless actual landscapes in rural America, private property is thought of in much different ways. Private property is the shield that landowners use to ward off claims that they ought to do better. Land degradation is the nagging problem; regulation is the proposed solution; and private property is the shield that keeps regulators at bay. Far from ensuring good land use, then, private property is used to protect present practices, good and bad alike.

No matter what standard one uses to measure the health of landscapes, there is little doubt that many owners fall below it. Somewhere, Hardin's privatization analysis contains flaws. To get at them, we need to return to the beginning of Hardin's story and look again at the process of dividing land into private shares. What does it mean to transform a commons into privately owned pieces? If we start with a common landscape and fragment it into individual parcels, in what way have we divided the commons?

First, assuming we have not erected fences or other barriers, we must recognize that privatization does nothing to the commons in any physical sense. The animals that scampered across it are still free to do so. The wind that blew across it still blows. The groundwater percolating beneath the surface, the birds that fly through, the insect populations that ebb and flow—none are affected by this intangible action called privatization. Nature is an integrated whole, and it remains integrated before privatization and after. Cattle will likely respect property lines (at least when bounded by barbed wire or electric fences), and so might other large mammals. But as for the latter, in what useful sense have they been privatized?

What has been divided, of course, is not the land but authority over the land, particularly the power to make decisions about it. Privatization is not chiefly a physical act but instead a matter of fragmenting rights and responsibilities among people. When a commons is intact and uncontrolled, no one has management power over it; it is an unmanaged free-for-all, precisely the kind of place that Hardin condemned. On the other hand, when a commons is well managed by all users collectively, rights and responsibilities are vested in the group as a whole. The users collectively have the power, if not to avoid the tragedy entirely, at least to diminish it considerably.

When Hardin proposed privatization as a solution, he assumed that what private owners did within their tracts would stay within those tracts. Harms associated with an owner's land use would be shouldered by the owner alone, perhaps not completely but to such a high degree that harms imposed on neighbors could be ignored. Privatizing solved the tragedy of the commons by bringing mismatched costs and benefits into alignment.

But is this so? What does happen, in terms of costs and benefits, when a natural commons is broken up?

The most obvious effect is that the scale of management becomes physically smaller. Instead of having a single management regime over a large area, there are lots of management regimes over smaller areas. And many consequences could flow from this change—some good but some definitely not so good. One not-so-good consequence is that the problem of management boundaries increases significantly. If boundaries provide incentive for land managers to ignore the effects that spill over onto neighbors, a vast increase in boundaries exacerbates the problem. When the grazing commons is intact, an effect that spreads from one part of the commons to another part remains within the same commons, and those who manage the commons are affected by it. But when the commons is divided into private shares, a boundary line might intervene between the one causing the harm and the one affected by it.

Related to the problem of harms that spill across property lines is a second problem exacerbated by the fragmentation that privatization creates: the increased difficulty of addressing ecological challenges that require planning at the landscape level. When a sound land-use plan is possible only on large spatial scales, successful planning becomes less and less likely as the land is divided into ever-smaller pieces.

Consider the case of downstream flooding caused by excessive upstream drainage. When an entire watershed is managed as a single commons, the group that drains is the group that suffers the flooding: costs and benefits are matched. When the commons is divided, however, with upstream and downstream lands separately owned, a mismatch is created. The upstream owner now has little incentive to reduce drainage. The downstream owner has reason to act but not the power; decisions about upstream drainage are not his or hers to make. The only recourse may be—as in the nineteenth-century cases of Palmer and Mrs. Sanderson—to file suit against the upstream owner and hope that the law offers relief.

The problem here is not only a matter of dividing land into private parcels. It is also a problem of dividing landscapes into smaller political units. Here, urban sprawl offers evidence. When a single governing unit controls all land planning around an urban area, it can control the rate and forms of expansion. When the political commons is divided into smaller legal entities, in contrast, externalities increase, and no person or group has the power to coordinate the whole. Division worsens the problem.

One might also consider the case of wildlife habitat, perhaps along a riparian corridor. To make the case realistic, pick one of the 99 percent of all species that lack market value. Most species today are declining in population because of habitat loss. When sufficient habitat exists within a single parcel, a parcel manager theoretically could prepare and execute a habitat-protection plan. But nearly always, critical habitat will be spread over many parcels. No single owner is able to develop a conservation plan. Once again, fragmentation of the whole gives rise to a crisis of management.

In these instances, fragmentation does not undercut all chance of cooperative management. Managers acting together can still make joint plans to remedy problems that transcend human-drawn lines on the map. But negotiations are costly, and many people balk at them for social and cultural reasons. They often do not occur, even when only two parties are involved. As the numbers increase above two, the chances of agreement fall quickly.

When Garrett Hardin and others viewed privatization as a solution to the tragedy of the commons, they implicitly embraced three assumptions that are crucial to their reasoning. They assumed that what a landowner did on his or her parcel would mostly stay within the bounds of that property; spillover effects or externalities would be minor or easily remedied. They assumed that the power of the market was sufficient to encourage owners within the bounds of their parcels to conserve what they owned. And they assumed that land-owners were able, acting alone or through easily arranged private transactions, to employ their lands in ways that amounted to good land use. It is now clear, or at least ought to be, that these assumptions are wrong to significant degrees.

It is clear, ecologically, that spillover effects are numerous, vital, and often hard to trace. Harms and benefits remain poorly matched, even when pollution laws curtail the obvious forms of air and water pollution. It is equally clear that, even within land boundaries, the market is not strong enough to promote sound, long-term land practices—as the widespread soil-erosion problem illustrates. Indeed, the competitive pressures of the market can push (or pull) landowners to embrace practices that are distinctly unwise. Finally, it is clear that much conservation work requires coordination of land uses on large spatial scales. Problems such as urban sprawl, excessive drainage, and wildlife habitat degradation are simply not matters that individual owners acting alone can handle.

If Hardin's privatization alternative has significant limitations, what of his other solution to the commons tragedy: mutual coercion, mutually agreed upon? What does it entail, and can it shed further light on the benefits and limits of privatization?

In the mutual coercion option, landowners collectively impose limits on the ways that each can use the commons. They might do so unwisely, of course, embracing rules that lead to the early destruction of the commons. But if they did their work well, what steps would they undertake? What work is needed to craft a coercive regime that successfully protects the land's vigor?

An indispensable first step is to settle upon the desired long-term condition of the land—to make a decision about what it means to take care. Once selected, this goal would set the overall limits on land use. In the case of a grazing pasture that can handle only a particular number of animals, overall animal numbers would need to stay below that. If parts of the pasture could handle more animals, if animals needed shifting from time to time, or if animal numbers required adjusting because of changed conditions, these matters too would go into the mix, affecting the total rights that users possessed.

Once overall limits were put in place, users of the commons could proceed in several ways. They could decide to use the commons together, perhaps managing their animals in communal herds or flocks. Alternatively, they could assign each user a share, allowing the user to pasture a specific number of animals, perhaps in specified locations and during specified seasons. Such rights could well be created as secure private property rights and be made fully transferable. Or the group could restrict the transfer of rights in the name of protecting the good of the whole. However this is done, private rights would be specifically designed to sustain the common good.

In all likelihood, the group of commons users would want to make its schemes more complex than this. In the real world, commons-management regimes tend to be highly sophisticated, whether they are grazing commons (which still exist), forests, or fisheries. Successful regimes provide for ongoing changes in the ways people can use the commons, mostly to respond to changes in the land itself and in its capacity to withstand use. Provision also needs to be made to bring in the next generation of users and to accommodate the shifting needs of current users. One fundamental precept: a commons regime can work only if the vast majority of local residents view it as fair and only if they sense that they have voices in its management.

We can now finally get to the bottom of Hardin's privatization alternative. What would it take for privatization to achieve the good results that commons management at its best can bring about? The overriding answer is straightforward. For privatization to work well, it must deal successfully with the same challenges that the common-property regime is forced to address. In a divided landscape as in a shared one, users need to tailor their actions to respect the well-being of the whole. In a divided landscape as in a shared one, uses need to be sensitive to nature's fluctuations. When private landowners are allowed to overuse their lands or to ignore the external effects of what they do, the private landscape can slide downward, ecologically and socially, just as an open-access commons can. Dividing the commons does not reduce the challenges of good land use; it merely divides up responsibility for achieving that goal. The challenges remain, and if information-gathering and administrative costs sometimes decline with privatization, other problems worsen: the transboundary problems, the costs of boundary enforcement, and the problems requiring landscape-scale coordination.

At root, perhaps the chief flaw in Hardin's reasoning was his failure to see that his two solutions were, in fact, variants on a single solution. He failed to note that private property itself, considered as a legal institution, is a form of mutual coercion, mutually agreed upon. When property law recognizes one person as owner, it prescribes limits on how the person can use what she owns. It sets even stricter limits on the ways that other people can use the owner's tract. Landowners agree to respect one another's rights, and nonowners accept the system's coercive limits because it benefits them as well. Mutual coercion, mutually agreed upon.

With little difficulty, one could create a private property regime and a common-property regime that are essentially identical. In both regimes, a user could hold the exclusive right to graze animals on some designated part of the grazing commons. The right could be transferable and even perpetual, though subject to the rights of the group as a whole to impose cutbacks (or increases) in usages when deemed necessary. In the common-property setting, the group typically has overt powers to limit uses patterns. But a similar lawmaking power is held in the private property setting by courts, legislatures, and city councils. In both instances, private rights evolve over time.

Centuries ago—back when land was relatively plentiful, land uses were not intensive, and actions on one parcel had few spillover effects—the categories of private and common property were more distinctly different. In such a world, private landowners could use their parcels as they saw fit; few overt problems arose, and hence

173

there was little need for coercion. But when landscapes became more congested, when land uses intensified, when spillover effects multiplied, and when social values shifted so that the public began to worry about subtle signs of long-term decline, the gap between the two options narrowed rapidly. Indeed, if the land community of the future is to remain healthy, the private property approach will need to take on even more of the trappings of a successful common-property regime. Landscapes everywhere will be made up not of two types of land—private and commons—but of a wide array of variants that blend the two.

Privatizing nature has become a cause célebrè for many harsh critics of government. Proponents portray it as a way of addressing land-use issues that is quite different from both government regulation and the management of lands as natural commons. But wherein lie the true differences? A law that precisely defines a private property right can look a great deal like a law that regulates private land use. A landscape that is divided into private tracts can remain subject to control at the level of the natural commons when lawmakers (or their private equivalents, such as homeowners' associations) limit how people can use what they own. What, then, are the practical differences between the alternative of privatization and the alternative of using government regulation?

To answer this question, one needs to get beneath the surface of the property-versus-regulation rhetoric. Under the rhetoric lie two important dichotomies or policy trade-offs. Once these two are identified, it becomes far easier to understand what the confusing privatization-versus-regulation conflict is really all about. The first dichotomy has to do with how often the legal rules of ownership get changed, the second with whether the governing legal rules will apply statewide or more locally.

Static Laws versus Dynamic Laws

Advocates of privatization recognize that detailed property laws are needed to prescribe what landowners can and cannot do; privatization is not a "no law, all market" alternative. Their assumption, though, is that such laws will remain relatively static or stable for a long period of time. Land-use regulations, in contrast, are viewed as more transient and changing; they are constantly in flux as regulators tinker with them. When property laws change only rarely, decisions about land uses are largely left to market forces to sort out—which is what privatization advocates prefer. When laws stay the same, an inefficient or unwise land use will continue until some market force brings about change (that is, until the owner either changes the land use in order to increase profits or sells the land to someone else who puts it to a new use). In a world of land-use regulations, on the other hand, government officials can get involved in dealing with such land-use decisions. They can force changes in existing or proposed land uses by rewriting regulations.

Widespread Laws versus Local Laws

When advocates of privatization talk about the laws that specify landowner rights, they also presume that such laws will apply over wide geographic regions—statewide, for instance. Such laws, because they apply widely, are usually written with a broad brush, ignoring local conditions and needs. Zoning laws and other land-use regulations, in contrast, are often more local in their reach; they are enacted by local lawmakers and vary greatly from community to community. Such regulations are often far more detailed than statewide laws. Just as with the first dichotomy, this difference between widespread and local laws carries important implications in terms of how land-use decisions are made. When local land-use regulation is involved, government officials exert more power; when statewide property laws govern (the position that privatization advocates prefer), the market does more.

These two dichotomies expose the real issues underlying the privatization debate. To uncover them is to see that this debate does, in fact, have something to do with the government's role vis-à-vis the market's. But the two alternatives (static and widespread versus dynamic and local) are not directly opposed on this issue; their outcomes overlap considerably and their differences are easily exaggerated. In any event, it is hard to know which to prefer—the private property approach or the regulation approach—without considering the relative advantages and disadvantages of each. And the best way to do that is to cut through the rhetoric and to ask directly: When is it wise to have private property laws that are relatively static and wide-ranging (the private property approach), and when is it better instead to have private property laws that are more dynamic and locally produced (the government regulation approach)? On the issue of widespread versus local laws, there is a related concern: Is it better to have property laws written by legislators who work at the state level (or at some other large spatial scale) or for local people to be more involved?

These questions are all good ones, and they have no easy answers. Indeed, one can readily list advantages and disadvantages to each position. Frequent changes in the law, for instance, can unsettle expectations, and the more often the law is changed, the greater the opportunity for changes that are misguided. On the other hand, static laws get out of date and, over time, can authorize landowners to engage in activities that bring net social costs. Local lawmakers can ignore the larger geographic contexts in which they live, and yet local laws can also be more responsive to local needs and local conditions. In short, it is impossible in the abstract to prefer either alternative.

The fair-minded position is to recognize that both involve trade-offs and that details are important.

In the popular rhetoric of recent years, these important policy issues have been reduced to slogans about market versus government or privatization versus regulation as solutions to land degradation. Like most slogans, these confuse more than they illuminate. They take difficult policy issues and recast them in simplistic terms. In reality, privatizing nature is such a vague idea as to have little clear meaning. Far better, in terms of promoting good discussions and clear public thought, is to focus squarely on the real issues at stake.

When all is said and done, privatization of a landscape is no silver bullet. It is no magic mechanism to turn land degraded by private greed into a healthy, beautiful place for people to live. A people who want to live in a place well, in high numbers, and with modern technology have no choice but to study the nature around them, to identify its limits, and to shape their activities to fit within those limits. Individual landowners could do some of this work, but many of them do not; and when they do not, they drag others down with them. Moreover, even well-meaning landowners cannot address by themselves such landscape-scale problems as urban sprawl and wildlife habitat protection.

Garrett Hardin was fundamentally right in his analysis of the unregulated commons. The open-access commons is a prescription for tragedy. But probably more important than the tragedy of the commons, in terms of the environmental predicament in the present-day United States, is the *tragedy of fragmentation:* the tragedy that occurs when landscapes are divided into small pieces with no mechanisms available to correct market failures and achieve landscape-scale goals. The more fragmented a landscape becomes, the harder it is to make sensible, large-scale plans. Externalities increase. Market imperfections rise. Transaction costs escalate. It becomes ever harder to identify sources of problems and trace their ripple effects. It becomes infeasible if not impossible for people to pursue goals that require coordinated action.

In the land-use arena, America's problem is not chiefly that the commons needs dividing; it is that the natural commons has been overly divided in terms of decision-making powers. Rather than needing stronger or clearer powers to act individually, landowners collectively need greater control over the landscapes they share. Without that control, their landscapes are tragically doomed.

CHAPTER SEVEN

The

MARKET TRAIN

Like many regions in the United States, south Texas faces a widening gap between its natural supply of fresh water and the demand for that water. In the San Antonio area, water comes from the Edwards aquifer, which is far from adequate to satisfy the demands made on it. When area residents were few, the aquifer was ample to irrigate farm fields and to meet household and urban needs. As populations rose and lifestyles became more water-intensive, shortages inevitably developed. To increase the supply, groundwater pumpers drilled wells deeper and extracted water faster than the aquifer's natural recharge rate. Predictably, groundwater tables declined steadily, threatening farms, cities, and natural areas. In one form or another, a legal regime was needed to limit who could withdraw water and how much.[1]

During the late 1990s, the Edwards Aquifer Authority crafted a set of rules to govern groundwater withdrawals. It then conducted public hearings to solicit comments on them. So evident was the water shortage that nearly everyone accepted both the need to limit pumping and the wisdom of using a permit scheme to do so. What the hearings came to focus on were the terms of the water rights that permit holders would receive. Would pumping rights be independent items of private property that an owner could sell to someone else, or would they—as in the past—be firmly attached to a tract of land, usable only on that land and salable only if the land itself was sold? Only if water rights could be severed from the land and sold separately could water become a tradable market commodity. And only if that happened could a regional water market develop—a market that, according to advocates, could satisfy all of the highest-valued water uses.

Under the proposed rules, pumping permits in the Edwards aquifer would largely be handed out to existing water users, based on historic water-use patterns. This meant that water would go mostly to irrigators, given the history of water use in the region. The growing demand for water, though, lay in the region's urban areas, particularly San Antonio. San Antonio needed water to keep expanding, and according to city officials it could only get that water by buying rights from farmers. So vital was the issue that the president of the San Antonio Water System appeared at one hearing to plead for rules that would transform groundwater into a marketable commodity. Urban users were willing to pay more for water than irrigators could possibly afford; in an open market, San Antonio could meet its needs.

The aquifer authority's proposed new rules significantly limited the amount of water that farmers could sell, and to whom. Irrigation water could only be used on farms, not held for speculation or diverted to golf courses and suburban lawns. Farmers could sell only the water that they conserved by irrigating more efficiently. Accordingly, San Antonio could not simply enter a farming community, buy its water, and leave the place dry. Strict limits on sale were needed, the aquifer authority announced, to protect rural economies and keep speculators from driving prices up. When one farmer sold out and ceased irrigating, the ecology of neighboring farms could be disturbed, given the interconnection among lands and land uses. If enough farmers in an area sold out, the infrastructure needed to support agriculture would erode, making it harder for remaining farmers to stay in business. To protect the farming economy, water needed to remain where it was.

San Antonio's objections to the proposed restrictions on water transfers were easy enough to understand: it needed water and had money to buy it. So too were the objections of large commercial farmers such as the Lone Star Growers, who knew that if water transfers were unrestricted, they could sell their water for top dollar. But joining the ranks of the objectors were the Environmental Defense Fund (now known simply as Environmental Defense) and the Sierra Club. In jointly filed comments, they also asked the aquifer authority to ease transfer limits so that a true market in water rights could develop. If cities wanted to buy and farmers wanted to sell, argued the conservation groups, the sales should go through. If speculators wanted to make money trading water, stimulating a more active market, that too would be fine under the circumstances. Farm-to-city transfers of water did not directly benefit the environment; urban uses were typically no less troubling than rural ones. But such transfers could avoid the need to build new reservoirs, diversion systems, and related environmentally damaging projects. Environmentally speaking, it was better for San Antonio to get its water from nearby farms than to drain a river or another aquifer hundreds of miles away.

Water marketing has gained popularity these days as a means of shifting water from low-valued uses such as irrigated farming to high-valued uses, including ski resorts (to make snow) and vineyards (to protect against frost). While the Texas hearings were taking place, Micron Technology in southeastern Utah was arranging a water-rights swap with the Bureau of Reclamation to gain secure access to the water it needed (2 million gallons per day) to clean and cool its silicon chips. At the same time, conservation interests in Nebraska were constructing an imaginative plan to create a water-rights "bank" to protect Platte River waterfowl. Under the plan, willing farmers would lease water to the bank during dry years, with the water then left in the river to support wildlife, public recreation, and other "in-streamflow" uses.

Among conservation groups, Environmental Defense has been the most active in its support of such deals, particularly in the noisiest of all water battlegrounds, southern California. For decades, California's thirsty coastal cities have turned desiring eyes on the massive water flows that invigorate the nearby desert. It was Environmental Defense that helped facilitate a deal by which Los Angeles paid desert irrigators to implement water-conserving measures, with Los Angeles, in exchange, gaining rights to use the water saved. San Diego, desperate for water, has tried similar arrangements, even as it looks for opportunities to buy up irrigated farmland, transfer the water, and leave the desert to reclaim its own.

Enthusiasm for water marketing builds upon a long and venerated American tradition of turning nature into a mart. Colonial Americans began buying and selling nature practically from the moment they stepped ashore. To do that, they first had to divide nature into commodities, such as acres of land, iron-ore mines, and waterwheel sites.[2] This decidedly utilitarian and individualistic mode of valuing nature has been dominant in American culture for a full two centuries. Nature has been a storehouse of resources that gain value only through human use, not an integrated ecological whole to be studied and valued as such.

For generations, enthusiasts have touted the market as an efficient mechanism for exploiting America's lands and waters. New today is the claim that markets are equally efficient in promoting far different goals: reducing pollution and fostering sustainable practices on private lands such as the Wisconsin wetlands that the Justs wanted to fill, for instance, or protecting the beaver lodges and dams that Barrett and his neighbors wanted to destroy to protect their trees. According to market advocates, environmental problems today arise in large part because pricing mechanisms are badly skewed. When polluters are allowed to externalize their harmful wastes, free of charge, their production costs are artificially lowered and they generate more wastes than they should. When natural resources are un-tradable, they get stuck in low-valued—often wasteful and damag-ing—uses. New, high-valued resource users then must scramble to meet their needs by increasing the overall supply of the resource. In the case of water, the search for new supplies has prompted costly new reservoirs and pipelines that carry water hundreds of miles. In the process, waterways and natural ecosystems have suffered. If the market worked better and if users of nature absorbed the full costs of their use, so the argument goes, new uses could typically be met by shifting resources among existing users, without need of squeezing nature harder to extract even more from it.

Properly structured, in short, and given free rein to operate, the market can bring significant conservation benefits to privately owned lands and landscapes, or so its defenders claim. And it can do so without the kind of moral reform that Aldo Leopold, Wendell Berry, and others have thought necessary and without having to craft a new understanding of private ownership. There is no need for much in the way of fundamental cultural or legal change, they assert; no need for heavy-handed restraints on how landowners act. Simply buy a ticket on the market train, and let the market do most of the work.[3]

Market enthusiasts have pushed hard to turn more of nature into private property, with resource rights defined in ways that facilitate markets. Limits on transferring such resources and on how and where resources can be used are regularly challenged. Also chal-lenged are the detailed bureaucratic rules that prescribe how pol-luters must cut back on their emissions. Too often, the argument goes, lawmakers have combated pollution by using "command-and-control" rules enforced by massive bureaucracies. Bureaucrats allegedly stifle technological ingenuity and raise pollution-control costs when they tell companies how to cut back their pollution and by how much. The more efficient approach, proponents say, is to discard such regulations and unleash the powerful market. If the market took the place of regulations, polluters would limit pollution whenever they could do so more cheaply than the industry-wide average.

In recent years, "free-market environmentalism" of this type has gained considerable intellectual momentum, led by conservative, probusiness think tanks. And although its history has been relatively brief, it has already scored important victories. None has been touted more than the 1990 revision of the federal Clean Air Act, in which Congress took its most forceful step in using market forces to control industrial pollution. Before then, tradable pollution rights were used only occasionally, in the phaseouts of leaded gasoline and ozone-depleting chlorofluorocarbons (CFCs). The 1990 act gave the technique its most challenging trial run, to bring about low-cost reductions in the emission of sulfur dioxide by coal-burning electric utilities.

Congress dealt with the 110 worst sulfur emitters in 1990 simply by ordering them to make prescribed reductions as a group. The law gave polluters flexibility in how to go about achieving these reductions and did not mandate the use of any particular pollution-control technology. In addition, the law allowed individual polluters to over-pollute, so long as they bought rights to do so from other utilities. By giving utilities tradable pollution rights (or allowances, as the law termed them), the law created an incentive for utilities to reduce pollution more than the required amounts. Utilities that did so could either save their unused allowances for later use or sell them for cash.

By all accounts, the sulfur-reduction program set up in 1990 has been a big success. Pollution has been reduced even below target levels. The costs of reduction have fallen far below the predicted costs of new scrubber technology. Flush with this success, market proponents have pushed for similar trading schemes for other air pollutants, such as nitrogen oxide, a precursor to ground-level ozone formation. Impatient with the pace of federal action, states have moved ahead with intrastate trading schemes covering nearly all of the half-dozen pollutants subject to national ambient air-quality standards. On the water-pollution front, several states have experimented with schemes that allow factories and other point-source polluters to avoid further pollution cutbacks if they can successfully pay farmers, timber harvesters, or other non-point-source polluters to reduce runoff pollution through better land-use practices. Finally and perhaps most conspicuously, there are proposals to address global climate change by creating systems of tradable pollution rights in carbon dioxide and other climate-changing gases.

Markets in pollution rights are credited with an impressive list of virtues, much like those credited to markets in water rights. They can reduce overall pollution rates at lower cost than bureaucratic alternatives. They entail less government involvement, thereby reducing tax expenditures and speeding the emergence of green technology. Unlike command-and-control methods, market approaches supply incentives for bad actors to do better than legal mandates: irrigators can sell every gallon conserved; polluters can do the same with unused pollution allowances.

So great are the market's virtues, according to some free-marketers, that it can even tell us what level of environmental amenities we really want. Properly functioning water markets can tell us how much water should remain in rivers to support crayfish and river rafters and how much should bathe golf courses and computer chips. Pollution-trading schemes can tell us whether the ill effects of nutrient-laden rivers are more or less tolerable, in dollar-cost terms, than the price tags for new sewage treatment facilities. The challenges of creating and operating such markets are often large. But when markets work well, so it is urged, they achieve wonders.

Free-market environmentalism aims to make decisions about resource uses responsive to the more disciplined signals of the market rather than to governmental mandates. To get the market train purring this well—to get the prices right, as the slogan goes—market proponents have assembled a large box of tools, some used to expand the market's reach, others to mimic market processes. A tax on pollution, for example, a powerful if politically awkward tool, helps correct market distortions that arise when polluters can push harms onto outsiders without cost to themselves. A tax on the use of new raw materials can have a similar effect: it pushes users of such materials to take into account the adverse environmental impacts that inevitably arise when minerals are extracted or trees are cut.

Mitigation requirements, another free-market tool, force developers to absorb the costs of harms caused when they destroy or consume ecologically valuable lands. They work by forcing a developer who destroys a valuable wetland or wildlife habitat to compensate for the loss by constructing a similar-sized wetland or habitat area nearby. Faced with such a requirement, the developer will consider the ecological damage before deciding whether and where to develop. Less complicated are liability rules, common law and statutory, that require polluters who cause harm to pay damages to those who are injured. Not much more complicated are volume-based garbage hauling schemes, which require people to pay for each bag of garbage they generate rather than a flat monthly fee; such a pricing scheme yields more sensitive price signals and provides incremental incentives to reduce waste. When regulations are needed to curtail environmental harms such as pollution, the market-oriented approach is simply to set performance standards, typically specific pollution maximums, leaving it to polluters themselves to figure out the cheapest way to comply.

As useful as these various tools are, they nonetheless stand at the edge of free-market environmental thought. At the center is the construction of actual markets in resources and environmental amenities, whether in water, pollution emissions, conservation easements, river rafting rights, scenic views, free-flowing river segments, or migratory bird nesting spots. Fundamentally, the market is about cutting deals. And when it comes to the environment, proponents say, that is just what needs doing. Markets mean efficiency. Efficiency means low cost. Low cost means that society can afford more of what it wants—including, if people choose, such things as clean rivers, grizzly bears, and mature forests filled with birdsong. If we would only hop aboard the market train, it would carry us to a healthy land.

The claims made by market enthusiasts are grand ones, so alluring in their advertised benefits that they need to be taken seriously. To make sense of them, though, one needs to get out another tool—a paring knife—to cut away the soft from the sound. In the case of free-market environmentalism, arguments are thick with exaggeration.

The market train, in truth, is less new and less powerful than its advocates claim. More vitally, the train needs a human engineer, along with attentive, disciplined passengers, people able to think clearly and talk sensibly about where the train ought to head. The market can be a potent tool, but only if it is well embedded in a communal order and in a sound ethical and ecological view of the human place in nature. Without that, the market can do what it has done for centuries: bring destruction to the land.

To begin with, most tools referred to as market-based have little to do with putting markets to work for good environmental ends. A standard story told about environmental degradation portrays the uncontrolled market largely as villain, rewarding polluters for externalizing their costs and providing incentives for clear-cutting forests and depleting fisheries. As it turns out, most of the free-marketers' tools are premised, however quietly, on the truth of this indictment.

Many free-market tools are used not to harness the market to achieve something good but to restrain the market from producing so much harm.[4]

Pollution taxes, raw-materials fees, liability rules, volume-based pricing schemes—these and related tools all have the modest aim of getting exploiters of the land to pay for what they damage or consume. That aim, to be sure, is a worthy one, but it leaves exploiters free to degrade as much as they can afford. Other tools in the free-market box involve the easing of regulatory requirements so that regulated parties can select less costly compliance methods. Again, the aim—saving money—is worthy enough, but no market is needed to create incentives of this type. Robinson Crusoe, alone on his island, had plenty of incentive to work efficiently in his marketless world; time that he did not spend harvesting food was time he could spend exploring or resting.

Flexibility in complying with a pollution-control law arises when a polluter is allowed to decide on its own how to achieve a particular pollution reduction target. All things being otherwise equal, laws ought to allow as much flexibility as possible in achieving a specified pollution-reduction or resource-use goal. But in the case of environmental laws, the advent of such flexibility in compliance has come about mostly because of a weakening of the original environmental vision that Congress endorsed a generation ago. When Congress told the Environmental Protection Agency (EPA) to identify the pollution-control technology that various industries should use, its long-term goal was to compel use of the technology that did the best job of protecting the environment, at least so long as most polluters could afford it. Federal statutes typically required (and still require) that pollution permits be based on the pollution-control technology that is the "best available" or "maximum achievable" for a given industry. The EPA stumbled, however, rarely pushing polluters as hard or as far as Congress originally intended. In the era of flexible compliance, the goal of using the best technology has largely disappeared. Flexibility in choosing technology arises precisely because polluters do not have to use the best. Performance goals are set low enough that polluters can often satisfy them using a variety of pollution-reduction methods, some more expensive and effective than others.

Only a few free-market tools have to do with using the market to achieve positive environmental gains or to avoid environmental harms. Markets in private water rights have that good outcome when they keep dams and long pipelines from being built. Pollution trading rights—a new form of private property—can have the same good result when pollution-reduction goals are ambitiously set. Even in such cases, however, it is easy to exaggerate the benefits of markets. Water markets merely divert water to the highest bidder; if top bidders (such as San Antonio or San Diego) want to drain a river dry, watering lawns and golf courses, the market is quick to comply. In the sulfur-emissions program, the actual costs saved in reducing sulfur emissions had only a little to do with the trading system itself, despite loose claims made to the contrary. Savings came largely because the law allowed utilities to reduce pollution by shifting to low-sulfur coal—a much cheaper method of reducing sulfur than using scrubbers. (The requirement to use scrubbers had been inserted years earlier not by environmentalists but by the high-sulfur coal industry to keep utilities buying their coal.) The sudden rise in using low-sulfur coal from the Rocky Mountains prompted railroads to upgrade their freight service, resulting in lower shipping rates and further reducing compliance costs. The trading scheme, in short, helped reduce pollution-control costs only modestly; as for the overall reduction in sulfur emissions, it was the result not of market forces but entirely of Congress's "command-and-control" order to cut back.

Having pared down the exaggerated claims about the benefits of market tools, one is left with a small but nonetheless valuable core of free-market claims. Resistance to environmental protection arises largely from concerns over cost, so the more cheaply it can be done, the more likely protection is to take place. If San Diego is going to get its water, come what may, it is better that the water come from efficiencies in irrigation than from pipelines snaking south from Oregon.

Proponents of any policy approach are prone to exaggeration, so it is only a mild rebuke of free-market advocates to point out that they overplay their hands. There are, however, deeper worries about the free-market approach that have to do with the dangers posed by the free-market tools themselves, by the assumptions that underlie them, and by the messages they convey.

The dangers of market approaches are most evident when the case for markets is presented in its strongest form: when enthusiasts claim that a well-functioning market can supply sufficient incentives for land conservation, including the conservation of endangered species, while remedying pollution and other harmful externalities. These are alluring claims, but they rest upon assumptions that are empirically weak and morally questionable. Beyond that, they convey messages that make it harder for people to perceive the land ecologically and to grasp the moral complexity of the human plight on earth.

Correcting Market Failures

For a market to function efficiently, whether in water rights, sulfur emissions, or wildlife habitat, the common failings of the market first need to be addressed. One of them, as market advocates understand, is the problem of externalities—the harms that one landowner imposes on others without incurring liability—and many of their tools are aimed at limiting it. But externalities are far easier to redress in economic models than they are in the real world, where they are numerous, complex, hard to trace, and often impossible or undesirable to reverse. Other well-known market failings also need to be addressed: for one, market participants often lack full information about options and costs; for another, market transactions can be costly and culturally awkward to undertake, particularly when many parties are involved and facts are complex. Some of these market failings worsen when, as in Garrett Hardin's grazing scenario, nature is divided into smaller pieces and boundaries correspondingly increase. To the extent that market failings remain uncorrected (as they always do to one degree or another), market decisions are flawed.

Variations in Local Effects

For markets to work well, buyers and sellers of goods (and of rights to commit environmental harms) need to be able to move resources around and to use them in different places, without significant legal restraints. For a water market to develop, for instance, purchasers need to be able to shift the water they buy to the place where they want to use it—perhaps hundreds of miles away. Similarly, for pollution permits to work, a buying polluter needs to be able to pollute at its own location, perhaps far distant from the seller's location. Land, of course, cannot be moved around, but if a market program in conservation easements is to work, there must be some rough equation in the benefits that come from conserving land in one place versus conserving it in another. In some settings, it does make little difference where a resource is used or where pollution is emitted. A water withdrawal from an aquifer could have the same affect on the aquifer without regard for where the water is withdrawn and where it is used. CFCs emitted from one location may have the same effect on the upper atmosphere as CFCs emitted from another location thousands of miles away. But in the case of most environmental problems, an activity's precise location does affect its environmental consequences, often greatly. When this is true, a shift in a resource (or pollution right) from seller A to buyer B could either improve or worsen environmental conditions, in ways that the market ignores. The mining-polluted water that affected Mrs. Sanderson, for instance, may have done far less damage if dumped into a waterway much larger than Meadow Brook.

Most water is extracted from rivers, and the effects of withdrawing and using the water vary significantly from place to place. A small stream suffers more than a large river when water is extracted or pollution is allowed to enter. How water is used and where it is used alters the amount and timing of the return flow and hence the welfare of the waterway to which the water returns. Shipping water outside its watershed of origin by long-distance pumping can prove particularly damaging to resident aquatic and human life. Trading rights to emit CFCs and greenhouse gases makes sense; trading water-use rights often does not (a fact that conservation groups understand but many trading-rights advocates do not).

While the Texas water-rights hearings were in progress, the problems of local pollution effects were brought to the fore in a California dispute. Communities for a Better Environment filed suit in Los Angeles, challenging a market-based pollution measure implemented by the South Coast Air Quality Management District. The group expressed concern about the emission of air pollution by oil tankers in neighborhoods around marine fuel-transfer terminals. Each unloading oil tanker emitted 6 tons of dangerous, volatile vapors—emissions easily controlled by installing vapor recovery systems. Air-quality managers, however, allowed fuel companies to forgo installing the recovery systems if they reduced regional pollution an equal or greater amount by purchasing old, polluting cars and taking them off the road, in effect pushing drivers to shift to less polluting modes of transport. The car-scrapping plan improved air quality regionally (in theory at least) and at lower cost to the fuel companies, but it created air-pollution "hot spots" around fuel terminals and nearby low-income communities. The trading scheme, in short, exacerbated localized pollution problems, to the considerable disadvantage of low-income neighborhoods.

Such variations in local effects could be taken into account by, for instance, a law restricting any market transfer of resources (or pollution rights) that would worsen the environmental outcomes. The problem with such a law is that the more restrictive the law is—the more it takes into account differences among local environmental effects—the harder it is for a market to work with any efficiency, because markets work best when goods are freely transferable from place to place. This problem of variations in local effects also crops up in a widely endorsed variant on true market mechanisms: government programs that pay private owners to use their property wisely. Incentive programs allow landowners to participate or not as they see fit; it is the lure of gain that brings action, not legal compulsion. A problem with such schemes is that they typically treat millions of acres as if they were alike in conservation terms, when they are not. The payments are the same, but the conservation benefits—the things that taxpayers are buying—vary greatly from place to place. Voluntary programs are also deficient in that they provide no means for achieving conservation goals that require the protection of particular lands. It is impossible, for instance, to assemble a contiguous corridor for migrating animals when each landowner along the corridor gets to decide whether or not to participate.

The Assumption of Accurate Valuation

Markets of all types are notorious for their ruthless assignments of value, and environmental markets are among the most heartless.

Free-market thought assumes the market's ability to place an accurate value on each commodity. In the case of nature, however, too many parts have little or no market value, even when their true value to society is vast. Species that humans do not make use of directly are pushed aside thoughtlessly, however important in sustaining ecosystem processes and providing a pleasing, diverse landscape. Ecological communities such as mature forests do have market value, and the market does supply an incentive to keep them productive. But the market values the individual trees, not the forest as an ecological whole. Managing for maximum timber production can degrade a forest's roles in protecting watersheds, cleaning air, and harboring wildlife, as residents of northern New England well knew a century ago. Indeed, managing land to maximize any crop—including such natural crops as elk or grouse for hunters—can derange the land ecologically.

The Market's Power to Cleanse

Implicit in the free-market emphasis on accurate pricing is the assertion that those who pay full value for a thing have adequately fulfilled their environmental duties, morally and legally. A person who pays full price for a can of tuna has no moral connection to the catching and processing of the tuna. If she also pays full price for garbage collection, she need not worry about the empty can once the garbage truck pulls away. The market, the claim goes, cleanses these transactions morally. If a half-filled can of dangerous weed killer is thrown into a leaky landfill, it is the landfill owner's fault, not the can owner's.

By embracing this perspective, the market promotes too simplistic a moral view. To buy a product is inevitably to become tied to its history and to accept a level of responsibility for its future.[5] In many legal settings, the market is not viewed as a complete cleansing agent.

For generations, civilized nations have objected to goods produced by slave labor and have viewed such goods as tainted in a way that the market cannot absolve. Similar objections have arisen over shoes and clothes made by children in unsafe factories; those who buy them are morally implicated in the mistreatment of the workers, particularly if they know of the mistreatment. For centuries, Anglo-American law has imposed liability on possessors of stolen goods; like goods produced by slaves, they remain tainted as they pass from hand to hand.

More than it has, conservation policy needs to connect people with their ecological footprints, making them aware of, and morally implicated by, the ecological costs incurred in supplying their goods and whisking away their wastes. So long as buyers are disconnected from environmental harms associated with their goods—as the market encourages them to be—they will reward sellers who keep market prices down, including sellers who take environmentally damaging shortcuts.

Consumer versus Citizen

In its moderate, useful forms, free-market thought acknowledges that the market's prime attribute—efficiency—is not a social goal. An efficient market is a means, not an end. An efficient market supplies individuals with whatever they want at lowest cost, be it healthy land abounding in biological diversity or chemically bathed blue-grass lawns. The market determines what people want, overall, by aggregating their dollar "votes" as individuals, then translating those votes into a low-cost stream of goods and services. But what people want as individuals is often quite different from what they want collectively as citizens and community members. A market that responds solely to aggregate consumer preferences (as markets typically do) will often give people, paradoxically, a community and a world that they do *not* really want.[6]

As individual consumers interacting with one another only through the market, residents of a region might choose to carve a wilderness area into individual homesites. If the same people instead came together as citizens, taking time to consider the wilderness and how they might best use it, their consensus decision might well differ. They might decide to protect the wilderness as a nature preserve, using it for recreation but keeping roads few and homes clustered around the edge.[7]

Free-market advocates in recent years have challenged this citizen-consumer dichotomy. Because self-interest always rules, they claim, individuals have the same policy preferences whether acting as consumers or as citizens—public opinion polls notwithstanding. As a factual matter, it is easy to counter this criticism. In fact, citizens often do support costly community programs that yield them few or no personal benefits. One need look no further than the many tax referenda that are approved by voters who enjoy no direct benefit from them. But even putting such evidence to one side and assuming that individual self-interest rules, there is a logical flaw in the argument. One can see it by returning to Garrett Hardin's tragedy of the commons. Hardin assumed that each grazier would act in his self-interest, grazing additional cows and bringing destruction to the communal whole. But what if the grazier had a chance to play a citizen role rather than the consumer role that Hardin assigned him? What if the grazier had a chance to get together with other users of the commons to make collective decisions about the pasture? Now self-interest would lead the grazier to vote for restrictions on additional grazing. As consumer, the grazier would add a cow; as citizen, the grazier would vote for a ban.

The difference in outcomes, of course, flows logically from a grazier's decision to promote self-interest when acting both as consumer and as citizen. In the open-access commons, the grazier who adds a cow gets all the benefits while sharing the costs. The grazier who forgoes adding cows in the open-access setting is in precisely the opposite situation: as consumer, he incurs all the costs of restraint, while the conservation benefits of his restraint are enjoyed by all. When the grazier acts instead as a citizen, the calculus shifts completely. Now self-interest dictates cooperation and legal restraint; the grazier who agrees to limit grazing benefits because the restraints imposed on everyone keep the pasture more productive. The same holds true in the case of people who deal with a wilderness as discrete consumers. As a consumer, a person might charge in and build a home, figuring that if he does not build, someone else will and the wilderness in any event will disappear. As a citizen, the same person, acting on self-interest, might logically vote to protect the wilderness.

To get to this point is to see why the market is far from a neutral institution and why unrestrained markets so often frustrate conservation. The market compels people to act alone or through voluntary alliances (which are costly and often impossible to arrange). As such, it competes directly with modes of decision-making in which people are allowed to act, directly or through representatives, as citizens. The market enhances the liberty of people to act as individual consumers; it undercuts severely their liberty to act otherwise.

The prime virtue of markets is that they do well in supplying people with goods and services that they can largely enjoy without sharing them with others. The downside of markets is that they do increasingly less well as more and more of the benefits are enjoyed by people who do not pay for them. When the benefits of a good (such as conservation) accrue to the community as a whole, market mechanisms fail almost entirely—unless a selfless citizen steps forward to contribute resources to benefit the community. One might hope, of course, that benevolent millionaires or billionaires will be around to do such a good thing, buying land or conservation easements for the public good. But to count on their presence is surely foolhardy, just as foolhardy as hoping that benevolent donors will fund national defense. Indeed, one might as well hope to solve the tragedy of the grazing commons by awaiting a wealthy patron who pays all graziers to refrain from overgrazing.

At bottom, the market is simply not a good mechanism for making many key decisions. The market's most exalted promise is merely efficiency—typically a good trait when selecting among means to achieve an end but hardly an end in and of itself. If a community desires to protect endangered species, it makes sense to find efficient ways to do so. But efficiency cannot tell people whether species are worth saving and, if so, how much they should spend on it. The decision to save species requires an all-things-considered judgment about how people ought to live. Sound judgments come out of collective processes that are informed, deliberative, and morally challenging—the kind of processes that the market undercuts.

The Market's Misguided Messages

Not the least of the problems markets present are the powerful messages they convey about the natural world, about how people ought to live in that world, and about how people ought to relate to one another. As portrayed by the market, nature is a collection of resources; a warehouse of parts and pieces that are available to buy and sell. To focus on nature's parts, however, is to overlook the interconnections that link the pieces together, the known connections as well as the unknown ones. By presenting nature in this way, the market pushes people to think of nature in purely utilitarian terms; to think of the potential homesites on a tract and forget the resident beaver and the ecological health of the waterways they help sustain. Value in the market means value to humans with money to spend, which in turn means purely human-centered value. Yet to value nature in this way—to let the market set value, that is—is to avoid grappling with tough moral questions, including questions about the intrinsic value of nonhuman nature and about duties owed to future generations, both nonhuman and human.

A related market message, equally troubling, is the stamp of legitimacy that the market imposes on individual self-centered behavior. The market encourages behavior by rewarding it financially. However effective economic incentives might be, they ultimately do not push people to look beyond their own personal self-interest; and healthy communities, in the end, will never come about so long as individuals look out only for themselves. As a short-term tactic, conservation policy can take advantage of individual greed. In the long term, it needs to lead people to care for what they possess in common as well as what they possess individually.

Along with sanctioning self-centered behavior, the market conveys unhelpful messages about the ways people properly relate to one another. In the market, people act as producers and consumers, not as citizens charged with considering the common good. To exalt the market, then, is to emphasize the role of consumer and to diminish and belittle one's calling as citizen. In the market, people often relate competitively rather than cooperatively; they strive like runners in a race, straining to get ahead, rarely coming together face to face to talk about connections and shared interests.

Perhaps the most troubling message of the market arises from its very ability to produce so many things so successfully. From comfortable cars to supersonic jets to bone-rattling home theaters, the market's accomplishments are impressive. A market that can do these things—so the implicit message suggests—is a market that can satisfy every want and need. But the truth is much to the contrary. The market has never given rise to a healthy land in which to live, and it is not on the verge of doing so today. When dealing with such collective goals, there is no substitute for rolling up the sleeves of citizenship and getting to work.

In his short story "The Celestial Rail-road," Nathaniel Hawthorne challenged the technological optimism of his day by retelling John Bunyan's classic tale, *Pilgrim's Progress*. Hawthorne's pilgrim Christian, removed from Puritan England and set down in America during the industrial revolution, chose to forgo his predecessor's arduous footpath toward the Celestial City, instead traveling in comfort by train. With technology carrying him onward and Mr. Smooth-it-away as his companion, the industrial-age pilgrim quickly bypassed the moral trials and pitfalls that so troubled his pedestrian ancestor. Technology, it seemed, had obviated the need for him to steel his heart and contain his pride, just as it had softened the rigors of winter and the toils of long-distance travel.

Hawthorne's allegory ends, predictably, with the train falling short of the Celestial City. The pilgrim must retrace his route and undergo the same moral challenges as his predecessor. Industrial technology, it turns out, provides only a facade of moral progress, however useful it is in satisfying more material needs.

The technological optimism of the nineteenth century finds its modern counterpart in the market enthusiasm of the early twenty-first century. The market as much as the railroad is a useful tool, but discipline is needed to use it well. It does not obviate the need to reshape values and visions, individually and collectively. Like the railroad, the market is no panacea. Indeed, when left alone, the market has brought considerable destruction—to the beavers of New York State and the rivers of Pennsylvania's coal districts, to the forests of New England and the aquifers of the American Southwest.

In the end, market-based tools need to fit into a larger scheme of environmental policy. Like Hardin's vision of privatization, the market is no simple tool to use to achieve healthy lands and communities. Healthy lands and communities can come only from public policies that have as their aim not the promotion of markets but something far different.

CHAPTER EIGHT

PRIVATE PROPERTY

for an

ECOLOGICAL AGE

It is hardly surprising that private land ownership as an institution is under such stress today. Pleas for conservation, the ardent cries of developers and extractive industries, and polemical calls for privatization and greater faith in the market—all are putting pressure on it. New values and circumstances have arisen in American culture, many conservation related, and they have pressed hard against industrial understandings of private rights. Most Americans now want landscapes that are ecologically healthy and pleasing places to live and work. What we are beginning to see is that we can create such landscapes only by making significant changes, both in the ways we understand private property—particularly in the simplistic ways we often talk about it—and in the specific rights and responsibilities that ownership entails. Also necessary and taken up in the next chapter is the need to reassert the public's varied interests in private lands by protecting water, wildlife, and other ecologically important resources; by rethinking landowner development rights; by identifying workable methods of reassembling fragmented landscapes; and by realigning private rights so as to promote overall ecological goals.

Portraying Law and Conflict Realistically

In popular talk about private rights, land-use disputes are often reduced to a simple portrait of conflict. An individual owner, desirous of using his land in some new way, engages in legal battle with a zoning board or conservation agency that resists the proposed activity. It is a stark, two-sided image, just the kind that many journalists find so appealing. Private interest lies on one side of the conflict; the public interest—or the government's claim of public interest—on the other. With such a simplistic portrayal, it is little wonder that debates about ownership are so often fruitless or that it is so difficult to envision how to promote conservation without sacrificing private property as an institution.

Among the ironies posed by this simplistic portrait is its sharp contrast with private property as John Locke defined it in writings that were so influential for America's founders. "Where there is no Law, there is no Freedom" Locke announced.[1] Freedom meant an immunity from outside interferences, particularly from neighbors and other private actors, not an immunity from all legal constraint. In a world where law was absent, a landowner was constantly at risk of having his land seized or invaded by others at any time. Only when law and government existed did an owner possess secure control of a sphere of free living. Locke's thinking permeated English law and was reflected in the American law of property, particularly the doctrine of do-no-harm. *Sic utere tuo* defined the scope of a landowner's personal enclave and gave rise to her freedom as it did so. A landowner who abided by the doctrine could turn to the courts for protection against any interference; without the doctrine, her quiet enjoyment was insecure.

Locke's reasoning on this issue is helpful in transforming the two-sided image of owner-government conflict into a more accurate and useful portrayal of ownership and ownership disputes. Private property is a creature of law, as Locke recognized; when the law protecting property disappears, so does private property itself. In the United States, the law that creates and defines property rights is made largely at the state level; landowner rights thus depend on the continuance of state law. The U.S. Constitution does provide protections for private property, including protections against improper shifts in state law, but it does so only for property that arises under some other body of law. The Constitution itself does not create property (as it does, for instance, the freedoms of speech and religion), nor does it explain where the rights of one owner end and the rights of neighbors and the community begin.[2]

Property law's role in creating private property (and thus landowner freedom) becomes easy to see when neighboring landowners are added to the crude portrayal of property rights conflict. Property law is regularly called upon to draw the line between one owner's right to act and a neighbor's right to complain. As we saw in the first chapter, private property would not exist in any meaningful sense without such a line. When government draws the line, it naturally needs to think about the public interest and how property law might best serve it. But the chief effect of drawing the line between landowners is to create and protect a sphere of private influence. In Locke's day, a landowner's quiet enjoyment was the ultimate element of private ownership. The more rigorously courts enforced *sic utere tuo*, the more they protected (and hence freed, in Locke's sense) the individual landowner within his personal sphere. It would take many generations to transform landowner freedom into an owner's right to use land intensively, regardless of how his actions might affect neighbors and surrounding communities.

Once we see how landowner freedom depends upon law, it also becomes easier to see why government is not aptly portrayed (as the simple image portrays it) as a force that promotes public interests at the expense of private ones. Government should always foster the public interest, but it often does that best by creating and protecting secure private rights. Moreover, when it regulates land uses, it typically protects the interests of some landowners even as it curtails the land-use options of others. As for the private side of the public-private clash, private owners may often look out only for themselves, but it is hardly true (despite what is sometimes said) that they want government to leave them completely alone. Owners want government to stand by their sides, protecting them with their police and courts. Private rights, in short, are fused with and made possible by public power. At bottom, a landowner is a person who draws upon state power to protect a sphere of personal liberty in a way that curtails the liberties of everyone else.

Adding Interdependence

Just as neighbors need to be brought into the portrayal of land-use conflict, so too does nature and the larger social world. Land-use dramas unfold in real-world settings where land parcels are interconnected—ecologically, socially, and economically. The privatization of a landscape divides managerial rights among individual owners but in itself leaves nature unaffected. Nature remains an integrated commons and hence is subject to the tragic dangers of overuse that afflict any natural commons. With interconnection comes interdependence. The humans who enact the unfolding land-use dramas depend for their sustenance and breath upon nature's ecological processes. Nature's processes, in turn, depend more than is commonly realized on the presence of an extraordinary number of life-forms, from complex soil microbes to nitrogen-fixing legumes to insect-eating birds. Land uses often disrupt these natural processes and displace these life-forms.

The natural interconnection of land parcels is closely related to their other interconnections. Economic interdependence is perhaps the easiest to see: as the Cathedral Mansion South–National Zoo case illustrates, the value of a land parcel depends heavily upon its proximity to other particular land uses. Lands are often valuable as residences, for instance, only when they are within commuting distances to workplaces and when homeowners can travel back and forth without undue annoyance. The value of a home, then, can depend on its proximity to work locations and on the quality of regional transportation systems—that is, on improvements made on other lands.

The flip side of interdependence is the fact that the actions of one landowner inevitably affect other landowners. Land uses that undermine nature's processes, diminish the values of surrounding lands, or undercut social communities (perhaps by pushing people to live farther from where they work) all exert a downward pull on the surrounding landscape. In contrast, good land uses can enhance the values of surrounding places. The landowner who practices sound conservation, for instance, creates benefits that spread through the surrounding community and into the future.

Linking Private Rights and Public Good

To make the simple portrait of landowner-government conflict useful, we must add not only the major elements just discussed but also a far clearer linkage between private rights and the public good. Private property promotes individual good to the degree that it enables individuals to thrive. Secure property helps individuals live "a fully human life," as legal scholar Joseph William Singer has put it:

> Access to material resources is a precondition, not only of subsistence, but of the capacity to shape one's life, to create a home, to develop relationships with others, and to engage in meaningful work. Access to

property promotes security by ensuring stable control over the resources needed for a dignified life.[3]

Even so (again to quote Singer), private property remains what it has always been: an "intensely social institution."[4] Particularly in the context of disputes about nature, private property is justified only insofar as it promotes the aggregate good of all. The communal good is fostered when people are able to thrive freely as individuals, but it is also often aided by laws that constrain individuals from acting in socially harmful ways.

Given the conflict between unlimited individual liberty on one side and the common good on the other, one is tempted to propose a centrist position, one that balances liberty and community. But it is a temptation that needs to be resisted, for private property is not a product of these two elements, brought into some sort of balance. Property draws its philosophic justification from the common good, which means that the common good should supply the polestar for crafting property law. Individual liberty, vital and necessary though it is, enters the picture only to the extent that its recognition promotes the good of people generally.

In real life, the common good is a messy, complex, shifting ideal, with many clashing components. Individual liberty is one of those components, and like the other components it conflicts with competing values and aims. For instance, unrestrained liberty regularly conflicts with the maintenance of public heath and order and with land-use goals that can be achieved only when landowner actions are somehow coordinated. Landowner liberty, accordingly, should be recognized in property law only when it helps promote the common good—as it often, but not always, does.

Once we see private property's link to conceptions of the collective good, it becomes easier to appreciate why property must remain an organic institution, forever in an incomplete state. In the eigh-

teenth century, prevailing values favored the settled life and opportunities for landowners to remain undisturbed within their private
spheres. Landowner independence was highly prized, in part because of its role in promoting civic virtue and good government—or
so people believed. In the nineteenth century, property-as-opportu-
nity continued to draw intellectual support, but conceptions of the
common good were shifting. Economic development was the goal of
the hour, and the common good took on a new shape. By the early
twentieth century, citizens were reasserting their desires for more
settled, peaceful lives. Quality-of-life issues gained in support. By
the end of the twentieth century, ecological degradation had become
a major concern.

Most people recognize that law changes over time; visibly and
constantly, legislators and regulators tinker with governing rules.
It can be unsettling nonetheless to realize that property law has
changed as dramatically as it has, to hear that lawmakers have significantly refashioned the rights and responsibilities of ownership
over the past two centuries. Private property is supposed to be a bul-
wark to protect civil society. It is vital ballast that keeps the nation
steady and individuals grounded and secure. Can it perform this
work if it does not stay put?

If the idea of past change is disturbing, even more unsettling is the
idea that further change might be in the offing—and that such
change might be not just legitimate but indispensable if private
property is to remain justified. Yet property law is a creation of the
majority—the demos—and should respond to its needs. To keep
property law from evolving along with the needs and wants of the
people is to turn property into something far different from what
it was originally. It can become (as it too often has been) a tool
that landowners use to resist change, to exert power unfairly, and to
insist on being paid to halt activities that clash with contemporary
needs.

Crafting an Ecological Message

In specifying a particular mix of landowner rights and responsibilities, property law always conveys messages to people about the land itself, about how they should perceive it, and about how private owners fit into it. Quietly but powerfully and for good or ill, the law supplies ways to see the landscape and ways to think about how its various parts do or do not fit together. It also conveys messages about where the private sphere ends and the public sphere begins, while educating us about what behaviors are deemed ecologically and ethically sound. These are influential messages—all the more so because they operate subtly.

The image of landownership that dominated in the late nineteenth century (and still carries weight today) might be termed an atomistic image. In such an image, the natural landscape comes divided into distinct parts, each part ecologically separate from the others and valued in isolation. The parts are legally identical in the sense that the rights and responsibilities of ownership are the same. By implication, if one part no longer functions well, it can be exchanged for another. A more tolerable variant of this image is the machinelike or mechanistic image of land and landownership. In it, nature is still made up of distinct parts, but this time the parts are not treated as identical. The image implicitly acknowledges that many parts are needed to keep the overall machine working, though replacement is still possible, just as a worn-out machine part can be replaced with a new one.[5]

Now, a more ecological image is very much needed, one that softens the boundaries on the landscape and diminishes their social and legal importance. A sound image would portray nature's parts as interrelated, with their values visibly dependent on the healthfulness of the links between and among them. A mechanistic image of prop-

erty is preferable to an atomistic one, in that a mechanistic view recognizes interdependence (even if it assumes that worn-out parts are
replaceable). But far better than a mechanical perspective would be
an ecological image: one that includes a sense of growth and change
over time, that would diminish the role of humans in creating and
managing nature, and that would draw attention to the fact that it is
life itself that courses throughout the whole.[6]

What, then, should be the terms of landownership today, given the
needs, values, and understandings of our time? What steps might be
taken to re-form private property so that it better serves communal
needs? And what particular ideas might help this process along by
supplying the vocabulary and intellectual tools for talking about
property's future? Broader senses of value; greater ecological awareness; heightened concerns over sprawl, aesthetics, land degradation,
and quality of life; desires for more settled lives—these motives and
others point toward a revitalized property system in which landowners are expected to use their lands in gentler and more communally responsive ways. At the same time, worries about government's
growth and the difficulties people experience in controlling their
lives give good cause to search for voluntary or market-based solutions to conservation challenges, whenever they work effectively and
treat taxpayers fairly.

We can turn to two further legal disputes for useful glimpses of
where private property needs to head.

Maine, 1989

Grant's Farm Associates, a development firm, owned 100 acres of
land in the town of Kittery, Maine, adjoining the town hall and

bounded by the tidal estuaries of Spruce Creek and Gerry Cove. Because of its waterfront location and the region's existing development, the land was particularly attractive for new residences. Local law zoned the tract as "urban residence." Land within 250 feet of the shore was subject to shoreland-protection restrictions, with additional protections covering the 100 feet closest to shore. In 1985, under the ordinance on new subdivisions, Grant's Farm Associates sought a permit to construct a 200-unit condominium complex. Even though the units would be clustered in a way that left 90 of the 100 acres open, the Kittery Planning Board refused the request, concluding that the project would cause unreasonable road congestion and unsafe traffic conditions, adversely affect the water quality of Spruce Creek, and place an "unreasonable burden" on the town's municipal and governmental services.

Ultimately, Grant's Farm Associates's challenge to the permit denial worked its way to the Supreme Judicial Court of Maine, which upheld the denial based on the traffic and water-quality problems.[7] Under the subdivision ordinance, the Kittery board could object to a subdivision only when it "caused" harmful traffic congestion. Grant's Farm Associates challenged the finding of causation, arguing that although its project would *worsen* already existing congestion, it would not *cause* it. The court, though, found the distinction meritless, at least when the worsening was material (here, 10 percent). As for the waterway issues, the town's ordinance barred development within 250 feet of any body of water if the development would harm water quality or "unreasonably affect the shoreline." After taking evidence, the board concluded

> that untreated surface water, possibly polluted, would run into Spruce Creek; that construction would change drainage patterns for the worse; that nesting and brooding areas for waterfowl and salt water wetland birds would be eliminated; and that the "critical edge" wildlife habitat along the shoreline would be damaged.[8]

Related to these problems were the expected harms caused during the construction period within the 100-foot shoreline setback area. Although the developers designed "extensive reclamation measures" to mitigate lasting adverse effects, the board was legitimately dubious that the measures would work. Moreover, the high court agreed, it made no difference that the land was zoned overall for residences: "It is simply not true that all parts of the urban residence zone must be regarded as equally well suited to high-density development."[9]

New Jersey, 1991

Since 1902, the Gardner family had owned a 217-acre farm in the Pinelands region of New Jersey, on which it cultivated sod and grain. In the fall of 1987, Hobart Gardner explored the possibility of selling off most of his property, dividing it into 10-acre "farmettes." While he considered the option, a new law took effect that was designed to protect the farmlands and unique ecological features of the Pinelands more strictly. Under it, Gardner could construct only one home per 40 acres, and even then he had to place 39 of the acres under perpetual deed restrictions limiting them to agricultural use. If Gardner did that, he would receive, for each 39 acres so restricted, two "Pinelands Development Credits," which he could sell to landowners elsewhere who wanted to increase development on their own lands. According to the Supreme Court of New Jersey, which ultimately resolved the case, the credits were worth at least $10,000 each. Unhappy with these tight land-use restrictions, Gardner sued to have them declared invalid as an unconstitutional taking of his property.[10]

The Pinelands was the largest undeveloped region within the sprawling metropolis that extended from Richmond to Boston. Long recognized for its unique ecological and cultural features, the Pinelands featured expansive pine-oak forests, wild and scenic rivers, important agricultural areas, and a "wide variety of rare, threatened, and endangered plant and animal species." Underlying the region was the vast, 17-trillion-gallon Cohansey aquifer, which constituted "one of the largest virtually untapped sources of pure water in the world." The aquifer was unusually sensitive because contamination of the region's sandy soils could easily pollute it.

Recognizing the region's ecological importance and seeking to protect its agriculture from piecemeal development, governments at various levels had imposed increasingly stringent regulatory controls. In 1978, Congress provided funds for planning and land acquisition on the condition that the state create a planning commission and prepare a comprehensive regional plan. The resulting Pinelands plan, which local governments were free to supplement, divided the Pinelands into eight land-use management areas with differing land uses allowed in each. Gardner's farm was located in the Uplands Agricultural Production Area.

In his suit, Gardner claimed that the Pinelands plan failed to advance substantially legitimate government objectives, particularly in its restriction of large-lot residences, long viewed as a benign if not desirable land-use type. The court dismissed the objection firmly. There was "not the slightest quarrel," it asserted, that the statute was proper in protecting the habitat of rare plant and animal species. Equally legitimate was the preservation of agriculture and farmland and the protection of the aquifer from contamination. That land itself was a diminishing resource could not be overemphasized, the court asserted, and environmentally sensitive land was "all the more precious.... Hence, a proposed development that may constitute only a small insult to the environment does not lessen the need to avoid such an offense. The cumulative detrimental impact of many small projects can be devastating."[11]

On his behalf, Gardner cited a 1963 ruling by the New Jersey court that had struck down, as an unconstitutional taking of property, a zoning ordinance that required "an entire swamp area" to be left in its natural state. That earlier ruling, however, was not apposite, the high court responded. Unlike the swampland owner, Gardner was allowed to continue economically valuable farming on his land. Moreover, times had changed since 1963, and the vitality of the ruling had "declined with the emerging priority accorded to the ecological integrity of the environment." The 1963 ruling "arose in a time before the environmental and social harms of indiscriminate and excessive development were widely understood or acknowledged." Had the same case arisen in 1991, the court hinted, the wetland law would have been upheld.

Grant's Farm Associates and Gardner provide good points of reference to explore where private property has headed in some places and where it needs to head in far more places if land conservation goals are to be achieved. Together, the two rulings illustrate the major steps that lie on the path to healthier lands and communities.

Redefining Land-Use Harm

One obvious step is to revise the idea of land-use harm further, vesting it with a content that matches today's circumstances and values. *Sic utere tuo* continues to be a firm limit on how landowners can use what they own, but its content remains open to change. Life in twenty-first-century America is far different from life a century ago—in terms of population, technology, modes of transportation, and the health of natural systems. Values and desires have shifted even more substantially. "Do no harm" needs updating to take into account a variety of ecological, aesthetic, and quality-of-life harms. In *Grant's Farm Associates,* governing law took into account such harms as water-quality degradation and loss of wildlife habitat, along with traffic congestion and excessive burdens on municipal systems.

In *Gardner,* the law recognized similar harms, including harms to the private land itself—to its value as farmland and to the quality of the water underlying the private land.

To chart this ongoing evolution in values, one need only note the rising percentage of Americans who sense a duty to protect rare species. Two centuries ago, Thomas Jefferson believed that the world still contained all the species that had ever lived. Jefferson could hardly conceive that human activities might bring a species to an end. By the late nineteenth century, people knew otherwise—they knew that species such as dinosaurs and ice-age mammals had come and gone—but few seemed to care about human-caused species losses. Not until the twentieth century did public sentiment shift substantially. Aldo Leopold marked an important event in that shift in an essay on a monument to the extinct passenger pigeon, erected in 1947 by the Wisconsin Society for Ornithology. It was a monument that symbolized our sorrow, Leopold recognized, our grief that "no living man will see again the onrushing phalanx of victorious birds, sweeping a path for spring across the March skies, chasing the defeated winter from all the woods and prairies of Wisconsin." It was "a new thing under the sun," Leopold observed, "for one species to mourn the death of another." In this mourning, Leopold claimed, "rather than in Mr. DuPont's nylons or Mr. Vannevar Bush's bombs, lies objective evidence of our superiority over the beasts."[12]

Many imperiled species are declining because of the ways private lands are used. By harming imperiled species, habitat destruction harms other landowners and the community at large. Given the harm, why should property law allow it? In what way is the common good served by allowing landowners to use their lands in communally harmful ways? Despite the profound shifts in public values, these questions are only now being raised.

To impose a new law restricting a landowner's ability to alter wildlife habitat is not to impose law where no law has been, for property law necessarily expresses a position as to whether a landowner can or cannot use land in this way. When property law allows a landowner to alter habitat (which it routinely does), it recognizes that right while withholding from neighbors and the community at large the reciprocal legal right to complain about the destruction. Were a new law to reverse that legal arrangement, curtailing the owner's right to alter habitat while expanding the rights of others to complain about the destruction, it would merely do what so many property laws over the decades have done: reconfigure the rights of land ownership by adding a bit here and pruning a bit there. Landowners and communities would gain greater rights to protect the wildlife that sustains natural systems and adds joy and beauty to the landscape; on the other side, landowners wanting to develop their lands would lose their right to develop in ways that destroyed important habitat.

One category of land-use harm that cries out for legal recognition is harm that occurs to the land itself, rather than to neighbors. Late in the nineteenth century, land was plentiful enough that its destruction seemed unimportant, and the law allowed it. Today, with land scarcer and more vulnerable to environmental insult, the landscape looks far different. Given the importance of fertile soil to community and society, why should landowners be allowed to erode it? Given the importance of vegetation along waterways in protecting stream banks from erosion and shading waterways, why should landowners have the right to cut, plow, or mow right up to the edge? Given the connections between natural hydrologic flows and healthy biotic communities, why should landowners be permitted to drain or dike in ways that cause ecological harm? There may be answers, but such questions can no longer be ignored if private property is to retain its necessary connection to the common good.

One argument used to resist new rules on land-use harms is the claim that government should act only when proof of harm is indisputable. In many settings, particularly ecological ones, evidence of harm will be merely suggestive until it is too late. Gathering detailed data, particularly local data, can be prohibitively expensive. To impose new restrictions when evidence of harm is incomplete is to employ a version of what is termed the precautionary rule, which counsels caution in the manipulation of nature when early evidence warns of harm. Is such a precautionary approach wise, or should government act only when evidence of harm is nearly certain?

In thinking about this issue, it is useful to understand clearly the approach now widely used. Err on the side of liberty, the current rule seems to advise, and restrict liberty only when the evidence is unassailable. Yet what is this approach itself but a precautionary rule? What is this but a rule that requires caution in interfering with an individual's freedom to act? To propose a precautionary rule in favor of nature, then, is not to interject a precautionary rule but instead to change its focus, to diminish the protection of liberty while increasing the protection of land. Libertarian political thought, which undergirds so much of the property rights rhetoric, is essentially a precautionary rule writ large. It holds liberty high above all competing values and seeks to protect it from interferences that do not, beyond all reasonable doubt, promote the welfare of all. Liberty is an important value, of course, yet so is the health of nature and of human communities. Even in terms of liberty, it is easy to forget (as popular thought often does) that liberty has an affirmative component as well as a negative or protective one. There is the liberty to achieve desired goals in concert with others (affirmative or positive liberty), as well as the (negative) liberty to act without restraint. Many conservation goals can be achieved only when people exercise the power of government, as the tragedy of fragmentation reveals. Only by exercising their positive liberties in this way, working with and through government, can people hope to nurture healthy and beautiful lands, control sprawl, contain traffic, and retain open spaces such as the New Jersey Pinelands.

At bottom, it is intellectually incoherent to allow landowners, in the name of liberty and private property, to strike down conservation laws on the ground that such laws improperly use government power to disrupt individual liberty. It is incoherent not because liberty is less important than conservation but because private property itself entails the exercise of government power by one citizen to curtail the liberties of others. Only by restricting the liberties of other citizens is a landowner able to carve out a sphere of personal liberty. When property rights trump conservation laws, they curtail the positive liberties of the majority.

Tailoring Rights to the Land

An important and much-needed trend in property law today—illustrated by *Grant's Farm Associates, Gardner,* and many other rulings—is the gradual tendency to define landowner rights in ways that take into account the land's natural features. *Just v. Marinette County,* the 1972 Wisconsin decision upholding a strict wetlands law and limiting owners to "natural uses" of their lands, remains a leading judicial step in this direction, largely because of the court's clear language and thought.

Many laws provide evidence of this trend: rules limiting the draining or filling of wetlands; laws prohibiting landowners from plowing steep hillsides without protective contour strips; laws that ban landowners from removing trees along stream banks; laws that require timber harvesters to formulate harvesting plans that pay attention to environmental effects. In *Grant's Farm Associates,* the owner's property rights varied based on whether the land was within the shoreland protection zones. In *Gardner,* the Gardners' entire farm was placed in a special agricultural area because of its natural features and historic uses, with rights throughout the region defined in ways that took into account the region's sensitive aquifer.

Considered in isolation, such laws appear to address only specific problems in specific natural settings. Taken as a whole, they trumpet a major change slowly taking place in landowner rights and responsibilities. How a landowner can use land is beginning to depend more and more on the land itself. Step by step, landowners are being asked to shape their visions to the land, rather than the land to their visions.

Once this idea is understood for what it is and is given the freedom to work its way throughout property law, the changes it brings about could be astonishing. Developers wanting to implement particular development visions already need to find land that is well suited for their projects in terms of proximity to people and to other land uses. Why not insist that they find lands that are also ecologically well suited? Given the diversity of land available in the country, why should homebuilders be allowed to situate new homes on fragile wetlands, in sensitive riparian corridors, or in scare wildlife habitat?

The typical answer to these last questions, of course, has been that such restrictions take away a landowner's development rights. And for lawmakers in most parts of the country, that answer has been persuasive. Yet that answer hearkens to an era when land development was the most important of all goals. It also looks back to a time when the ecological differences among land parcels were poorly understood or ignored. In a day when development pressures are greater and more sensitive land uses are desirable, it makes sense to restrict land uses to those that are ecologically sound. Landowners can rightly insist on fair treatment vis-à-vis other landowners. But ecological differences among land parcels are real differences that lawmakers should take into account to prescribe differing packages of landowner rights. In a legal system that took ecological harm seriously, land-use options would vary considerably from natural setting to natural setting. The land itself would have gained a voice in the lawmaking process.

A particular form of land-use harm that cries out for attention is the harm that comes from land uses that do not create problems in isolation but do create problems when too many landowners engage in them. When too many fields in a watershed are plowed, or too many fields are drained, or too much wildlife habitat is altered, or too many homes are built in an area, or too much impervious pavement distorts hydrologic patterns, the ecological status of entire landscapes can be degraded. The actions of each landowner in isolation —such as building a home on 10 acres, as Gardner wanted to do in the Pinelands—might seem reasonable, but collectively they may cause severe decline.

Many communal harms today are of this type: harms that arise because the land's capacity is overloaded by a particular type of activity, whether ecologically or (as in *Grant's Farm Associates*) in terms of the capacities of roads and municipal services. In fairness to everyone, landowners included, property law needs to respond. The situation cries out for mutual coercion, mutually agreed upon. If such a carrying-capacity problem can be anticipated and restrictions implemented in advance, before the land's capacity is reached, many remedial options are available, some quite fair. When no action is taken and the problem builds, reaching or exceeding the point where all further development is harmful, the only feasible option may be to halt further development—and then find ways to respond to landowners' cries of unfairness.

In thinking about land-use harms, one temptation is to assume that harm occurs whenever a land use gives rise to an externality— an effect that spills across property boundaries. Market theorists, out to remedy defects in market pricing methods, have encouraged lawmakers to find ways to internalize the external harms that land uses sometimes impose on neighbors (such as the water pollution that destroyed Mrs. Sanderson's pond and the gaseous fumes that turned the Washaks' home black). When landowners are barred from pushing their harms onto others, when they are forced to absorb or otherwise take into account all the harms they generate, they will make more economically sound decisions—often decisions good for the land.

The danger of externalities analysis applied in this way is that it fails to consider the ecological interdependence of land parcels. In simplistic externalities analysis, parcels are portrayed as distinct except for the external harms and benefits they generate; these externalities skew decision-making and are thus economically undesirable. Ideally, this analysis hints, land parcels ought to be fully isolated, so that one owner's acts never cross property lines. Decision-making then would be perfect and resource-allocation decisions would be optimal.

If such a world of disconnected parcels existed, it would not sustain life for long. On healthy lands, life courses through the landscape. Animals need to inhabit the land, including animals that routinely ignore land boundaries. Soil fertility cycles need to be maintained across boundaries if terrestrial life is to flourish. Natural links between and among land parcels are not just desirable, they are essential. Halting pollution, soil erosion, and certain other externalities is clearly beneficial; halting many others is neither desirable nor possible.

Standard externalities analysis is also misguided because it suggests that a landowner acts well so long as he causes no externalities. But this assertion also is far from true. A landowner can cause harm simply by disrupting a natural externality that helps sustain life. A dam that blocks the passage of fish or a vast farm field too wide for animals to cross can cause harm, even when an owner's activities stay entirely within his property lines. In the old common law, harm was usually equated with some action a landowner took that physically invaded or otherwise disrupted actions taking place on other lands. That preecological understanding is overdue for revision.

In an ecological age, property law should *promote* healthy connections between and among land parcels, socially, economically, and ecologically.

Making Room for Conservation Goals

Property law needs to change today largely to accommodate new demands for the conservation of lands, communities, and beautiful surroundings. Yet it needs to do so, to the extent possible, in ways that allow private ownership to continue serving its core older goals. Private property has brought great economic prosperity by helping citizens achieve their economic aspirations. It has encouraged planting in the spring by promising a right to harvest in the fall. Markets have played a key role in this prosperity, and what makes markets possible are reasonably secure, transferable private rights. Private property, particularly private land, also plays a central role in protecting personal and family privacy. Less important but by no means gone is private property's role in dispersing power within society, facilitating individual independence, and providing stability and virtue for the civic state.

Today's challenge, then, is (1) to promote conservation; (2) to do so while still respecting property's other goals, to the extent possible and desirable; and (3) to do so in ways that are fair, both to taxpayers generally and to the vast majority of citizens who own little or no land. To lay out these three key points is to see both the magnitude of the challenge and why conservation strategies commonly talked about today suffer from defects. Ardent conservation measures do well at achieving point (1) but usually ignore point (2) and are indifferent to point (3). Ardent property rights advocates, in contrast, typically labor to achieve (2) while shortchanging (1) and (3). Free-market conservation writers do better than that, working to achieve (1) as well as (2)—though stumbling on (1) with respect to landscape-scale goals—but they fail completely in dealing with (3). Given the politics of the day and the influence of money in it, we should not be surprised that it is point (3) that is so routinely downplayed. The public as such too often counts for little. One rarely hears the question: Is a particular ownership system or conservation program fair to taxpayers and to people who own no land?

Much of the work that needs to be done in revising property law ought to focus on clarifying these broad goals and applying them to particular landscapes. The goals, easy to state in the abstract, will always be hard to apply in practice. And the work of refining and applying them will never end. The goals themselves will evolve, along with the lawmaking community, and landscapes will meanwhile also continue to change, calling for yet further adjustments in property law.

Ownership Duties and the Fair Share

Lurking beneath many land-use disputes, better known to lawyers than to the public, is the so-called harm-benefit test, long used to help decide whether a land-use regulation amounts to an unconstitutional taking of private land without the payment of just compensation. The test asks a simple, two-part question: Does a particular land-use regulation ban a landowner from engaging in a harmful land use? Or does it instead ask the landowner to use what he owns in ways that confer a benefit on the public? If a law bans a harmful land use, it is a proper exercise of the police power, and the owner is not entitled to compensation. If a law asks the owner to confer a public benefit, singling him out for an extra burden, it is more suspect and may amount to an unlawful taking.

Scholarly commentary on this harm-benefit test over the past decade has tended to challenge its usefulness in resolving takings disputes. As Supreme Court Justice Antonin Scalia put it in a highly contentious ruling, whether one sees a law one way or the other seems to depend on one's point of view. A law banning wetlands draining could appear to halt a harm to one observer, while another observer might see it as a mandate that the owner use the land to provide ecological services for surrounding lands.[13] A law that bars wildlife habitat destruction could appear as halting a harm; it could also appear as an order directing an owner to use her land as a wildlife refuge for the public good.

Justice Scalia is right in noting that pure logic does not allow one to take sides in such a dispute. But then the law has never operated on pure logic—that is, in a social and cultural vacuum. Harm-benefit is a workable, useful test when it operates in a communal setting where citizens have shared ideas of what is and is not acceptable. Harm is clear when a landowner falls below community standards. Benefit is also clear when a landowner is being unfairly singled out to carry a particularly heavy burden. To apply the harm-benefit test, in short, a baseline of socially acceptable conduct is needed. What can society reasonably expect of a landowner? Lawmakers can treat landowners unfairly by setting the bar of ownership duties too high. But it can also treat neighbors, community member, taxpayers, and others unfairly when it sets the bar of landowner duties too low. By most appearances, the danger of the latter is the greater one. Embedded in farm programs is the view that every act of conservation confers public benefits and hence deserves payment. Strongly pushing this line of thought have been advocates for industrial agriculture, who insist that all conservation must be voluntary. When all conservation is voluntary, landowners are obligated to do nothing—unless and until they are paid. The baseline is rock bottom.

Are such incentive payments wise, even if they last only a few years? This was a question that Aldo Leopold openly wondered about in his later years. Such programs worked well, Leopold believed, only if they encouraged landowners and others to embrace new ideas of right and wrong land use. To pay people to use lands conservatively was sound policy if conservative land use then became an accepted norm—if, that is, landowners thereafter followed the norm without continuing payments. But after observing incentive payments in operation, Leopold decided they had no such good effect. In fact, they seemed to do just the opposite. Payments told a landowner that conservation was optional and that the wise owner should conserve only if and so long as the money flowed. In practice, landowners reverted to old habits when payments ended.

Not just incentive payment programs but land trusts and easement-purchase programs, useful though they are, often have the similar, unintended effect of pushing the bar of landowner duties downward. To pay landowners to give up their development rights is to confirm loudly that they do, and should, possess such rights. To purchase easements in which landowners pledge to refrain from damaging activities sends a similar, unhelpful message about the meaning of ownership. When one landowner sees a neighbor get paid to conserve, what incentive does the first owner have to conserve voluntarily? And what of the landowner who conserves voluntarily and who then sees a neighbor getting paid to do what she is already doing?

The conservation movement has paid too little attention to the ill effects of landowner payments. It has spent too little time thinking about what it ought to mean to own land. When, late in his life, Leopold wrote a simple two-point national conservation platform, he tellingly put landowner responsibilities first, ahead even of his overall conservation goal of land health: "The average citizen, especially the landowner," he urged, had "an obligation to manage his land in the interest of the community, as well as in his own interest." To water down this duty was to stifle progress in bringing about a new way of thinking about land and land ownership.

So long as conservation is paid for by government, land trusts, and taxpayer-funded public purchase programs, landowner duties will likely remain more or less where they were a century ago. Landowners will continue to hold rights to use their lands in ways that damage the common good, and taxpayers and others will be expected to pay them to stop. However politically attractive this approach might be, it allows landowners to extract money in settings where they do not deserve to, it treats taxpayers and conservation-minded citizens unfairly, and it frustrates much-needed efforts to rethink what land-ownership ought to entail, today. Payment can be easier politically, particularly when landowners scream. But the easy route is often not the fair one. Nor is it the one that moves society in the right direction.

In an ecological age, then, an age in which the common good included a sense of ecological interconnection, key elements of land-owner rights would be reworked, particularly elements that arise from the long-standing *sic utere tuo* doctrine. Yet more change than that is needed to bring private property to the point where it effectively serves contemporary needs. Another, related piece needs to be put in place: the public needs to recognize and protect more forcefully its essential interests in all lands, private and public.

CHAPTER NINE

The

PUBLIC'S INTEREST

in

PRIVATE LAND

Although a new, ecological approach to private landownership will carry forward important elements of its immediate predecessor, the industrial approach of a century and more ago, it will apply the elements in distinctly new ways. As before, landowners could complain about being unfairly singled out for excessive burdens, but private rights will nonetheless be tailored to take into account the natural variations among land parcels. Landowners will still be expected to use their lands in ways that harm neither neighbors nor the surrounding community, but land-use harm will include alterations of nature itself when the alterations disrupt ecological processes, overburden the land's carrying capacity, or otherwise interfere with conservation aims. With land-use harm thus redefined, landowners will be expected to use their lands in ways that keep landscapes healthier and better suited for human life. Because good land use will be more of an expectation than it has been in the past, landowners will not be paid to do it. Instead, incentive programs will compensate landowners only for doing more than their fair share.

Related to this new ecological orientation for private property will be increased protections for the public's direct interests in private land. Those interests arise both because of the interconnections of lands and land uses and because private property rights are justified and limited by their ability to promote the public good. The public's interests are particularly clear when the private land includes water and wildlife—parts of nature that visibly ignore property boundaries. So important are water and wildlife that they require special attention. So too do development rights, whose value is directly linked to a community's history and whose exercise so affects the entire landscape. In addition, protecting the public's interest in private land will mean addressing head-on the tragedy of fragmentation, sometimes through affirmative public steps to reassemble fragmented landscapes. Thus, methods of land reassembly will also be part of a new, ecological understanding of private property, in urban areas as well as rural ones. Finally, there is the looming challenge posed by such ecological goals as Aldo Leopold's land health—perhaps the ultimate public interest in private lands. What changes might such a goal bring to the rights and responsibilities of private ownership?

These various issues, which we take up in this chapter, pave the way for consideration in the final chapter of important questions about government and its land-related lawmaking work. If government is to wield its power to redefine property rights, how might it best do so, and what recourse will landowners have if it acts badly?

Reclaiming Public Rights in Water

Water plays a greater role in property law than is commonly understood. Along with air, water is the most obvious force that integrates nature's parts. Falling from the sky, it runs over and under land, is drawn into plants and then animals, makes its way into waterways, and ultimately returns skyward. Of the many highly visible lawsuits in which landowners have complained that laws have allegedly taken their property, a sizable majority have dealt with the places where land and water come together: wetlands, barrier islands, floodplains, ocean beaches, and fields washed with rain. Such lands are often fragile ecologically, and their alteration visibly affects surrounding lands—as illustrated by *Grant's Farm Associates* (tidal estuaries in Maine) and *Gardner* (groundwater beneath the Pinelands). In addition, there are the contentious disputes that center on fresh water itself as a valuable resource: disputes about declining aquifers and polluted lakes and rivers. Holders of water rights often use their water in ways that degrade waterways, whether by diverting too much water, disrupting the timing of the flow, or polluting the water that percolates back to the waterway. Such degradation is harmful ecologically, aesthetically, and to other waterway users, including recreational users.

Under long-standing American law, water belongs to the people collectively, whether it is underground, in lakes and streams, or simply running over the surface. What private owners possess are merely conditional rights to use the resource. By law, their rights are limited by an obligation to use their water in ways that are "beneficial" and (in most places) "reasonable," at the risk of forfeiting those rights. Because of these related obligations, owners of water not only must engage in a *type* of water use that is deemed "beneficial" (household use, stock watering, industrial uses) but also must conduct that use in a way that, under the circumstances and in light of competing demands for the same water, is deemed "reasonable."[1]

One of the most disheartening aspects of property law today is the failure of so many courts to enforce these long-standing limits on private water rights. Courts have surrendered to the insistent demands of many owners to be free of the limits, thereby silently expanding the rights of such water users while shortchanging the public's own rights. Irrigators in the West commonly claim that a water use is beneficial so long as it was deemed beneficial when it was begun, perhaps a century or more ago. Or they claim that the benefits of irrigation should be decided in the abstract, so that all irrigation uses stand together, the wise and the unwise, in terms of their benefits to society. Neither claim makes good sense. "Beneficial" and "reasonable" plainly refer to what is beneficial to society as a whole and what is reasonable in light of today's values and circumstances. They cannot sensibly mean reasonable and beneficial to the water user alone or to an era that is long past.[2]

Even if these two express limits on water usage did not exist, lawmakers would possess ample power to reformulate water laws to force owners to act responsibly. Private rights in water are no stronger than property rights in land, which means that they too are subject to the do-no-harm, *sic utere tuo* rule. Owners of water, like owners of land, must avoid causing harm. When water supplies are short, inefficient uses ought to be deemed harmful *per se*. Using scarce water to grow overabundant crops also should be unreasonable per se. Irrigation practices that yield low-valued crops while producing return flows heavy in salts and chemicals might be viewed in the same way.

Two centuries ago, lawmakers protected the public's interests in water by embracing the natural-flow rule of surface water usage, under which landowners could use surface water so long as they did not diminish its quality or quantity (the rule applied, and modified, in *Palmer v. Mulligan* in 1805). That rule makes considerable ecological sense, given that its protections for downstream owners also protect waterways as ecosystems. If it was legitimate for the law to drift away from the natural-flow rule in the nineteenth century, it should be equally legitimate for the law to move back toward it now, given that public values have shifted again. Whether it would be wise to embrace natural flow fully is harder to say, given that its full embrace could restrict economically productive uses. But with so many water-ways in ill health, substantial change is clearly in order. To pay water users to halt bad practices is unfair to the taxpaying public: it denies their existing ownership rights in the water while perpetuating an understanding of private rights that is no longer legitimate. Even worse is to expect some charitable subset of citizens—such as con-servation organizations—to step forward and pay water users to halt their bad practices.

A handful of far-sighted state court justices—even one highly articulate judge—could go far toward realigning private rights and public interests in American water law. Major change is sometimes best undertaken slowly, step by step. But the time to begin that reform is decades past; now the need to act is urgent.

Water disputes in the western United States are particularly knotty because of the long-standing legal rule that any water applied to a nonbeneficial use is subject to the harsh penalty of automatic forfeiture.[3] So harsh is the penalty that courts are reluctant to impose it and hence are reluctant to conclude that a particular use is nonbeneficial. If lesser penalties were available, courts might more freely consider whether particular water uses really are socially ben-eficial, using the law to pressure water users to mend their ways. Bet-ter than automatic forfeiture would be forfeiture only in cases in which water users plainly should have known that their uses were nonbeneficial. In less serious cases, water users could be given the chance to shift to a sound use or sell their water to someone else who can use it soundly. Such a legal change, easy to make, would help courts bring the beneficial-reasonable use rule up to date. It would also stimulate water markets by pushing inefficient users to sell their rights.

Another useful water-law reform would be a rule allowing courts to order cutbacks among entire classes of water users, to deal with the many situations in which the public harm arises simply because too many people are using a waterway. State water officials possess plenty of power to disallow new uses in waterways that are already fully used. What they lack, and very much need, are ways to curtail existing uses to fit the system's capacity, without having to compensate property owners. Every water use that contributes to a systemic problem is, to that extent, unreasonable.

When Aldo Leopold looked across the landscapes of the Southwest and Midwest, cataloging the signs of land sickness, he always brought up the issue of deranged hydrologic systems. He usually listed the symptom as second in gravity behind disruptions of soil fertility cycles (to which it was, and is, closely related).[4] Today, as waterway restoration efforts intensify, it would prove useful to take a look back to the natural-flow rule, not just as a practical rule of law but as an expression of the public's interest in maintaining waterways in close to their natural conditions. Given technology now available, water users could significantly reduce their alterations of water flows. When they cannot, it is worth asking: Is the private activity in fact socially useful, and is it being conducted in an ecologically reasonable location?

Reclaiming Rights in Wildlife

In addition to water, the public also owns wild animals, game and nongame. As with its water rights, the public's wildlife rights need greater protection than they now receive. If these rights received greater protection, entire landscapes would become ecologically healthier, benefiting humans and animals alike.

American law vests ownership of wildlife in the state, as the courts in *Barrett v. State* (1917) and *Cawsey v. Bricker* (1914) explained. But the state owns wildlife in a special trustee capacity: not as it would a building or piece of land but in trust for the benefit of the people as a whole.[5] The state's power to ban the killing or harassing of wild animals is unquestioned. Less clear is how the state as trustee might, and perhaps even must, take action to protect wildlife habitat when habitat loss is destroying trust property (that is, the wildlife). The law on this subject is undeveloped and may take decades to unfold.

Areas of law dealing with other natural resources offer help on this issue. Often, land is owned by one person while another person holds title to a particular resource located on or under that land. Oil and mineral rights, for instance, are commonly severed from ownership of the surface and held by someone other than the landowner. Rights to cut timber, to graze animals, or to enter land to hunt are also held separately. Further examples are rights of way and the ubiquitous easements for roads and utility lines. Indeed, in urban areas, it is more the norm than the exception for an owner of land to have his use of it curtailed because someone else holds rights in the same land.

Bodies of law have arisen in all these settings to deal with situations where the owner of the underlying land proposes to act in a way that conflicts with the interests of those holding separate rights in the same land—in its minerals, trees, forage or the like. In some of these legal settings, the holder of the separate right is given the upper hand: an owner of oil and gas rights, for instance, can do pretty much whatever he wants in the exercise of his rights, with little regard for the effects on the surface owner (unless the parties have agreed otherwise). In other legal settings, the surface owner holds equal or even greater rights; then, it is the holder of the separate right that must reasonably accommodate the surface owner's desires.

What, then, might be done to protect the public's interest in wildlife located on private lands, without unduly burdening the owner of the private land? Because property rights, public and private, reside on both sides of this issue, there is no "pro-property" position that one can take on it; landowner property rights clash with the public's property rights.

The federal Endangered Species Act represents an initial effort at addressing this issue. On paper, the act restrains landowners from destroying valuable habitat when the destruction would kill or injure imperiled animals. As applied by federal agencies, the restriction is weaker than that formulation, but the law nevertheless does affect landowner actions and has introduced into the national discourse important ideas about wildlife and private land. Behind the Endangered Species Act is a long line of statutes and regulations, enacted mostly at the state level, that have protected wildlife habitat on private land. The New York court's 1917 ruling in *Barrett*, for instance, firmly upheld a state statute that restricted a landowner's ability to alter beaver dams and lodges, even when the beavers were destroying valuable trees. Wildlife habitat is also protected by more general land-use laws, such as subdivision-approval ordinances (as in *Grant's Farm Associates*) and regional land-use plans (as in *Gardner*). Legal precedents protecting habitat exist far back in English law as well. A 1692 statute prescribed imprisonment of 10 days to 1 month ("there to be whipt, and kept to hard labour") for anyone who between February 2 and June 24 burned the habitats of "the red and black game of grouse, commonly called heath-cocks, or heath-polts."[6]

Some complaints leveled against the Endangered Species Act are based on the erroneous assumption that private ownership necessarily includes a right to kill or drive away every living thing on a person's land. More legitimate is the complaint that the act operates erratically and thus unfairly; it applies to only a tiny proportion of the nation's landowners, seriously restricting them while leaving other landowners unaffected.

This latter complaint, though often voiced, is easy to exaggerate. Many land-use laws apply only to small numbers of landowners. Historic preservation laws apply only to owners of historic structures; laws dealing with dry-cleaning establishments or gas stations apply only to those activities. To determine whether a landowner is being singled out unfairly, one needs to look not just at one law in isolation but at the full range of laws that define what landowners can do. One landowner will be restricted by one law, the next landowner by another: both, though, are expected to use what they own in communally beneficial ways. Then, too, as understanding of conservation grows, nature itself is coming to play a larger role in defining landowner rights. Land that includes rare wildlife habitat is, by definition, ecologically different from other lands and therefore can entail different ownership rights, just as the court in *Cawsey* announced in 1914.

Even with these points in mind, however, the Endangered Species Act does raise issues of fairness, particularly when political squabbles in Congress make its implementation so erratic. Aside from the act's spotty enforcement, the burdens imposed on landowners are not well thought out in terms of what lands are restricted and in what ways, at least not in the statute itself. (Regulations diminish the problem by allowing landowners to negotiate fairer arrangements with the Fish and Wildlife Service.) The burdens can be severe—as when the act bans all construction or tells landowners they cannot harvest their trees—and the act does seem to strike like lightning, applying only to the tiny percentage of landowners whose land includes designated critical habitat. On the other hand (and in fairness to lawmakers), the act is little more than an early, tentative step to protect wildlife of national significance. Lessons can be learned from it and used to craft better codes.

The Endangered Species Act affects only a small number of landowners because it covers only rare species. To protect wildlife better and make the law fairer, the idea embedded in the act must be expanded to include more species and more habitat types. Wildlife law generally, that is, should recognize overtly the public's legitimate interest in wildlife habitat on private land as well as in the wildlife itself. That public interest ought to be described as a type of publicly owned easement, one that allows wildlife within reasonable limits to use private land without being harmed, either directly or by having their habitats destroyed. What should the scope of that easement be, given the corresponding rights held by the landowner? How far would it restrict landowners from using their lands intensively? These questions have not been asked, so answers are not yet available. But similar questions have arisen in analogous legal settings involving mineral rights, hunting easements, and other natural resources. There, courts have fashioned rules that call for reasonable accommodation between competing interests. Drawing upon such precedents, it would make sense to proclaim that landowners are obliged to make reasonable accommodations on their lands for wildlife. That obligation should apply broadly and treat all ecologically similar lands alike. Private ownership, in short, would include a specific duty for each owner to do his respective fair share in providing home and food for resident wild animals. Fair-share burdens widely applied could work far better than the well-intended but erratic burdens imposed today by the Endangered Species Act. In implementing this idea, much of the work would be done by the states rather than by the federal government, given the state's special trustee duties over wildlife. The federal government's role might remain focused on imperiled species and migratory wildlife, leaving all other wildlife to the states.

Beyond Water and Wildlife

As important as water and wildlife are, many conservation writers have focused their greatest attention on another component of terrestrial systems: the soil. The soil is the fund of all life, the great medium, as Wendell Berry has put it, through which old life passes by death and decay and is transformed into new life. Whenever Aldo Leopold listed signs of land sickness, he always began with soil loss and degradation. In doing so, Leopold joined such contemporaries as Hugh Hammond Bennett and Sir Albert Howard, who viewed soil as the critical component in all natural systems. Given this role, is there a reason that soil should not also be viewed as common property, a part of nature that landowners can use so long as they take good care of it?

This conception of private property as merely a use right characterized the ownership systems of many early peoples (as noted in Chapter 2). Tribal cultures tended (and still tend) to think of private rights in terms of particular use rights, with the tribe itself owning the land. American water law overtly incorporates this reasoning. Logically, the idea applies equally to wildlife, soil, and many other parts of nature. Oil and gas leases give only limited use rights to lessees, as do agreements covering timber cutting, grazing, and hunting easements. Owners of condominium units often possess carefully tailored easements (or use rights) to use lands that the unit owners own collectively. Tenants in shopping malls enjoy similar tailored arrangements. Indeed, property law is full of legal arrangements that recognize ownership in one party and use rights in another. It would be a significant step, but hardly unprecedented, for lawmakers to declare that the public owns all of nature, with private owners holding something akin to use rights, tailored to respect the common good.

This use-rights approach to land is imperfectly illustrated by the laws governing the multiple-use lands of the federal government— lands that are managed for such various uses as timber harvesting, grazing, watershed protection, mineral development, and (most valuable) recreation. Extractive activities such as grazing and timber harvesting on these public (federal) lands are done by private companies that have purchased or leased specific use rights from the government. These rights are clearly private property; they can be bought, sold, and renewed to varying degrees. The public still owns the lands and sets limits on the land uses. Public-lands management, to be sure, has its problems, largely because decision-making is skewed by the ardent external pressures that federal agencies face. But the underlying arrangement is sound: the public owns the land, whereas private users have tailored, secure, transferable rights to make use of it.

Water law, wildlife law, public-lands management—all highlight how artificial it is to think about land as fitting into one of two distinct categories, either publicly owned or privately owned. To be sure, there are some lands so completely controlled and used by government (high-security defense installations, for instance) that it seems apt to call them entirely public. On the other hand, there are rural lands in scarcely inhabited regions that are so immune to land-use controls that they might be deemed fully private. But such lands provide not the norms but the poles of public and private ownership, with the vast majority of all lands in between.

Many benefits would come from recognizing public ownership and private ownership as a smooth continuum, with private influence rising as one moves one way and public interest rising as one moves the other. It would become easier to imagine more flexible ways of protecting the public's interest in private land. In addition, the never-ending controversy over public lands would be easier to address if a full suite of options were open to discussion. Already, federal lands mix elements of the public and private, but a variety of public-private mixes could be tried, with the lessons learned perhaps being used to reshape thinking about predominantly private lands.

Rethinking Development Rights

Like all property rights, the rights of landowners to begin new land uses or intensify existing ones are legitimate only insofar as such rights do not undermine the common good. To the extent that they do, the rights should be diminished or even ended, ideally in ways that treat landowners (and taxpayers) fairly and that avoid undue disruptions of economic activities.

The current confused situation of landowner development rights is easy to summarize:

1. Development rights generally receive far too much respect, in the law and in popular culture, particularly in physical settings where development would be harmful.
2. When governments do curtail development rights, they often have trouble treating landowners fairly and reducing the economic disruptions they cause.
3. Point 2 is more closely linked with point 1 than one might first imagine. Indeed, the key to resolving point 2 might well be to deal more forcefully with point 1.

So entrenched is the idea that landowners everywhere have a right to develop, and so economically valuable are many development rights, that rethinking this issue is not easy. But it needs to be done. Conservation on a large scale is simply not possible unless and until that rethinking occurs. Sound conservation will require vast tracts of land to remain undeveloped. The public could not reasonably afford to purchase development rights on all such lands, and it would be unfair to expect them to do so. To address this issue, we need to recall private property's legal origins and why private property exists, and then use that knowledge to examine the arguments for and against development rights.

In many settings, the value of a land parcel results from the expected profit that its owner can make when putting it to a new use. When the right to put the land to that new use is legally secure, the market price of the land will fully reflect the expected profit. When the legal right is insecure, however, the land's market price will be discounted accordingly; the profit will be contingent on the land-owner's legal ability to engage in the new land use when the time is ripe for it. Land's market price is based on an expectation—or more aptly, a hope—that a given land use will be legally permitted when development time comes around. The more secure the expectation, the higher the land value; the less secure the expectation, the lower the value. The issue, then, from the viewpoint of public policy, is whether such landowner expectations deserve legal protection. Should the law tell landowners that they have secure rights to develop their land in the future, even if the development when undertaken might harm the public? Or should the law tell them instead that their right to develop is contingent upon the law in effect at the time of development?

Overall, there is little reason to recognize secure, future development rights. Property law protects buildings and other improvements for two reasons: to encourage their construction and (less importantly) to recognize the moral claim of the builder to the labor invested in it. Both rationales kick in, however, only when construction begins or perhaps a bit earlier, when work on the project commences behind the scenes. Until then, the landowner has a moral claim only to fair treatment and due process of law. Money spent to buy land (or water or other parts of nature), is not, in Lockean terms, a morally worthy investment, for it creates no value. Society has an interest in keeping homes and buildings valuable; it has no such interest in elevating market prices of bare land, which comes from nature alone. Land values based on proposed new or expanded uses are merely speculative, resting on guesses about future events in the market and at law. Society has no greater interest in protecting such values than it does in protecting speculative investments in gold or medieval paintings.

It is instructive here to compare the case of vacant land that awaits a valuable use with the related case of future human labor that similarly awaits use. What people produce with their labor is entitled to after-the-fact legal protection. But what legal protection does labor have prospectively, before the laborer has expended it? What protection, that is, does the law give to a person's desire to exert labor in a particular way next year or 5 or 20 years hence? The answer is: practically none. Laws governing the practice of a profession are subject to change at any time. A person planning to enter a profession in the future can hardly claim an immunity from new rules simply because she had preexisting hopes to enter the profession (or, even more extreme, simply because she was alive). Laws do sometimes contain grandfather clauses that protect people who have already expended labor preparing for a profession; new education rules on entering the bar, for instance, often apply only to people who have not yet begun law school. But such protection is akin to protecting a homebuilder against new rules that take effect when a project is half-constructed. It is not akin to allowing an owner of vacant land to challenge building restrictions that took effect years earlier.

Not just morally but in practical terms, having to do with property law's role in encouraging enterprise, there is a big difference between protecting *existing* land uses and protecting *prospective* ones. When the law allowed existing uses to begin, it implicitly promised a degree of protection. To go against that promise is to unsettle future development projects. No such worry arises, however, in the case of a landowner's hope to engage in a future project.

Whatever level of development lawmakers allow, individual landowners always have a moral claim to fair treatment in comparison with other landowners. Too often, governments have trouble respecting this entitlement when they control development: they allow one landowner to develop and then deny the same right to a neighbor, whose planned activity is essentially the same and whose lands are ecologically similar. The problem is posed starkly by the case where a lawmaking community wants to limit overall development in a region. How can it do so and achieve its conservation goals while treating landowners fairly?

One approach widely used for years was the minimum lot-size requirement, which limits home construction to one home per 10 acres, for instance, or per 40 acres. Such laws treat landowners equally and do succeed in capping overall construction. But the new development typically ends up in the wrong places. Minimum lot-size rules, meant to control sprawling development, can actually stimulate it by forcing developers to consume more space. New Jersey had this experience under its Pinelands comprehensive plan at issue in *Gardner;* because of it, the 10-acre development option was dropped.

A second-generation legal approach to this problem, also illustrated by the Pinelands plan, has been to make use of transferable development rights, or TDRs. Under a TDR scheme (called Pinelands Development Credits in the Pinelands plan), lawmakers decide upon the maximum amount of development to allow and where it ought to take place. Landowners then receive development rights that are similar to those used in minimum lot-size schemes; they can build one structure for every 10 acres or 40 acres that they own (two per 39 acres in *Gardner*). But the TDR scheme includes an additional limitation: the development rights can be exercised only in specifically designated locations, and a landowner may or may not own land in such an area (the Gardners did not). Two elements combine to make the scheme fair. First, the development rights are transferable, so that a person who owns rights and either does not want to use them or lacks the right land to use them can sell them for cash, thereby gaining from regional development without personally undertaking it. Second, areas designated for development allow development at relatively high densities. The owners of such lands, however, are allocated only the same modest development rights as other landowners. To develop up to the maximum allowed density, the owner must buy development rights from other landowners. The developing landowner gains because her land rises in value as more development rights are acquired and exercised. Nondeveloping owners share in that gain because the developer pays cash for their transferable rights.

When they work, TDR schemes help to achieve conservation goals because they divert development into those areas where it is believed to be good for the community. In practice, however, most citizens view TDR schemes as alien creatures, and so far such schemes have been nearly impossible to set up. The fairness elements are present only when a workable market arises in the development rights, so that the market prices of the rights really allow nondeveloping landowners to participate fairly in the gains of development. An even bigger problem is the practical reality that TDR schemes work best when imposed before substantial development has occurred. Lawmakers need to look ahead and respond to a problem while it is in its early stages. Governments have shown an ability to do so only in places of exceptional ecological value (such as the Pinelands, parts of Long Island, and Lake Tahoe on the California-Nevada border). Instead, most governments wait until problems become acute and then try to draw a line halting all future development—as Kittery, Maine, did when it banned the condominium project proposed by Grant's Farm Associates. That more common approach in essence uses a first-in-time method of handing out development rights. Landowners who develop early get to do so; those who wait too long get hit with the ban. First-in-time is not the least-fair method of allocating valuable property rights, but it is harsh and easily criticized all the same.

Moreover, governments that draw lines to halt further development have trouble sticking with them under pressure from landowners who have powerful economic incentives to keep pushing against legal limits. The first-in-time method is also weak in that it typically produces haphazard development.

What, then, might be done to achieve conservation while treating landowners fairly?

Surprisingly, a fairer approach would be to eliminate nearly all development rights. Landowners would then have no protected right to develop. Instead, they could develop only with permission from community leaders, who would act, ideally, in accordance with a well-considered development plan. Those receiving permission to develop would be understood as receiving a benefit from the public. In exchange for that benefit, they would be expected to compensate the community in some manner commensurate with the economic value of their gain.

At first glance, such an approach will seem unfair, if not profoundly misguided, to most Americans. But the unfairness arises only if we assume that landowners deserve a right to develop in the first place. But why should they, when the community itself largely created the development value? Why should they, when property law can stimulate enterprise perfectly well without secure development rights? Since World War II, this basic approach has been successfully followed in Great Britain, where landed property rights rest on the same common law that applies in the United States.

When a development permit is viewed as a publicly conferred benefit that a landowner should pay for, taxpayers are the ones who capture the community-created increases in land value. What the landowner loses, the taxpayer gains. This shift in economic benefit, though, is not the main virtue of this approach. Its main virtue is that landowners lose much of their incentive to push hard against government to gain a right to develop. When a right to develop comes free of charge and is worth thousands or even hundreds of thousands of dollars, landowners can spend a great deal to get it, manipulating zoning processes, working political angles, and pressing incessantly against development limits. In addition, cries of unfairness are loud when government decisions allow some landowners to gain hugely and others not at all. Take away the rise in value of the underlying vacant land, created by the community rather than the landowner, and the picture changes profoundly. Development can still bring gains, but the gains take the form of return on labor and enterprise, not a rise in bare land values. Land speculation would decrease sig-nif-icantly, leaving prices more affordable for people who want to devote land to farming, conservation, or other less intensive uses. Public programs requiring new land would also become less expensive. Cities would find it easier to promote "in-fill" development on sites within existing city boundaries that developers now bypass in the rush to build on the fringe. Landowners would be the losers, but they would be losing market values that they did not create.

What, then, of the effects on potential home buyers? Would they pay higher prices because of such a scheme? The answer would depend largely on the amount of development that a community per-mits. A government could allow expansive development, thereby keeping home prices low while still channeling development into areas where it yielded the greatest social benefit. Clustered develop-ment reduces the costs of such infrastructure elements as roads, schools, utility lines, and public transportation routes. When devel-opment everywhere is sharply limited, of course, home prices can rise. But sharp limits on development could make good policy sense in some situations. When new development would in fact harm the community, lawmakers might wisely divert it elsewhere.

So long as landowners possess secure development rights, com-munities may have no choice but to purchase them to keep harmful development from taking place. The community creates the value and then finds itself having to buy it back. Taxpayers are the obvious, if easily ignored, losers. Increasing this unfairness is the economic reality that as more development rights are purchased, prices rise on remaining development lands. Thus, as a community (or conservation group) buys development rights, it raises the prices that it must pay when it next goes out to buy more.

Land Reassembly

Some conservation goals can be achieved only when fragmented landscapes are reassembled into common ownership or management. Regulation alone is not always adequate to coordinate land uses in needed ways. The survival of wildlife populations, for instance, may depend on their ability to migrate across landscapes to reach seasonal habitats. A migration corridor may work only if it contains particular vegetation and connects distant locations without a break. Similarly, a hiking trail will typically succeed only if it contains no gaps. Government, of course, has long held the power of eminent domain to buy land without an owner's consent. In the nineteenth century, state governments exercised that power freely to buy land for roads and other public projects. They also used it to aid private development activities that in their view promoted the public interest. But government purchases today often stimulate resentment, and governments have trouble buying land at prices fair to taxpayers. Indeed, some government bodies go out of their way to avoid exercising eminent domain, paying prices far above the market, as if keeping a few landowners happy is more important than treating the mass of taxpayers fairly.

Eminent domain is constitutionally permissible only when the property is taken for a "public use," but public use does not mean that the public must have access to the land acquired. Public use, according to the Supreme Court, means little more than public benefit.[7] Governments have often taken land and then sold it to private parties for private use, when the private use arguably brought public gains. In the eighteenth and nineteenth centuries, governments allowed miners, irrigators, and others to undertake what could fairly be called private condemnation—buying land despite the seller's resistance—when doing so served the public. What characterized the private condemnation cases was the need of the private buyer for a particular property interest and no other: Nature itself prescribed where a ditch or right of way needed to go.

Given the challenges that governments face today in reassembling land, might it make sense to revive nineteenth-century precedents and update them to present needs? If it made sense a century ago to allow private irrigators to condemn lengthy corridors to construct private irrigation ditches, is it any less legitimate today to allow a conservation organization to exercise similar powers to assemble a valuable wildlife corridor or to help preserve a historic urban neighborhood? Going a step further, if the purchased property interests would directly benefit the public at large, might government even put up some of the funding to make the purchases possible—paying half the price, for instance, of any conservation interest or historic-preservation easement that a certified organization acquired, on the condition that the interest be used in ways benefiting the public? In terms of constitutional law, the case would seem an easy one to resolve: the judicial precedents upholding nineteenth-century condemnation statutes would seem to apply to their twenty-first-century counterparts. Indeed, recent Supreme Court precedents on "public use" have relaxed the limit considerably, allowing governments to condemn land for almost any purpose that plausibly benefits the public.

If government were paying only half the purchase price, private interests would need to cover the rest. And in doing so, they would have adequate incentive to go after lands that yielded the highest conservation benefits. Private groups can often act more quickly than governments, and they are less swayed by political considerations.

Private condemnation under carefully prescribed legal limits could be one of the new generation of legal tools that harness private initiative to achieve sound public aims. As such, it might be just the kind of mixed private-public effort that free-market environmentalists would find appealing.

The Right to Exclude

Few property-law issues arouse more passion than the right of landowners to exclude people from their lands. Private property has long included that right, but it has been subject to important limits. In colonial and early federal times, it was particularly weak with respect to unimproved rural land. Not until late in the twentieth century did the right to exclude vault to the status it now enjoys in the minds of many as the most important of all landowner rights.[8] Why it now stands so high is unclear. The right to exclude is valuable when it allows a landowner to halt disruptive intrusions. But what about the right to exclude people who are merely passing across the land in ways that do not disrupt, do not invade privacy, and cause no physical harm? In such cases, the right to exclude is of trivial importance. Why honor completely a landowner's right to keep out harmless trespassers, when, for instance, the owner may have only limited power to halt a neighboring land use that disrupts what he wants to do? The rational owner would readily give up the first to get more of the second.

The right to exclude is no better grounded, legally or philosophically, than any other landowner right. It too needs to be justified in terms of the common good. If the public owns the wildlife on private land, is it wrong for citizens to want to see what they own and interact with it? In Lockean terms, landowners have no moral claim on nature itself or on the benefits that nature yields. Landowners do have legitimate worries about interferences, damage to their lands, and possible liability for injuries. But these worries can be resolved, as they have been in other countries (for instance, by limits on public hikers getting close to homes, disturbing livestock or gardens, leaving gates open, or hiking during times when they might disturb nesting game).

It is on the issue of public wandering rights, where access would cause no harm, that one sees perhaps the greatest incongruity in contemporary libertarian thought. According to libertarians, expansive private property rights foster liberty, and the more expansive the rights, the greater the liberty. But what about the liberty of citizens generally? In this setting, libertarian thought would seem to call for a curtailment of private rights. When landowners close off their lands, using state power to do so, they limit the liberties of citizens to wander at will. A right-to-roam statute would, in practice, significantly expand the physical liberties of the public at the cost of a much lesser restriction on landowners.

Land Health and Private Property

Perhaps the ultimate issue in redefining private property—and certainly the most enigmatic—is the public's interest in promoting the well-being of landscapes as a whole. Aldo Leopold's vision of land health was and is a deceptively simple idea. By land, Leopold meant the entire community of life, humans included. By health he meant a mode of functioning that allows life to flourish indefinitely. To Leopold, it seemed obvious to put the two ideas together; it seemed incontrovertible that humans ought to live in ways that nourish the entire community of life.

Leopold's idea, though, did not catch on in his day, and it still has not, mostly for cultural reasons. Americans continue to have trouble with the idea that nature imposes constraints. Nature is still something to conquer, and the conquest continues, particularly at the genetic level. Decision-making processes tend to take into account only what we know and to ignore the vast amounts that we do not. Desirous of protecting individual liberty over nature, we charge ahead, presuming that we can do what we want until contrary proof is overwhelming. Viewing society (as we largely do) as merely a collection of individual humans and nature as a mass of discrete parts, we have trouble understanding the world as an integrated community in which the well-being of the parts depends on the well-being of the whole.

As commonly understood today in the United States, private property stands starkly opposed to holistic, ecological goals such as land health. And little wonder, given that the main strands of contemporary ownership came together at a time when the liberated entrepreneur, not the healthy community, was the symbol of progress. Centuries ago, citizens would likely have responded to Leopold's thinking better than the average modern of his day did, for people then took holistic visions more seriously. They saw themselves, as Leopold came to see himself, as a part of something larger. Holistic thinking has had its past; particularly in our dealings with nature, it deserves also to have its future.

Should the day come when land health is taken seriously as a public goal, private property could be put to good use achieving it. When American law banned slavery, market participants could no longer use slave labor to produce goods for the market. The legal bar took effect, and the national economy charged on. A generation or two later, public sentiment similarly turned against the use of child labor and the use of laborers for excessive hours under dangerous conditions. Again the market accommodated the change without noticeable cost. In recent years, developers have been told to steer clear of wetlands, and they have responded by looking for more ecologically suitable lands. The market has not suffered, nor has the economy. The cost of realizing land health might, in fact, be quite modest in economic terms. It would certainly *not* be modest, however, in terms of cultural values and perceptions. We would need to cast aside old ways of seeing the land, curb our human arrogance, and reduce our detachment from nature and our belief in our superiority. Land health would entail giving up many old values. But the long-term gains would be immeasurable.

Not economics, then, but cultural values stand in the way of a transition to a more ecologically and ethically sound way of life. Private property as now configured is an obstacle to the achievement of land health. But it is an obstacle that is highly flexible; with the right kind of pruning and reshaping, it could be readily transformed into a useful tool to heal the land.

CHAPTER TEN

FAIR GOVERNANCE

South Carolina, 1818

Astride his horse and in search of deer, one Singleton entered into the unenclosed and unimproved land owned by M'Conico. M'Conico ordered him to leave, Singleton refused, and M'Conico sued for trespass. A local jury ruled in favor of the wandering hunter, and the landowner appealed to the South Carolina Supreme Court. The rule of law that should govern the case, M'Conico argued to the court, was that a trespass occurred whenever a hunter failed to depart private land when ordered to do so, even if the land was unenclosed and the hunter caused no harm.

In a 5–1 ruling, the Court rejected the idea:

> Until the bringing of this action, the right to hunt on unenclosed and uncultivated lands has never been disputed, and it is well known that it has been universally exercised from the first settlement of the country up to the present; and the time has been, when, in all probability, obedient as our ancestors were to the law of the country, a civil war would have been the consequence of such an attempt, even by the legislature, to enforce a restraint on this privilege.[1]

"The forest was regarded as a common" into which hunters had the right to enter at their pleasure, Justice Johnson explained. Forests served as a source of food for many of the state's citizens. In addition, public hunting on unenclosed lands allowed citizens to learn "the dexterous use and consequent certainty of firearms." Thus trained, citizens could ably serve as militia men, thereby allowing the state to avoid the costs and dangers of a large standing army. Open hunting, in short, promoted the common good.

Given Singleton's right to hunt on unenclosed lands, it seemed obvious, Justice Johnson concluded, "that the dissent or disapprobation of the owner cannot deprive him of it; for I am sure it never yet entered the mind of any man, that a right which the law gives, can be defeated at the mere will and caprice of an individual."[2]

New York, 2000

Sour Mountain Realty, Inc., owned 213 acres of "rugged, rocky, and undeveloped land" on the slopes of Fishkill Ridge in Dutchess County, New York. The land abutted the Fishkill Ridge Conservation Area, which a conservation group, Scenic Hudson, Inc., had purchased and which was managed as part of Hudson Highlands State Park. In the early 1990s, Sour Mountain Realty sought approval to quarry gravel from its property. The town of Fishkill, supportive of the mining, rezoned the tract from residential to planned industry. Objecting to this rezoning were both nearby homeowners, who claimed that blasting and rock crushing would disturb their residential life, and Scenic Hudson, Inc, which pointed out that the quarry would be an eyesore and harm the region's tourist trade.

As the rezoning was taking place and mining permits were being sought, biologists located a den of timber rattlesnakes 250 feet from the edge of the Sour Mountain tract. The timber rattler was a threatened species under New York's endangered species act, and because of that the state Department of Environmental Conservation insisted that mining be delayed until environmental studies could gauge its likely effects. In January 1999, after unsuccessfully challenging the department's order, Sour Mountain announced plans to construct a 3,500-foot-long snake-proof fence to keep the rattlers from entering its land. Although the state objected, pointing out that the fence would likely violate the endangered species act by disrupting the rattlers' essential behavior and habitat, Sour Mountain nonetheless went ahead. New York then sought a court order compelling the fence's removal.

At the ensuing trial, state biologists Theodore Kerpez and William Brown testified that timber rattlers had only a limited number of suitable dens in New York State where they could survive the winter months and that the snakes living in the Sour Mountain den regularly migrated across the Sour Mountain site and used it for summer foraging. "The snakes were not really dangerous to people," Kerpez testified; indeed, a person was more likely to be struck by lightning than bitten by a rattlesnake. According to Brown, the rattler was an ecologically important predator in the "'food web of the deciduous forest.'" Sour Mountain's fence, the scientists concluded, interfered with the rattlers' migratory movements. It also constricted its summer habitat and exposed individual snakes to harm by diverting or shunting them along the fence.

In court, the key legal issue was whether the fence amounted to an unlawful "taking" of the threatened species because it curtailed the snakes' habitat and blocked their migrations. The New York statute that prohibited unlawful takings defined the term broadly, including within its reach not just pursuing, shooting, hunting, and killing the species but "all lesser acts such as disturbing, harrying, or worrying" it. Because the fence disturbed the snakes, the court concluded, it violated the law. As for the effect of the statute on Sour Mountain's property rights, it was not so excessive as to amount to a constitutional infringement. The state had not "physically occupied or appropriated any portion of the parcel," the appellate court observed, but had instead merely restricted use of it, and the economic effect of the law was at best "tenuous" given the proposed use (gravel mining) and the low danger that the snakes posed.[3]

While Sour Mountain Realty was losing its endangered species case, it was similarly losing in its attempt to gain a permit to mine. State authorities denied the permit because of the expected harm that mining would cause to surrounding lands and the local economy.

To study the history of property law in America is to see reflections of major currents in the country's culture and economy. At first glance and despite their separation in time, *M'Conico v. Singleton* and *State v. Sour Mountain Realty, Inc.*, display intriguing continuities. In each case, a landowner seeks to exercise a right to exclude and fails because of a conflict with another activity that society deems more important. Yet much had happened in the decades that separated the two rulings. Few citizens in 1818 could have comprehended a public policy that protected rattlesnakes. Perhaps no one then would have worried about the loss of rattler habitat or known how a fence might disrupt the snakes' behavior. Hunting, however, they did know about, and they viewed it as important enough to warrant protection. At the modern end, state law in 2000 was willing and constitutionally able to protect rattlesnakes entering Sour Mountain's land, at least when the landowner's intended activity could still proceed. Yet by then courts would have promptly struck down any statute that tried to open rural lands to human hunters—or even to hikers—against the landowner's will. Recreational pursuits could be conducted elsewhere, people had come to believe, and protecting them was less important than protecting the landowner's desire to control physical access. Both eras respected private property, yet in different ways both made ownership rights subordinate to competing public interests.

A variety of narratives can be constructed to connect and interpret these two revealing rulings. One story would be about the rise in American culture of ecological knowledge and new understandings of nature's value and about the increased role of experts and scientific knowledge in resolving courtroom disputes. Another would explore the decline of subsistence hunting in the nation's economy and the law's tendency over time to discount the importance, or even the possibility, of a person's gaining sustenance directly from the land. A third story might dwell upon the rise of government bureaucracy and the increase in litigation that featured, not one private citizen squaring off against another, with a court looking after the common good, but instead citizen versus the state, with a state agency expected to assert the public's needs. Related to this third story would be one about the declining importance of the common law and about the gradual shift of policy-making power from judges to legislatures and regulatory agencies.

Private property, plainly, has not been an unchanging arrangement: It is an organic, flexible institution, capable of taking many forms and responding to diverse aims. This very flexibility, however, has been as much a source of anxiety as it has been a comfort, for if property law can be reworked in ways that take into account changing conditions, so too can it be reworked in ways that grant owners too much power or that undercut the institution's ability to foster enterprise. To guard against perceived dangers, one is tempted to limit or even halt the law's evolution, perhaps by interpreting the Constitution as a severe limit on the powers of lawmakers to make changes. But to do so would be to sever property's link to the culture that it serves. In time, a static property regime would inevitably become an anachronism and would gradually be perceived as an obstacle to progress.

For the institution of private property to be vital, it must remain flexible. It also needs to be well tended by lawmakers. High courts can supply the needed flexibility by interpreting the Constitution in ways that constrain legislatures and ordinance drafters only min-imally. The "well tended" part of the equation, however, is not so easily accomplished. "Well tended" means cared for by seasoned lawmakers who are thoughtful and competent, who are responsive to public needs over private power interests, and who recognize how private property might help to achieve the public good.

What might be done to reduce worries that the institution of pri-vate property will be manipulated in damaging ways? And short of the miraculous rise of a new breed of omniscient, ethical lawmaker, what institutional steps might be taken to help ordinary humans reach better decisions?

Update the Common Law and the Overall Meaning of Ownership

One of the great failings of the past century has been the lack of guid-ance from state supreme courts on the rights and responsibilities of owning land and other parts of nature. Courts do more than resolve particular disputes. They explain key legal institutions and educate the public about them. One reason absolutist images of ownership have gained such currency is that contemporary courts have said so little about what it means to own nature today. Courts have in-terpreted statutes, applied regulations, and occasionally fine-tuned common law rules. But they have done little to describe how state, federal, and local laws work together to define a sphere of landowner independence. The public is without moorings on the subject, but hardly more so than most lawyers. What does it mean today to own land? When the common law enjoyed its golden age (as historians have termed it) during the antebellum era, nationally prominent state jurists such as Lemuel Shaw of Massachusetts skillfully per-formed the task of describing property broadly and situating it within American values and institutions. A few latter-day Lemuel Shaws would be welcome today.

If they were here, what could they do?

To begin with, courts could explain that land ownership is no longer defined entirely or even largely by the judge-made common law. In the mid–nineteenth century, when Lemuel Shaw and other jurists talked about private land, federal and state statutes had little effect on how owners of nature could use what they owned. Now statutes play key roles. Shaw was familiar with local land-use ordinances, but since his day they have become more widespread and detailed and they need to be better integrated into the overall picture. Private property is a creature of law, as Benjamin Franklin explained, and it is the sum total of all applicable laws, not merely a subset of them, that shapes it. This point ought to be clear—and certainly land developers know it from experience—but commentators on the subject often cling to more simplistic views. They assume that it is the old common law that defines ownership and that later statutes and regulations merely distort that ownership. That perspective is plainly wrong. State legislatures have broad power to revise the common law, and they have exercised it often. Congress, in turn, has the power to override state law, including the state common law, which it has also exercised. But the aura of the common law lives on, particularly among those who prefer the prodevelopment slant of the late nineteenth century.

State courts could perform a valuable service by explaining how common law, statutes, and regulations all fit together. As they do that, they could also bring the common law into better alignment with present-day needs and values. Late in the nineteenth century, courts began to defer more and more to legislatures and regulatory bodies, so much so that some wondered whether courts had any continuing lawmaking role. The powers of courts, of course, are limited in that they cannot overrule statutes unless they conflict with the federal or state constitutions. But the common law has always been a judicial creation. It remains the courts' job to keep it up to date.

Even with the modern era's flurry of statutes and regulations, the common law of private property remains important. It resolves cases where no statute or ordinance governs. It supplies the background principles and ideas of ownership that give shape to an overall organizing vision of what ownership means. When a new statute or regulation comes along, its effect is commonly measured by how much it changes these background principles. The more outdated the principles, the greater the change that a statute appears to make.

Critics of present-era conservation laws often portray them as severe interferences with private property rights, pointing out (and usually decrying) how different they are from the common law of a century ago. Or even more extremely, they measure a new law's effects by contrasting it with private property rights in an imagined world in which landowners can do whatever they like, so long as they do not physically invade neighboring land. When examined in this way, present-day conservation laws appear more suspect, their economic effects become more acute, and the demand for landowner compensation grows louder.

The flaws in this reasoning would be easier to see if courts updated the common law principles of landownership. The *sic utere tuo* doctrine remains a guiding principle of ownership. Landowners have no rights to use what they own in ways that cause harm to neighbors or the community at large. When this principle is kept front and center, it becomes easier to see that a statute banning a new type of land-use harm may not curtail landowner rights in any material new way; it might instead merely give specific application to an already existing limit on those rights. Along with the venerable concept of *sic utere tuo*, courts should revive the phrase once firmly linked to it: *salus populi suprema lex est*, the good of the people is the supreme law. As

Lemuel Shaw and other antebellum judges made clear, landowners have their rights, but the public itself and communities as such also have rights. When rights clash, it is the courts' job to reconcile them.

Updating the common law and applying it to current circumstances (in terms of specifying what land-use activities are deemed harmful, for instance) would yield many benefits. The meaning of ownership would gain greater focus. The public could measure the effects of new statutes on private rights more accurately. Beyond that, the common law itself would not be the problem it is now in many legal settings. For example, the long-standing "beneficial use" and "reasonable use" limits on private water rights in the West too often retain meanings that date from a century ago. If the common law were more in tune with the times—if it reflected better the widespread public demand for conservation—the pressure on legislatures to address conservation problems could lessen. If the common law banned many of the land-use practices that are widely viewed today as harmful—destroying wetlands, allowing soil to erode, draining aquifers, leaving dilapidated buildings dangerously unattended—the need for lawmakers to do so would diminish. The stakes would decline in the legislative arena, with big money perhaps wielding less influence.

Recognize Openly the Task of Redefining Landowner Rights

Not just courts but legislatures, city councils, regional planning agencies, and administrative bodies of all types could improve their work if they thought more broadly about what they were doing when they tinkered with the rights and responsibilities of owning nature. Private property is not a God-given bundle of rights, nor does the Constitution set forth minimal standards for it. It is up to lawmakers to decide what it means, generation upon generation. Collectively they have vast powers, matched with far-reaching responsibilities.

Because private property is an institution that serves vital social aims, lawmakers need to see clearly what they are doing when they alter the rights and responsibilities of ownership. They must keep in mind the institution and all its goals and recognize clearly how legal changes would affect those goals.

Lawmakers need to attend particularly to the tensions among private property's various aims, making sensible compromises and ensuring that no single goal receives undue emphasis. Lawmakers commonly overemphasize the goal of fostering enterprise; they give too much weight to the desire of landowners to retain expansive development rights, thereby discounting other social goals. On the other hand, regulatory agencies created solely to deal with conservation issues sometimes fail to think clearly about how particular regulatory measures affect the achievement of property's other public aims.

Property law should not be called upon to deal with social problems that are better dealt with in other ways. For instance, a shortage in low- or moderate-income housing should not lead to an expansion of the development rights of landowners living on a community's fringe if added sprawl would otherwise be imprudent. Instead, housing needs should be met by promoting more efficient housing patterns within already developed areas.

When resolving issues about single parcels of land, lawmakers need to resist the temptation to frame their role as merely balancing public interests against private desires in the context of that single parcel. Neighbors as well as owners of similar lands elsewhere always need to be taken into account. Taxpayers and their fair treatment also deserve consideration, and so do the larger landscape's ecological functioning and the reality that new land uses add to cumulative burdens. Only by considering all these matters can lawmakers ensure that a landowner's rights fit together with the rights of neighbors, compare fairly to the rights of owners of similar lands, treat tax-payers fairly, and sustain the landscape as a whole.

Sound decisions arise from good reasoning. Good reasoning is often stimulated when lawmakers take the time to explain why they did what they did and why they thought a decision best served the public interest. Courts write lengthy judicial opinions for just this reason, and the court system is better because of it. If lawmakers would talk more about big-picture issues, the parties pushing against the laws might do so as well. If legislatures openly considered broader goals and implications in their processes and ultimate deci-sions, landowners who disliked their decisions would be less inclined simply to echo the refrain, "My rights have been violated."

Engage and Coordinate All Levels of Government

Sound land uses and conservation can be achieved only when all levels of government, from local to national, get involved in the work. Local governments can fairly address some challenges but not others. More regional planning is needed, as well as forceful tools to ensure that the plans have teeth. Inevitably, a greater federal role will be necessary to deal with many large-scale land-use issues, simply because states and local governments too often lack the independence to resist the coordinated, well-funded demands of big industry.

To the extent feasible, land-related problems should be addressed by the government that is closest to the landowner and the land. Local people often know the land best and usually have the most at stake. On the other hand, the tragedy of fragmentation can work at large scales as well as small ones: sometimes local communities ignore the ill effects that their actions have downstream or down-wind. Higher levels of government need to help in such situations—

as they did in conserving the Pinelands of New Jersey—and they need to coordinate their actions with one another.

The Fishkill–Sour Mountain case is similar to countless other land-use disputes around the country and illustrates the need for coordination among levels of government. The town of Fishkill, New York, moved quickly to rezone Sour Mountain to allow gravel quarrying because the mining operation would add local jobs and pay local taxes. Fishkill was parochially concerned about its town alone. It took higher levels of government to see that the broader public interest was better served by having the mining take place elsewhere. To halt a gravel mine in one place is simply to make room for another mine elsewhere or to add business to other existing mines. The decision to ban the mining at Sour Mountain probably had no ill effects on mining in the larger region, while it aided tourism and protected neighbors. To study this dispute is to see why industrial groups and developers typically press hard to get conservation issues decided at the local level. Parochial interests are more likely to predominate there, and local decision-makers are more prone to ignore larger contexts. (The exception is when a land use is widely viewed as undesirable; a landfill, for instance, or a mega hog farm. In such cases, industries typically want regulatory authority elevated to higher levels and turned over to agencies—such as state departments of agriculture—that they are better able to control.)

Involve Citizens More Meaningfully

Lawmakers need to do better at drawing citizens into their processes, eliciting their views about the public interest and how private property can best serve it. They should do so in ways that encourage people to attend to the larger issues. Why not overtly encourage citizens to think about private property as an institution and to reflect on how it might best serve the common good? Citizen advisory groups sometimes participate usefully in land-planning processes, although they are rarely asked to think about the institutional aspects of ownership. Less formal groups could also work well, particularly as part of a government-led goal-setting process. Too often, citizens are treated as annoyances, their capabilities underestimated.[4]

In the typical government process, citizens are merely given the chance to submit comments in writing or to show up at public hearings and present testimony. But how much hearing takes place at the usual hearing? Speakers arrive with ideas firmly set; indeed, the more firmly they are set and the more passionately they are held, the more likely a person is to testify. Attendees at hearings rarely engage one another. Physically, they speak not to their fellow citizens but to a panel or hearing officer in the front of the room. Matters are even worse when comments are submitted in writing and the citizens who comment are isolated from one another; at least in a hearing, those speaking later can respond to what has already been said. Surely, better participatory processes are possible—processes that engage and educate interested citizens and that encourage them, as they participate, to rise above self-interest.

For government to succeed, Thomas Jefferson believed, people had to rise above self-interest and reflect on the good of the whole. Some citizens, of course, were better able to do this than others. But participants who showed up to promote their economic interests in an issue were *prima facie* ill-suited to participate. Comments by such "stakeholder groups" are not public comments; they express private interests that may or may not overlap with the good of the whole, and they should be labeled as such. Indeed, the most vociferous groups at public hearings often represent no more than a small fraction of 1 percent of the citizenry. Why should a homebuilders' association get away with the claim that it is the voice of prospective homeowners? At a gathering called to consider a plan limiting development, how different would the sense of the public be if "the public" excluded developers, homebuilders, and landowners poised to sell their lands at great gain?

In addition, more needs to be done to reconnect people to their governments, to the places they inhabit, and to their neighbors. A politics of engagement is needed, one in which people are drawn to listen to one another, to hammer out differences, and to reflect on the ways that their fates are intertwined. Engagement, it should be emphasized, is not the same as tolerance, nor is it the same as honoring cultural differences. One can tolerate by ignoring; one can honor cultural differences by viewing them from afar for their curiosity or entertainment value. Engagement is far more demanding. To engage is to seek to reconcile differences, not to leave them unresolved. To engage is to look for common ground while recognizing that one person's view might be far more sound than another's. To engage is to question, challenge, and even criticize one another, respectfully but nonetheless firmly, when the good of the whole requires it.

In the present age, tolerance has been elevated to the status of a prime virtue, a position that it never held in centuries past. With tolerance has come a lessened willingness to talk about responsibilities and to criticize one another for failing to fulfill them. Inevitably, the trend has proved harmful to institutions such as private property, which work well only when they include a careful calibration of rights and responsibilities. Property rights without responsibilities are virtual nonsense. Is it any wonder that the present era, more than any other, has seen a flourishing of the selfish assertion that a landowner can do whatever he wants, so long as he avoids overt harm? When it is viewed as impolite or politically incorrect to criticize neighbors and fellow citizens, one is apt to disengage and leave all problems at the doorstep of government. Individualism leads to stronger demands for tolerance; tolerance undercuts engagement and mutual criticism; the decline of criticism leads to increased government bureaucracy (as people turn problems over to government); and bureaucracy, operating in seclusion, fosters alienation and even more individualism.

Understand the Market's Strengths and Weaknesses

An essential need, not just for lawmakers but for engaged citizens, is to understand clearly the market's strengths and weaknesses and to use that knowledge when tinkering with property rights and promoting conservation. All citizens need to know, for instance, how to analyze the misleading claim that markets merely give people what they want, as well as the related mistaken claim that people vote most honestly when they act as independent consumers rather than as voting citizens.

The truth is, the market is the prime engine of landscape destruction, and the now-widespread talk about "harnessing the market" to achieve conservation cries out for challenge. To pay people to act right is not to use the market to promote conservation; it is to draw on the market's aura to sugarcoat what could well be an unfair raid on the public treasury. Similarly, to advocate freeing conservation groups so that they can enter the market and protect species or wildlife habitat is to dump onto a small number of people duties that in fairness should be borne by all. If conservation is to be left to private contributors, why not national defense? Markets do poorly at achieving such public goals as conservation (and national defense), and we need to know why.

For governance to be fair, it needs to include ways for individual landowners to seek redress when government goes awry and they are mistreated. The legal grounds on which they can legitimately complain make up an important part of private property as an institution. Claims of mistreatment first need to be presented to the lawmakers who caused the alleged mistreatment: The politics of engagement would require it. If not satisfied, though, owners deserve a chance to ask for a second opinion, by going to court and claiming that their rights have been constitutionally infringed. Their ability to do so gets courts involved and provides a useful check on the decisions of legislatures and regulatory bodies.

The idea that a land-use regulation could amount to an unlawful taking of property is largely a product of the twentieth century, beginning with the Supreme Court's 1922 ruling in *Pennsylvania Coal v. Mahon* (discussed in Chapter 3). Despite recent high-profile takings decisions hailed as victories by advocates of intensive property rights, takings law today remains highly deferential to lawmaking bodies. A law or regulation amounts to a taking only in rare, extreme circumstances—when it authorizes a permanent physical invasion of a private land parcel or deprives a land parcel of literally all its value. For landowners, it is modest protection indeed except for the issue of the landowner's right to exclude unwanted people and objects, which the Supreme Court has inexplicably rewarded with special status.[5]

Conservationists have largely viewed this lax takings doctrine as a good thing, because it gives lawmakers substantial discretion in going about their work. But is this so? Current takings law, to be sure, is not a serious roadblock to new conservation laws. But might it be causing trouble in other ways?

The Supreme Court's task, when resolving takings disputes, has been to decide when a regulation cuts so deeply into property rights that a landowner should get paid. The question of whether a taking has occurred is entirely one of constitutional law. But to decide what has been taken, one needs to know first what property rights the landowner possesses; and that initial question, the Court has said for generations, is not an issue of constitutional law. What property a person owns is determined by looking to other bodies of law, mostly state law.

The trouble with this approach or, more aptly, the awkwardness of it, is that property law itself is subject to change; it is a tool that the public uses to promote its evolving needs. It would be decidedly wrong to interpret the Constitution in a way that halted that necessary change. On the other side, the law of takings—the just-compensation clause of the Constitution—exists to protect the individual landowner against the abusive actions of the lawmaking majority. It would therefore also be wrong to interpret the Constitution in a way that gave lawmakers unlimited power to rewrite property laws, for they could then eliminate all rights that an owner possessed.

A powerful tension thus exists between the majority and the individual, a tension that the Supreme Court is called upon to resolve. The awkward question that the Supreme Court faces is this: When have lawmakers, in the process of changing an institution (private property) that properly responds to the majority will, acted in a way that is so unjust to individual owners that it should, in fairness, pay them? A more confusing question could hardly be asked.

The Supreme Court has had trouble answering this question, and its decisions have drawn a great deal of criticism. An important cause of the trouble, although one that is rarely noted, has been the Supreme Court's failure to think clearly about the first of the two issues that routinely arise in regulatory takings disputes. The Supreme Court, supreme and authoritative on issues of federal law, rarely addresses issues of state law in the course of its work. It is far less familiar with them than are state courts. For that reason (and no doubt others), the Court has had trouble identifying the precise property rights that a given landowner holds at the time a challenged law has allegedly interfered with them. Prone to focus only on the federal issue in any dispute, the Court has routinely rushed to the second issue—whether or not the law or regulation amounts to a taking. As the Court has done this, trying to protect landowners while at the same time giving lawmakers ample freedom to protect public interests, it has produced an oddly configured body of judicial precedent. Its decisions are fiercely protective of landowners, but they protect only a small portion or core of a landowner's rights. Where that core comes from in a legal sense is not at all clear. The right to exclude, the Court has said, is the chief attribute of ownership that the Constitution protects, yet state property law has never exalted this element of ownership. Is the Court championing the right to exclude so that it can appear to care about landowners without materially restraining the power of regulators to halt undesired land uses? And what about the other rights of landowners? The Court says that regulators cannot deprive land of all value (the test applied in the Cathedral Mansion South–National Zoo case), but regulators can mistreat landowners quite seriously without running afoul of that modest limit.

A better approach would be to view the just-compensation clause as protecting not merely some constitutionally defined core of rights but rather the full range of rights that a landowner possesses: the full array of rights that are recognized, at a given time and place, by the various laws that collectively prescribe what ownership means. The rights thus defined by the intersection of these laws are what the Constitution means, or ought to mean, by "property." These rights are what the Constitution should protect, not some core or residue of them. Property owners, in short, deserve broader protection than they now receive.

Having said that, though, one must go on to ask: How much protection should these more broadly defined property rights enjoy? Protection against what? Private rights cannot enjoy full protection against all shifts in property laws, for to provide such protection would be to kill, stuff, and mount on the wall a distinctly living institution.

So confusing is this entire subject that it is easy for observers to run aground logically at this point. If property law is an organic institution, with lawmakers having the power to rewrite laws, then what exactly does the just-compensation clause protect? If shifts in the law, even major ones, are permissible, could lawmakers not completely undercut a landowner's rights simply by rewriting the law? Could they not reduce private rights to the point where a landowner owned nothing? Many observers, reaching this point and unable to see a way ahead, have backed up and pushed legislatures to adopt a seemingly simpler test (though it would prove unsimple to apply in practice): a law amounts to a taking if it diminishes a land parcel's value by a specified percentage (for example, 50 percent).

The key to answering these legitimate questions is not to escape into a formulaic, market-value test but to think more clearly about why the just-compensation clause exists. The clause, like the other rights set forth in the Bill of Rights, is aimed at protecting landowners against mistreatment by government. Landowners get mistreated when governments make bad decisions, so the question becomes: When and in what way are land-related decisions sometimes bad? In the regulatory context (as opposed to physical confiscations), the possibilities fall into two overlapping categories.

One way landowners are treated badly is by being singled out for burdens materially different from those shouldered by other landowners whose lands are similar. The second, more subtle way is by having their rights as landowners altered by a shift or revision in property laws that is illegitimate in some significant way; that is, by a new law that is something other than a true revision in the rights and responsibilities of ownership. Legitimate changes in the prevailing laws of ownership—even new laws that fundamentally revise the rights and responsibilities of ownership—are proper and often necessary legal acts that landowners simply must accept. What landowners ought to have opportunity to complain about are curtailments of their rights that arise from government acts that are not justified as legitimate changes.

A landowner is improperly singled out for an extra burden when he is treated unfairly in comparison to other landowners who are similarly situated. In *Just v. Marinette County*, the celebrated Wisconsin decision from 1972, the Justs challenged a shoreland-protection law that applied to all shorelands in the county, and the court upheld it as a valid revision of landowner rights. If the law instead had applied only to the Justs' property or only to a small number of parcels—leaving other, essentially identical shoreland properties unaffected—the law would not have been a generally applicable revision of landowner rights and might well have been unconstitutional. In *Bormann v. Board of Supervisors*, as another example, had the Iowa legislature changed nuisance law statewide, the Bormanns and McGuires might have had no recourse. But the statute did not do that; it removed the rights of only the few landowners unfortunate enough to have neighbors who wanted to operate mega hog farms. The statute was therefore not a revision of landowner rights generally; it singled out landowners for special burdens that were not based on an ecological feature of their lands or on any harm that they personally were causing.

When deciding whether a landowner has been singled out, courts will face tough questions. Has the burden been severe enough to amount to a constitutional deprivation? Which other landowners, if any, are in the same situation as the plaintiff landowner, so that their treatment can be used as a comparison? Ecological differences are certainly proper for lawmakers to consider. Differences arise, too, from the surrounding human context; adjacent land uses and the spillover effects of a proposed use will vary from place to place. And there is a big difference between an existing use and a proposed new use. Lawmakers are likely to defend their work by pointing to some unique factor about an owner's land that justifies special treatment.

But they should be allowed to do that only when the factor really accounts for the differential treatment and is not merely a pretext. More can be said on this issue, of course, but in general, a new law that specially burdens a landowner (or a small group of owners) should be valid only when (1) the regulation bans an activity that lawmakers genuinely deem harmful, or (2) the burden is roughly proportional either to burdens that the landowner's activities are imposing on the public or to special benefits that the landowner has received from the public.

In addition to protecting landowners against being singled out, takings law should protect them against legal changes that are illegitimate in some general way. Here, too, the element of singling out is important, for illegitimate laws, regulations, and other government actions tend to affect only small numbers of landowners, but illegitimacy can come in other ways. The key question here: Is the new law intended to promote the public health, safety, or general welfare, and is it reasonably calculated to do so? If not, it is suspect. Does it apply to landowners similarly situated? Again, the more broadly a law applies, the more likely it is to be a change in the meaning of ownership, rather than a questionable effort by lawmakers to force particular landowners to act in ways that government prefers. Even a widely applicable law, however, can be illegitimate if its burdens on landowners are not matched by corresponding public benefits. Many new laws will implement evolving ideas about carrying capacity and land-use harm. They should not be struck down simply because they identify as harmful an activity that earlier generations saw differently.

For new laws to be legitimate, though, they need not always be based on a finding of harm. They need not, that is, draw inspiration from the *sic utere tuo* doctrine. New laws can promote the public health, safety, and welfare in various ways. Laws can impose affirmative duties on landowners to use their lands to promote the common good, including duties rooted in ethics, ecology, and even aesthetics, so long as they apply broadly and represent a real, legitimate shift in the way a community envisions private ownership. Communities, too, have rights, as courts used to announce regularly. The good of the people—*salus populi*—has been and should remain the supreme law.

Two pairs of decisions can usefully illustrate this issue of legitimate versus illegitimate change. The Pinelands conservation plan challenged in *Gardner* was plainly a wide-ranging, regional plan carefully calibrated to achieve its goals with burdens distributed among all landowners. Its legitimacy seems evident. More suspect was the regulatory decision-making by the Kittery, Maine, planning board in *Grant's Farm Associates*. There, the board made a decision about a single land parcel. Its reasons for restricting development were sound on their face, but the reported court decision leaves important facts unmentioned. Did the board apply its ordinances to other landowners just as rigorously? Had the board made a settled determination that specific types of land-use activities were harmful, or was it simply expressing a desire that a certain tract remain open? Shifting to the wildlife setting, the New York statute in *Barrett* that protected beaver was plainly a revision of statewide landowner rights, based on a newly identified form of harm. But what about the no-hunting ban that was challenged by the hunting club in *Cawsey v. Bricker*? Again, the court reasoned soundly when it said that the Skagit County, Washington, game commission could distinguish among land parcels based on their ecological suitability as game preserves. One wonders, though, whether all ecologically similar lands were constrained. If not, there was an element of unfairness, along with opportunities for favoritism. Did the game commission consider how it might have achieved its goals more fairly —for instance, by having the no-hunting zone rotate among all ecologically similar landowners over a period of years, so that owners were treated more evenly?

The Supreme Court has had trouble squarely facing this question of legal legitimacy because it has focused too much on the individual land parcel owned by the plaintiff in a suit, largely ignoring how the challenged law applies to other landowners. It has also ignored how the lawmakers went about crafting the challenged law or regulation. Did they pay attention to the effects of what they were doing on private property as an institution? Did they consider the larger landscape? Did they think seriously about how their proposed action would affect the ability of private property to serve its various aims? All these issues would seem relevant to whether a landowner received due process of law.

What the Supreme Court says about property rights and land-use regulation obviously carries a great deal of weight. Lawmakers everywhere pay attention, and what they have learned, unfortunately, is not particularly good. The Supreme Court suggests that they need worry only about infringing the small, constitutionally protected core of landowner rights; all other rights can be sacrificed. The Court seems to say that it is perfectly fine to make land-use decisions one parcel at a time, or at least to respond to complaints by looking only at individual parcels. Finally, the Court seems to say that it—and by implication, everyone else—can adequately protect private property without really thinking about property's various goals and about how a given law affects them. These are not good signals, and they have no doubt had bad effects on zoning boards and other regulatory bodies. Aggravating these problems has been the penchant of states (and other governments) to create regulatory agencies that have only narrow charters and that are told to pay attention only to a narrow range of policy concerns (for example, historic preservation, traffic patterns, or open-space protection). Such regulatory bodies are apt to ignore private property as an overall institution. Also problematic are regulatory agencies that control only small geographic areas (such as the planning board in Kittery, Maine), which can too easily ignore the surrounding landscape.

The stark truth is that the Supreme Court has not been doing its job very well on this issue. It has said precious little about why the Constitution protects private property, in what ways, and for what purposes. It has sent poorly considered signals to the country at large about how one decides whether a property owner has or has not been fairly treated. And it has said almost nothing about the processes and methods that lawmakers might use when tinkering with private rights. Better decisions would explain clearly the power that lawmakers have to adjust property rights while emphasizing also the responsibilities that go along with that power.

No doubt many conservationists will cringe at the thought of a regulatory takings jurisprudence that is *more* protective of landowner rights than current law. But current law is not nearly as helpful to conservation as they imagine. In the long run, conservation is not going to succeed if it unduly disrupts private property. In the short run, conservationists might get regulators to impose all manner of severe restrictions, but the laws of one day are subject to revision in the next. Unfair or unwise laws are particularly apt to be swept away. Conservationists would do better to stick to a path that treats private property with proper (though not undue) respect. Already public support for conservation is weakening because many citizens are unsure about how conservation measures affect private rights. When lawmaking is done in fair, open, and thoughtful ways, the public is more accepting and the legal results are more likely to last.

Just as much as lawmakers, conservationists and their organizations need to pay conscious attention to the larger landscape. They need to think about the bigger issues, such as the mix of rights and responsibilities that land ownership ought to entail. What should it mean to own nature in an age of growing ecological awareness? What should ownership mean in a time when more and more people are worried about the health of social and natural communities? If wetlands-protection laws and habitat-protection provisions are consistent with a new, conservative understanding of landownership, what is that understanding, and how consistent is it with America's core values? If conservationists would talk openly about such issues—and so far they have not—they might find that their work becomes easier. They might also find it feasible to take on bigger issues, getting state legislatures to rework the meaning of ownership overtly and thereby achieving success on a large scale. Why work parcel by parcel when a big shift could generate far more conservation benefits while treating landowners more equally?

It can be done. Private property can be modified in ways that promote conservative land uses and that add health to lands and social communities, without undercutting its long-standing purposes.

The problem with the Supreme Court's approach to takings jurisprudence is merely a variant on the problem that has corroded clear thinking about private property generally. It is too influenced by the liberal individualism of the modern era, by the tendency of Americans to think about social problems in terms of how they affect the individual and to see that individual as pitted in conflict against a bureaucratic state. Private property has become the special emblem of the strand of liberal individualism that seeks maximum freedom from government restraints, including restraints that fairly call citizens to perform their civic responsibilities.

For private property to serve contemporary society, it needs to move in a far different direction: the direction of community, responsibility, and social connection. In one of his final works, political commentator Christopher Lasch summed up this need:

> A public philosophy for the twenty-first century will have to give more weight to the community than to the right of private decision. It will have to emphasize responsibilities rather than rights. It will have to find a better expression of the community than the welfare state. It will have to limit the scope of the market and the power of corporations without replacing them with a centralized state bureaucracy.[6]

In addition to Lasch's criteria for a new civic vision, we need a new, ecologically and ethically guided attitude toward private land, a less domineering attitude that honors interdependence and recognizes the benefits of giving nature a role in the lawmaking process—particularly the process of deciding how private landowners can use what they own.

Few observers ruminated on the need for such a new attitude more than Aldo Leopold. He did so publicly in 1934, in an address delivered at the dedication of the University of Wisconsin's arboretum, which he had helped found. Leopold chose the occasion to bemoan the "iron-heel attitude" that had guided land-use practices over the previous century, "reduc[ing] by half the ability of Wisconsin [land] to support a cooperative community of men, animals, and plants." The appropriate response to such devastation was to rise up in protest, yet few citizens were doing it, in Wisconsin or elsewhere:

> If some foreign invader attempted such loot, the whole nation would resist to the last man and the last dollar. But as long as we loot ourselves, we charge the indignity to "rugged individualism," and try to forget it. But we cannot quite.[7]

Decades earlier, Leopold recounted, conservationists had begun their work expecting early success, only to realize in time the magnitude of the job: nothing short of "the reorganization of society. . . . We started to move a straw," he observed, "and end up with the job of moving a mountain."[8]

So far as Leopold could tell, no element of society was more in need of reorganization than private property, both as an institution and as a way of connecting people to the land and to one another. A legal reorganization, he knew in the 1920s and 1930s, would necessarily be a long way off. But it was not too early to pave the way for it. New ideas were needed; more ecological, ethical, and community-focused ideas; ideas phrased in terms of morality and collective responsibility; ideas that drew strength and inspiration from nature itself. "When land does well for its owner, and the owner does well by his land; when both end up better by reason of their partnership," Leopold would sum up, "we have conservation. When one of the other grows poorer, we do not."[9] Thoughtfully reshaped, private property could help make conservation a reality, in Leopold's day and in ours. It could bring within reach that lofty goal of land health, in which the entire community of life, humans included, flourishes and grows. It was an alluring goal and it retains its allure today, awaiting still the collective commitment and effort needed to achieve it.

Introduction

1. Echeverria and Eby, *Let the People Judge;* Helvarg, *War Against the Greens;* Sax, "Using Property Rights."

2. Fox, *American Conservation Movement;* Glanz, James, *Saving Our Soil;* Hays, *Beauty, Health, Permanence;* Rome, *Bulldozer in the Countryside;* Becker, Elizabeth, "Two Acres of Farm Lost to Sprawl Each Minute, New Study Says," *New York Times* (4 Oct. 2002); U.S. Department of Agriculture, Natural Resources Conservation Service, *1997 National Resources Inventory* (revision December 2000); U.S. Census Bureau, *Census 2000;* Street, John F., "Philadelphia's Neighborhood Initiative (NTI)," (15 April 2002) (available at www.usmayors.org).

3. de Crèvecoeur, *Letters from an American Farmer,* 20.

4. Rousseau, Jean-Jacques, *The Origin of Inequality,* quoted in MacPherson, *Mainstream and Critical Positions,* 31.

5. Quoted in McElfish, "Property Rights, Property Roots," 10234.

6. Quoted in Scott, *In Pursuit of Happiness,* 21.

7. Bentham, Jeremy, *The Theory of Legislation,* Chap. VIII ("On Property"), quoted in MacPherson, *Mainstream and Critical Positions,* 52.

8. Scott, *In Pursuit of Happiness,* 41–43, 57–58; Katz, "Thomas Jefferson."

9. Quoted in Katz, "Thomas Jefferson," 480 (from letter dated October 28, 1785).

10. Charles River Bridge v. Warren Bridge, 36 U.S. (11 Pet.) 420, 548 (1837).

11. Novak, *The People's Welfare,* 19–50.

Chapter 1

1. Bormann v. Board of Supervisors of Kossuth County, 584 N.W. 2d 306 (Iowa Supreme Court, 1998).

2. Echeverria and Eby, *Let the People Judge;* Helvarg, *War Against the Greens;* Sax, "Using Property Rights."

3. 33 United States Code §1344(a).

4. 16 United States Code §1538(a)(1).

5. Sax, "Using Property Rights."

6. Penner, *Property in Law;* Arnold, "Reconstitution of Property"; Duncan, "Reconceiving the Bundle of Sticks."

7. Fox, *American Conservation Movement;* Graham, *Man's Dominion;* Hays, *Gospel of Efficiency;* Judd, *Common Lands;* Lowenthal, *George Perkins Marsh;* Miller, *Gifford Pinchot;* Reiger, *American Sportsmen;* Trefethen, *Crusade for Wildlife;* Worster, *River Running West;* Bates, "Fulfilling American Democracy."

8. Judd, *Common Lands;* Cumbler, *Reasonable Use;* Steinberg, *Nature Incorporated.*

9. Goble and Freyfogle, *Wildlife Law,* 136–141; Tober, *Who Owns Wildlife,* 57–60, 119–123, 143–144.

10. Cumbler, *Reasonable Use;* Judd, *Common Lands,* 28–56; Mitchell, *Trespassing.*

11. Judd, *Common Lands,* 58–120.

12. In re Opinion of the Justices, 69 A. 627 (Maine Supreme Court, 1908).

13. Ibid., 629.

14. Judd, *Common Lands,* 118–120.

15. Barrett v. State, 220 N.Y. 423, 116 N.E. 99 (New York Court of Appeals, 1917).

16. 220 N.Y. at 427, 116 N.E. at 100.

17. Ibid.

18. 220 N.Y. at 430, 116 N.E. at 101.

19. Cawsey v. Brickey, 82 Wash. 653, 144 P. 938 (Supreme Court of Washington, 1914).

20. 82 Wash. at 658, 114 P. at 940.

Chapter 2

1. Garland, *Son of the Middle Border,* 195.

2. Ibid., 286.

3. Quoted in MacKaye, *The New Exploration,* 75.

4. Ibid., 160.

5. Anderson, *Benton MacKaye*, 211–227.

6. Berry, *Jayber Crow*, 194.

7. Schlatter, *Private Property*, 261–269.

8. Ibid., 265–269; Freyfogle, "Ethics," 632–635.

9. Schlatter, *Private Property*, 267; Philbrick, "Changing Conceptions," 692; Rose, "Keystone Right," 363.

10. A prominent study, citing anthropological literature, is Cronon, *Changes in the Land*, 34–67.

11. Polanyi, *Great Transformation*, 69–70.

12. Much of this paragraph and the next two are drawn from Gies, *Life in a Medieval Village*, supplemented by Hanawalt, *The Ties That Bound;* Pirenne, *Economic and Social History of Medieval Europe;* Rösener, *Peasants in the Middle Ages.*

13. Gies, *Life in Medieval Village*, 133.

14. The legal incidents of feudal landholding in England are considered in Baker, *Introduction to English Legal History*, 193–219; Milsom, *Historical Foundations of Common Law*, 99–165.

15. Fischer, *Albion's Seed;* Freyfogle, "Land Use"; Horn, *Adapting to the New World;* Lockridge, *A New England Town;* Morgan, *From Slavery to Freedom;* Pomfret, *Founding the American Colonies, 1583–1660;* Powell, *Puritan Village;* Taylor, Alan, *American Colonies.*

16. Bond, *Quit Rent System;* Crowley, *This Sheba;* Fisher, *Law of the Land;* Hoffer, *Law and People;* Isaac, *Transformation of Virginia;* Katz, "Thomas Jefferson"; Kulikoff, *Agrarian Origins;* Mensch, "Colonial Origins"; Nelson, *Americanization of Common Law;* Scott, *In Pursuit of Happiness;* Taylor, Alan, *American Colonies.*

17. Scott, *In Pursuit of Happiness*, 36–58.

18. Alexander, *Commodity and Propriety*, 33–36; Katz, "Thomas Jefferson."

19. Quoted in Katz, "Thomas Jefferson," 471.

20. Quoted in Katz, "Thomas Jefferson," 470.

21. Quoted in Scott, *In Pursuit of Happiness*, 41.

22. Quoted in Hart, "Land Use Law in the Early Republic," 1135.

23. Quoted in Scott, *In Pursuit of Happiness*, 19.

24. Hart, "Colonial Land Use Law," 1259–1263; Hart, "Forfeiture of Unimproved Land in the Early Republic"; Hart, "Land Use Law in the Early Republic," 1123–1130, 1137.

25. More, *Utopia*, 76.

26. Quoted in Hart, "Land Use Law in the Early Republic," 1126.
27. Quoted in Scott, *In Pursuit of Happiness*, 18.
28. Quoted in Scott, *In Pursuit of Happiness*, 20.
29. Alexander, *Commodity and Propriety*; Bailyn, *Ideological Origins*; Fisher, *Law of the Land*; Scott, *In Pursuit of Happiness*; Wood, *Creation of the American Republic*.
30. Alexander, *Commodity and Propriety*, 36–37; Scott, *In Pursuit of Happiness*, 24–28.
31. McCoy, *Elusive Republic*, 68.
32. Alexander, *Commodity and Propriety*, 29.
33. Ibid., 36.
34. Alexander, *Commodity and Propriety*; Bailyn, *Ideological Origins*; Ely, *Guardian of Every Other Right*; Fisher, *Law of the Land*; Scott, *In Pursuit of Happiness*; Wood, *Creation of the American Republic*.
35. Hart, "Colonial Land Use Law," 1259–1280; Hart, "Land Use Law in the Early Republic," 1107–1131; Hart, "Maryland Mill Act"; Hart, "Property Rights, Costs, and Welfare"; Hart "Takings and Compensation"; Horwitz, *Transformation of American Law, 1780–1860*, 64; Treanor, "Original Understanding."
36. Scott, *In Pursuit of Happiness*, 54–55.
37. Alexander, *Commodity and Propriety*, 26–71; Hart, "Colonial Land Use Law"; Hart, "Land Use Law in the Early Republic"; Maier, *American Scripture*, 146–147, passim.
38. Quoted in Scott, *In Pursuit of Happiness*, 21–22.
39. Novak, *The People's Welfare*, 11.
40. Hart, "Colonial Land Use"; Hart, "Land Use Law in the Early Republic."
41. Hart, "Colonial Land Use": Kinney, *Forest Legislation in America*.
42. Hart, "Colonial Land Use," 1273; Hart, "Land Use Law in the Early Republic," 1122–1123, 1145–1146.
43. Hart, "Colonial Land Use," 1281.

Chapter 3

1. Palmer v. Mulligan, 3 Cai. R. 307, 1 Am. Dec. 270 (N.Y. Sup. 1805).
2. For example, Horwitz, *Transformation of American Law, 1780–1860*, 2–3, 37–38.

3. 3 Cai. at 314.

4. Blackstone, *Commentaries*, 217–218; Boorstin, *Mysterious Science of Law*, 167–180; Burns, "Blackstone's Theory," 76–79; Horwitz, *Transformation of American Law, 1780–1860*, 31.

5. Pennsylvania Coal Co. v. Sanderson, 113 Pa. 126, 6 A. 453 (1886).

6. 113 Pa. at 145; 6 A. at 456.

7. 113 Pa. at 146; 6 A. at 457.

8. Major works covering this shift include Alexander, *Commodity and Propriety;* Cumbler, *Reasonable Use;* Fisher, *Law of the Land;* Friedman, *History of American Law;* Hall, *Magic Mirror;* Halper, "Nuisance, Courts and Markets"; Halper, "Untangling the Nuisance Knot"; Horwitz, *Transformation of American Law, 1780–1860;* Horwitz, *Transformation of American Law, 1870–1960;* Hovenkamp, *Enterprise and American Law;* Hurst, *Law and Conditions of Freedom;* Kurtz, "Anti-Entrepreneurial Nuisance Injunctions"; Kutler, *Privilege and Creative Destruction;* Novak, *The People's Welfare;* Opie, *Nature's Nation;* and Steinberg, *Nature Incorporated.*

9. Losee v. Buchanan, 51 N.Y. 476, 484 (1873); quoted in Horwitz, *Transformation of American Law, 1780–1860*, 71.

10. Lexington and Ohio Rail Road v. Applegate, 8 Dana 289, 309 (Ky. 1839); quoted in Horwitz, *Transformation of American Law, 1780–1860*, 75.

11. This paragraph and the next two draw upon the writings of Harry Schreiber cited in the bibliography, as well as Friedman, *History of American Law;* Hurst, *Law and Conditions of Freedom;* Light, *Industrializing America;* Opie, *Nature's Nation;* and Steinberg, *Nature, Incorporated.*

12. Hurst, *Law and Conditions of Freedom*, 6–7.

13. Horwitz, *Transformation of American Law, 1780–1860*, xiv–xvi.

14. Novak, *The People's Welfare*, 11.

15. Commonwealth v. Alger, 7 Cush. 53, 84–85 (Mass., 1851); Duncan, "Property as a Public Conversation," 1144–1152; Levy, *Law of the Commonwealth*, 247–254.

16. Vanderbilt v. Adams, 7 Cow. 349, 351–352 (N.Y., 1827).

17. Novak, *The People's Welfare*, 47.

18. Quoted in Novak, *The People's Welfare*, 34.

19. This paragraph and the ensuing ones draw chiefly upon Alexander, *Commodity and Propriety;* Fine, *Laissez-Faire and the General Welfare State;* Fisher, *Law of the Land;* Friedman, *History of American Law;* Horwitz,

Transformation of American Law, 1870–1960; Novak, *The People's Welfare;* Schreiber, "Instrumentalism and Property Rights"; Scott, *In Pursuit of Happiness;* Urofsky, "State Courts and Protective Legislation"; and Vandevelde, "New Property in the Nineteenth Century."

20. Pennsylvania Coal Co. v. Mahon, 260 U.S. 393 (1922).

21. Euclid v. Ambler Realty, 272 U.S. 365 (1926).

22. Zoning before *Euclid* is considered in Lees, "Preserving Property Values."

23. Chused, *"Euclid's Historical Imagery."*

24. 272 U.S. at 395.

25. Cohen, "Property and Sovereignty," 12.

26. Ibid., 21.

27. Ibid., 26.

28. Waschak v. Moffat, 379 Pa. 441, 109 A.2d 310 (1954).

29. 109 A.2d at 318.

30. 109 A.2d 321–322.

31. Hays, *Beauty, Health, Permanence;* Rome, *Bulldozer in the Countryside;* Steinberg, *Down to Earth.*

32. Just v. Marinette County, 56 Wis.2d 7, 201 N.W.2d 761 (1972).

33. 201 N.W.2d at 767.

34. 201 N.W.2d at 768.

35. Rome, *Bulldozer in the Countryside,* 234–236.

36. Horwitz, *Transformation of American Law, 1780–1860,* 46.

37. Prah v. Maretti, 108 Wis.2d 223, 321 N.W.2d 182 (1982).

38. 108 Wis.2d at 236, 321 N.W.2d at 189.

Chapter 4

1. Dana and Merrill, *Property: Takings.*

2. District Intown Properties Limited Partnership v. District of Columbia, 198 F.3d 874 (D.C. Cir. 1999).

3. Duncan, "Property as a Public Conversation"; MacPherson, *Mainstream and Critical Positions;* Philbrick, "Changing Conceptions"; Schlatter, *Private Property.*

4. Locke's ideas of property are expressed principally in Chapter V of his *Second Treatise of Government.* Locke, *Two Treatises,* 303–320. They are assessed in Laslett's useful introduction to *Two Treatises* and in Becker,

Property Rights, 32–56; Duncan, "Property as a Public Conversation," 1120–1127; Ryan, *Property and Political Theory,* 14–48; Schlatter, *Private Property,* 151–161; and Sreenivasan, *Limits of Lockean Rights.*

5. Locke, *Two Treatises,* 287–299; Becker, *Property Rights,* 32–56; Rose, "'Enough, and as Good' of What?"

6. Scott, *In Pursuit of Happiness,* 15–17; "Dispossessing the Indians."

7. Schlatter, *Private Property,* 255–261.

8. Ibid., 239–255.

9. Duncan, "Property as a Public Conversation," 1134.

10. Freyfogle, "Land Use," 725–728.

11. Hurst, *Law and Conditions of Freedom,* 74.

12. Garland, *Son of the Middle Border,* 252.

13. George, *Progress and Poverty,* ix.

14. Thomas, *Alternative America.*

Chapter 5

1. The original pencil draft is located in the Leopold papers at the University of Wisconsin Archives, Madison, Wisconsin, Leopold Papers, Series 10-6, box 16.

2. Ehrenfeld, *Arrogance of Humanism.*

3. Leopold, Aldo, "The Conservation Ethic," in Flader and Callicott, *River of the Mother of God,* 184 (entire essay is 181–192; originally published 1933).

4. Leopold, Aldo, "Conservation: In Whole or in Part?" in Flader and Callicott, *River of the Mother of God,* 311 (entire essay is 310–319; originally written 1944).

5. Leopold, *Sand County Almanac,* 224–225.

6. Leopold, Aldo, "Conservation Economics," in Flader and Callicott, *River of the Mother of God,* 197 (entire essay is 193–202; originally published 1934).

7. Leopold, Aldo, "Engineering and Conservation," in Flader and Callicott, *River of the Mother of God,* 254 (entire essay is 249–254; originally written 1938).

8. Leopold, Aldo, "The Ecological Conscience," in Flader and Callicott, *River of the Mother of God,* 340 (entire essay is 338–346; originally published 1947).

9. Leopold, "Conservation Ethic," 191.

10. Leopold, "Ecological Conscience," 338.

11. Leopold, *Sand County Almanac,* viii.

12. Leopold, Aldo, "The Role of Wildlife in Education," unpublished, undated manuscript, Leopold Papers, Series 10-6, box 16.

13. Leopold, Aldo, "The Conservation League," unpublished manuscript (1940), Leopold Papers, Series 10-6, box 16.

14. Leopold, Aldo, "Ecology, Philosophy, and Conservation," unpublished, undated manuscript, Leopold Papers, Series 10-6, box 16.

15. Leopold, "Conservation Ethic,"187.

16. Leopold, Aldo, "Land Pathology," in Flader and Callicott, *River of the Mother of God,* 300 (entire essay is 212–217; originally published 1942).

17. Leopold, "Conservation: In Whole or in Part," 318.

18. Leopold, Aldo, "Land-Use and Democracy," in Flader and Callicott, *River of the Mother of God,* 300 (entire essay is 295–300, originally published 1942).

19. "Biotic Land-Use," in Leopold, *For the Health of the Land,* 201 (entire essay is 198–207; originally written circa 1942).

20. Ibid., 205.

21. "The Land-Health Concept and Conservation," in Leopold, *For the Health of the Land,* 219 (entire essay is 218–226; originally written 1946).

22. Leopold, "Land-Use and Democracy," 300.

23. Leopold, Aldo, "A Biotic View of Land," in Flader and Callicott, *River of the Mother of God,* 270 (entire essay is 266–273; originally published 1939).

24. Leopold, "Conservation Ethic," 187.

25. Leopold's writings on economics include "The Conservation Ethic," " Conservation Economics," and "Land Pathology," all in Flader and Callicott, *River of the Mother of God,* as well as many unpublished essays, including "Armaments for Conservation," "Conservation and Politics," "Motives for Conservation," "Economics of the Wild," "Ecology and Economics and Land Use," and "Economics, Philosophy, and Land," all in the Leopold Papers, Series 10-6, box 16.

26. Leopold, "Land Pathology," 214.

27. Leopold, Aldo, *Round River* (New York: Oxford University Press, 1953), 156.

28. Leopold, Aldo, "Farmer-Sportsman, A Partnership for Wildlife Restoration," *Transactions of the 4th North American Wildlife Conference* (13–15 Feb. 1939): 146–147.

29. Leopold, Aldo, "The Farm Wildlife Program: A Self-Scrutiny," unpublished, undated manuscript, Leopold Papers, Series 10-6, box 16.

30. Leopold, Aldo, "Conservation," unpublished manuscript attached to letter to Aldo Leopold from Horace S. Fries, 8 Aug. 1946, Leopold Papers, Series 10-1, box 1.

31. Berry, *A Continuous Harmony*, 86, 164; Berry, *Sex, Economy, Freedom and Community*, 14–15, 40; Berry, *What Are People For?* 149, 206–207.

32. Howard, *Soil and Health*, 11.

33. Berry, *Another Turn of the Crank*, 90.

34. Berry, *Sex, Economy, Freedom and Community*, 14.

35. Berry, *What Are People For?* 157.

36. Berry, *Another Turn of the Crank*, 50.

37. Ibid., 52.

38. Berry, "Whose Head is the Farmer Using?" 30.

39. Ibid.

Chapter 6

1. Hardin, Garrett, "Tragedy of the Commons." Science 162 (1968): 1243–1248.

2. Ostrom, *Governing the Commons*, 2.

3. Quoted in Montmarquet, *Idea of Agrarianism*, 73–74.

4. Baden, Noonan, and Ruckelshaus, *Managing the Commons;* Baland and Platteau, *Halting Degradation;* Ostrom, *Governing the Commons;* Swaney, "Common Property, Reciprocity, and Community."

5. Kempton, Boaster, and Hartley, *Environmental Values*, 109–114 (showing 87 percent public support for the idea that "all species have a right to evolve without human interference" and 90 percent support for the idea that "preventing species extinction should be our highest environmental policy.")

6. World Commission on Environment and Development, *Our Common Future*.

7. Thoughtful critiques are offered in Callicott, *Beyond the Land Ethic*, 365–380; and Worster, *Wealth of Nature*, 142–155.

8. Callicott et al., "Normative Concepts in Conservation."

9. Worster, *Dust Bowl*.

10. Lehman, *Public Values, Private Lands*, 5–42.

11. Wilcove, *Condor's Shadow*, 106–108.

12. Freyfogle, *Bounded People, Boundless Lands,* 151–170.
13. Wilcover, *Condor's Shadow,* 106–108.

Chapter 7

1. Glennon, *Water Follies,* 87–97; Votteler, "Raiders of the Lost Aquifer?"
2. Cronon, *Changes in the Land,* 159–170.
3. Anderson, Terry L. and Donald R. Leal, *Free Market Environmentalism.* rev. ed. (New York: Palgrave Macmillan, 2000).
4. Field, *Environmental Economics,* 63–105.
5. Berry, *What Are People For?* 145–152; Berry, *Art of the Commonplace,* 236–248.
6. Sagoff, *Economy of the Earth,* 7–8, 51–53, 65–67.
7. Odum, "Environmental Degradation."

Chapter 8

1. Locke, *Two Treatises,* 306.
2. Board of Regents v. Roth, 408 U.S. 564, 577 (1972) ("property interests . . . are not created by the Constitution.")
3. Singer, *Edges of the Field,* 27.
4. Ibid., 3; Munzer, "Property as Social Relations"; Singer and Beerman, "Social Origins of Property."
5. Duncan, "Property as a Public Conversation," 1112–1118, 1127–1133.
6. Caldwell, "Rights of Ownership or Rights of Use?"; Large, "This Land is Whose Land?"; Sax, "The Economy of Nature"; Sax, "Takings, Private Property and Public Rights."
7. Grant's Farm Associates, Inc. v. Town of Kittery, 554 A.2d 799 (Maine, 1989).
8. 554 A. 2d at 802.
9. Ibid.
10. Gardner v. New Jersey Pinelands Commission, 125 N.J. 193, 593 A.2d 251 (1991).
11. 125 N.J. at 208; 593 A.2d at 258.
12. Leopold, *Sand County Almanac,* 110.
13. Lucas v. South Carolina Coastal Council, 505 U.S. 1003, 1024 (1992).

Chapter 9

1. Tarlock, *Law of Water Rights and Resources*, §§ 3.10, 3.60, 5.66–5.70.
2. Freyfogle, "Water Rights and the Common Wealth"; Neuman, "Beneficial Use."
3. Tarlock, *Law of Water Rights and Resources*, § 5.66.
4. Freyfogle, "A Sand County Almanac at 50," 10064–10066.
5. Goble and Freyfogle, *Wildlife Law*, 380–457.
6. Quoted in Goble and Freyfogle, *Wildlife Law*, 212–213.
7. Dana and Merrill, *Property: Takings*, 191–209.
8. Ibid., 72–75, 94–99.

Chapter 10

1. M'Conico v. Singleton, 9 S.C.L. (2 Mill) 244 (South Carolina, 1818).
2. 9 S.C.L. (2 Mill.) at 246.
3. State v. Sour Mountain Realty, Inc., 276 A.D.2d 8, 714 N.Y.S.2d 78 (N.Y. App. Div., 2000); *In re* Sour Mountain Realty, 260 A.D.2d 920, 688 N.Y.S.2d 842 (N.Y. App. Div., 1999); Parisella v. Town of Fishkill, 260 A.D.2d 620, 688 N.Y.S.2d 694 (N.Y. App. Div., 1999).
4. My discussion of this issue draws upon Barber, *Strong Democracy*, and Kemmis, *Community and the Politics of Place*.
5. Dana and Merrill, *Property: Takings*, 72–75, 94–99; Freyfogle, "Regulatory Takings, Methodically," 10315, 10319–10321.
6. Lasch, *Revolt of the Elites*, 113.
7. Leopold, Aldo, "The Arboretum and the University," in Flader and Callicott, *River of the Mother of God*, 210.
8. Leopold, Aldo, "The State of the Profession," in Flader and Callicott, *River of the Mother of God*, 280.
9. Leopold, Aldo, "The Farmer as a Conservationist," in Flader and Callicott, *River of the Mother of God*, 255.

Abraham, David. "Liberty and Property: Lord Bramwell and the Political Economy of Liberal Jurisprudence, Individualism, Freedom and Utility." *American Journal of Legal History* 38 (1994): 288–321.

Ackerman, Bruce A. *Private Property and the Constitution.* New Haven: Yale University Press, 1977.

Adams, W. M. *Future Nature: A Vision for Conservation.* London: Earthscan Publications Limited, 1996.

Adler, Robert. "Addressing the Barriers to Watershed Protection." *Environmental Law* 25 (1995): 973–1106.

———. "Fresh Water–Toward a Sustainable Future." *Environmental Law Reporter* 32 (2002): 10167–10189.

Agar, Herbert, and Allen Tate, eds. *Who Owns America: A New Declaration of Independence.* Wilmington, Del. ISI Books, 1999.

Alexander, Gregory S. *Commodity and Propriety: Competing Visions of Property in American Legal Thought, 1776–1970.* Chicago: University of Chicago Press, 1997.

Anderson, Jerry L. "Takings and Expectations: Toward a 'Broader Vision' of Property Rights." *University of Kansas Law Review* 37 (1989): 529–562.

Anderson, Larry. *Benton MacKaye: Conservationist, Planner, and Creator of the Appalachian Trail.* Baltimore: Johns Hopkins University Press, 2002.

Anderson, Terry L., and Donald R. Leal, *Free Market Environmentalism.* New York: Palgrave Macmillan, rev. ed., 2000.

Appleby, Joyce. *Inheriting the Revolution: The First Generation of Americans.* Cambridge: Harvard University Press, 2000.

Arnold, Craig A. "The Reconstitution of Property: Property as a Web of Interests." *Harvard Environmental Law Review* 26 (2002): 281–364.

Babcock, Richard F., and Duane A. Feurer, "Land as a Commodity 'Affected with a Public Interest'." *Washington Law Review* 52 (1977): 289–334.

Baden, John A., Douglas S. Noonan, and William D. Ruckelshaus, eds. *Managing the Commons.* Bloomington: Indiana University Press, 2d ed., 1998.

Baden, John A., and Donald Snow, eds. *The Next West: Public Lands, Community, and Economy in the American West.* Washington, D.C.: Island Press, 1997.

Bailyn, Bernard. *The Ideological Origins of the American Revolution.* Cambridge: Harvard University Press.

Baker, C. Edwin. "Property and Its Relation to Constitutionally Protected Liberty." *University of Pennsylvania Law Review* 134 (1986): 741–816.

Baker, J. H. *An Introduction to English Legal History.* London: Butterworths, 2d ed., 1979.

Baland, Jean-Marie, and Jean-Phillipe Platteau. *Halting Degradation of Natural Resources: Is There a Role for Rural Communities?* Oxford: Clarendon Press, 1996.

Baldwin, A. Dwight, Judith De Luce, and Carl Pletsch, eds. *Beyond Preservation: Restoring and Inventing Landscapes.* Minneapolis: University of Minnesota Press, 1994.

Barber, Benjamin. *Strong Democracy: Participatory Politics for a New Age.* Berkeley: University of California Press, 1984.

Bates, J. Leonard. "Fulfilling American Democracy: The Conservation Movement, 1907–1921." *Mississippi Valley Historical Review* 44 (June 1957): 29–57.

Bates, Sarah F., David H. Getches, Lawrence J. MacDonnell, and Charles F. Wilkinson. *Searching Out the Headwaters: Change and Rediscovery in Western Water Policy.* Washington, D.C.: Island Press, 1993.

Beatley, Timothy. *Ethical Land Use: Principles of Policy and Planning.* Baltimore: Johns Hopkins University Press, 1994.

———. *Habitat Conservation Planning: Endangered Species and Urban Growth.* Austin: University of Texas Press, 1994.

———. "Preserving Biodiversity: Challenges for Planners." *Journal of the American Planning Association* 66 (2000): 5–20.

Beatley, Timothy, and Kristy Manning. *The Ecology of Place: Planning for Environment, Economy, and Community.* Washington, D.C.: Island Press, 1997.

Becker, Lawrence C. *Property Rights: Philosophic Foundations.* London: Routledge & Kegan Paul, Ltd., 1977.

Beeman, Randal A., and James A. Pritchard. *A Green and Permanent Land: Ecology and Agriculture in the Twentieth Century.* Lawrence: University Press of Kansas, 2001.

Bell, Daniel. *The Cultural Contradictions of Capitalism.* New York: Basic Books, 1976.

Berger, Jonathan, and John W. Sinton. *Water, Earth, and Fire: Land Use and Environmental Planning in the New Jersey Pine Barrens.* Baltimore: Johns Hopkins University Press, 1985.

Berry, Wendell. *A Continuous Harmony: Essays Cultural and Agricultural.* New York: Harcourt Brace Jovanovich, 1972.

———. "Whose Head is the Farmer Using? Whose Head is Using the Farmer?" In Wes Jackson, Wendell Berry, Bruce Colman, eds. *Meeting the Expectations of the Land,* 18–30. San Francisco: North Point Press, 1984.

———. *The Art of the Commonplace: The Agrarian Essays of Wendell Berry.* Washington, D.C.: Counterpoint Press, 2002.

———. *The Unsettling of America: Culture and Agriculture.* San Francisco: Sierra Club Books, 1977.

———. *The Gift of Good Land: Further Essays Cultural and Agricultural.* San Francisco: North Point Press, 1981.

———. "People, Land, and Community." In *Standing By Words,* 64–79. San Francisco: North Point Press, 1983.

———. *Home Economics.* San Francisco: North Point Press, 1987.

———. *What Are People For?* San Francisco: North Point Press, 1990.

———. *Sex, Economy, Freedom and Community.* New York: Pantheon Books, 1993.

———. *Another Turn of the Crank.* Washington, D.C.: Counterpoint, 1995.

———. *Jayber Crow.* Washington, D.C.: Counterpoint, 2000.

Berthoff, Rowland, and John M. Murrin. "Feudalism, Communalism, and the Yeoman Freeholder: The American Revolution Considered as a Social Accident." In Stephen G. Kurtz and James H. Hutson, eds. *Essays on the American Revolution,* 256–288. New York: W. W. Norton, 1973.

Blackstone, William. *Commentaries on the Laws of England.* Chicago: University of Chicago Press, volume III, 1979.

Bogue, Allan G. *From Prairie to Cornbelt: Farming on the Illinois and Iowa Prairies in the Nineteenth Century.* Chicago: University of Chicago Press, 1963.

Bond, Beverly W., Jr. *The Quit Rent System in the American Colonies.* New Haven: Yale University Press, 1919.

Boorstin, Daniel J. *The Mysterious Science of the Law: An Essay on Blackstone's Commentaries.* Cambridge: Harvard University Press, 1941.

Bormann, F. Herbert, and Stephen R. Kellert, eds. *Ecology, Economics, Ethics: The Broken Circle*. New Haven: Yale University Press, 1991.

Bosselman, Fred. "Four Land Ethics: Order, Reform, Responsibility, Opportunity." *Environmental Law* 24 (1994) 1439–1511.

Botkin, Daniel B. *Discordant Harmonies: A New Ecology for the Twenty-First Century*. New York: Oxford University Press, 1990.

Bowers, William L. *The Country Life Movement in America, 1900–1920*. Port Washington, N.Y.: Kennikat Press, 1974.

Bowles, Samuel, and Herbert Gintis. *Democracy & Capitalism: Property, Community, and the Contradictions of Modern Social Thought*. New York: Basic Books, 1987.

Breckenridge, Lee P. "Reweaving the Landscape: The Institutional Challenges of Ecosystem Management for Lands in Private Ownership." *Vermont Law Review* 19 (1995): 363–422.

———. "Nonprofit Environmental Organizations and the Restructuring of Institutions for Ecosystem Management." *Ecology Law Quarterly* 25 (1999): 692–706.

Brewer, John, and Susan Staves, eds. *Early Modern Conceptions of Property*. London: Routledge, 1995.

Bromley, Daniel W. *Environment and Economy: Property Rights and Public Policy*. Oxford: Blackwell, 1991.

———. "Regulatory Takings: Coherent Concept or Logical Contradiction?" *Vermont Law Review* 17 (1993): 647–682.

———. "Constitutional Political Economy: Property Claims in a Dynamic World." *Contemporary Economic Policy* 15 (1997): 43–54.

———. "Property Regimes for Sustainable Resource Management." In John F. Richards, ed. *Land, Property, and the Environment*, 338–354. Oakland, CA: ICS Press, 2002.

Brown, Lester. *Eco-Economy: Building an Economy for the Earth*. New York: Norton, 2001.

Buell, Lawrence. *The Environmental Imagination: Thoreau, Nature Writing, and the Formation of American Culture*. Cambridge: Harvard University Press, 1995.

Bunce, Arthur C. *Economics of Soil Conservation*. Ames: Iowa State Press, 1942.

Burns, Robert P. "Blackstone's Theory of the 'Absolute' Rights of Property." *Cincinnati Law Review* 54 (1985): 67–86.

Butler, Lynda L. "The Pathology of Property Norms: Living Within Nature's Boundaries." *Southern California Law Review* 73 (2000): 927–1015.

Calabresi, Guido, and A. Douglas Melamed. "Property Rules, Liability Rules, and Inalienability: One View of the Cathedral." *Harvard Law Review* 85 (1972): 1089–1128.

Caldwell, Lynton K. "Rights of Ownership or Rights of Use?–The Need for a New Conceptual Basis for Land use Policy." *William and Mary Law Review* 15 (1974): 759–775.

Caldwell, Lynton Keith, and Kristin Shrader-Frechette. *Policy for Land: Law and Ethics.* Landham, Md.: Rowman & Littlefield, 1993.

Callicott, J. Baird. *In Defense of the Land Ethic: Essays in Environmental Philosophy.* Albany: State University of New York Press, 1989.

———. *Beyond the Land Ethic: More Essays in Environmental Philosophy.* Albany: State University of New York Press, 1999.

Callicott, J. Baird, ed. *Companion to* A Sand County Almanac: *Interpretive & Critical Essays.* Madison: University of Wisconsin Press, 1987.

Callicott, J. Baird, Crowder, Larry B., and Mumford, Karen. "Current Normative Concepts in Conservation." *Conservation Biology* 13 (1999): 22–35.

Callies, David, ed. *After "Lucas": Land Use Regulation and the Taking of Property Without Compensation.* Chicago: American Bar Association, 1993.

Caudill, Harry M. *Night Comes to the Cumberlands.* Boston: Atlantic Monthly, 1962.

Christman, John. *The Myth of Property: Toward an Egalitarian Theory of Ownership.* New York: Oxford University Press, 1994.

Chused, Richard H. "*Euclid's* Historical Imagery." *Case Western Reserve Law Review* 51 (2001): 597–616.

Ciricy-Wantrup, S. V., and Richard C. Bishop. "'Common Property' as a Concept in Natural Resources Policy." *Natural Resources Journal* 15 (1975): 713–727.

Coase, Ronald. "The Problem of Social Cost." *Journal of Law and Economics* 3 (1960) 1–44.

Cohen, Morris. "Property and Sovereignty." *Cornell Law Quarterly* 13 (1927): 8–30.

Cole, Daniel H. *Pollution & Property: Comparing Ownership Institutions for Environmental Protection.* Cambridge: Cambridge University Press, 2002.

Commons, John R. *Legal Foundations of Capitalism.* New York: MacMillan, 1924.

Conkin, Paul. *The Southern Agrarians.* Knoxville: University of Tennessee Press, 1988.

Cooter, Robert, and Thomas Ulen. *Law and Economics.* 3d ed. Reading, Mass.: Addison-Wesley, 2000.

Costanza, Robert, ed. *Ecological Economics: The Science and Management of Sustainability.* New York: Columbia University Press, 1991.

Costanza, Robert, Bryan G. Norton, and Benjamin D. Haskells, eds. *Ecosystem Health: New Goals for Environmental Management.* Washington, D.C.: Island Press, 1992.

Cronon, William. *Changes in the Land: Indians, Colonists, and the Ecology of New England.* New York: Hill and Wang, 1983.

———. *Nature's Metropolis: Chicago and the Great West.* New York: W. W. Norton, 1991.

Cronon, William, ed. *Uncommon Ground: Rethinking the Human Place in Nature.* New York: W. W. Norton, 1996.

Crowley, J. E. *This Sheba, Self: The Conceptualization of Economic Life in Eighteenth-Century America.* Baltimore: Johns Hopkins University Press, 1974.

Cumbler, John T. *Reasonable Use: The People, the Environment, and the State, New England 1790–1930.* New York: Oxford University Press, 2001.

Dagan, Hanoch, and Michael E. Heller. "The Liberal Commons." *Yale Law Journal* 110 (2001): 549–623.

Daly, Herman E. *Beyond Growth: The Economics of Sustainable Development.* Boston: Beacon Press, 1996.

———. *Ecological Economics and the Ecology of Economics.* Cheltenham, England: Edward Elgar, 1999.

Daly, Herman E., and John B. Cobb, Jr. *For the Common Good: Redirecting the Economy Toward Community, the Environment, and a Sustainable Future.* Boston: Beacon Press, 1989.

Dana, David A. "Natural Preservation and the Race to Develop." *University of Pennsylvania Law Review* 143 (1995) 655–708.

Dana, David A., and Thomas W. Merrill. *Takings.* New York: Foundation Press, 2002.

Davidson, Eric A. *You Can't Eat GNP: Economics as if Ecology Mattered.* Cambridge, Mass.: Perseus Publishing, 2000.

Davidson, John H. "Conservation Plans in Agriculture." *Environmental Law Reporter* 31 (2001): 10501–10507.

deBuys, William, ed. *Seeing Things Whole: The Essential John Wesley Powell.* Washington, D.C.: Island Press, 2001.

de Crèvecoeur, J. Hector St. John. *Letters from an American Farmer.* New York: E. P. Dutton, 1957.

Demsetz, Harold. "Toward a Theory of Property Rights." *American Economic Review* 57 (1967): 347–359.

Donahue, Brian. *Reclaiming the Commons: Community Farms and Forests in a New England Town.* New Haven: Yale University Press, 1999.

Doremus, Holly. "The Special Importance of Ordinary Places." *Environs Environmental Law and Policy Journal* 23 (Spring 2000): 3–16.

Dubos, René. *A God Within.* New York: Scribners, 1972.

———. *The Wooing of Earth: New Perspectives on Man's Use of Nature.* London: Athlone Press, 1980.

Duncan, Myrl L. "Property as a Public Conversation, Not a Lockean Soliloquy: A Role for Intellectual and Legal History in Takings Analysis." *Environmental Law* 26 (1996): 1095–1160.

———. "Reconceiving the Bundle of Sticks: Land as a Community-Based Resource." *Environmental Law* 32 (2002): 773–807.

Durning, Alan Thein. *This Place on Earth: Home and the Practice of Permanence.* Seattle: Sasquatch Books, 1996.

Echeverria, John, and Raymond Booth Eby, eds. *Let the People Judge: Wise Use and the Private Property Rights Movement.* Washington, D.C.: Island Press, 1995.

Ehrenfeld, David. *The Arrogance of Humanism.* New York: Oxford University Press, 1981.

———. *Beginning Again: People & Nature in the New Millennium.* New York: Oxford University Press, 1993.

———. *Swimming Lessons: Keeping Afloat in the Age of Technology.* New York: Oxford University Press, 2002.

Ellickson, Robert C. "Alternatives to Zoning: Covenants, Nuisance Rules, and Fines as Land Use Controls." *University of Chicago Law Review* 40 (1973): 681–750.

———. "Property in Land." *Yale Law Journal* 102 (1993): 1315–1400.

Ellickson, Robert C., Carol M. Rose, and Bruce A. Ackerman. *Perspectives on Property Law.* 3d ed. Boston: Aspen Law & Business, 2002.

Elmendorf, Christopher S. "Ideas, Incentives, Gifts, and Governance: Toward Conservation Stewardship of Private Land, in Cultural and Psychological Perspective." *University of Illinois Law Review.* Forthcoming.

Ely, John W., Jr. *The Guardian of Every Other Right: A Constitutional History of Property Rights.* New York: Oxford University Press, 1992.

Ely, Richard T. *Property and Contract in Their Relations to the Distribution of Wealth.* 2 vols. New York: Macmillian, 1922.

Ely, Richard T., and George S. Wehrwein. *Land Economics.* Madison: University of Wisconsin Press, 1964.

Endicott, Eve, ed. *Land Conservation Through Public/Private Partnerships.* Washington, D.C.: Island Press, 1993.

Epstein, Richard A. *Takings: Private Property and the Power of Eminent Domain.* Cambridge: Harvard University Press, 1985.

Evernden, Neil. *The Natural Alien: Humankind and Environment.* Toronto: University of Toronto, 1985.

———. *The Social Creation of Nature.* Baltimore: Johns Hopkins University Press, 1992.

Farber, Daniel A., and Paul A Memmersbaugh. "The Shadow of the Future: Discount Rates, Later Generations, and the Environment." *Vanderbilt Law Review* 46 (1993): 267–304.

Field, Barry C. *Environmental Economics: An Introduction.* 2d ed. Boston: McGraw-Hill, 1997.

Fine, Sidney. *Laissez-Faire and the General-Welfare State: A Study of Conflict in American Thought, 1865–1901.* Ann Arbor: University of Michigan Press, 1956.

Fischel, William A. *Regulatory Takings: Law, Economics, and Politics.* Cambridge: Harvard University Press, 1995.

Fischer, David Hackett. *Albion's Seed: Four British Folkways to America.* New York: Oxford University Press, 1989.

Fisher, William Weston III. "*The Law of the Land: An Intellectual History of American Property Doctrine, 1776–1880.*" Ph.D. diss., Harvard University, 1991.

Fishman, Robert, ed. *The American Planning Tradition: Culture and Policy.* Washington, D.C.: Woodrow Wilson Center Press, 2000.

Flader, Susan L. *Thinking Like a Mountain: Aldo Leopold and the Evolution of an Ecological Attitude Toward Deer, Wolves, and Forests.* Columbia: University of Missouri Press, 1974.

Flader, Susan L., and J. Baird Callicott. *The River of the Mother of God and Other Essays by Aldo Leopold.* Madison: University of Wisconsin Press, 1991.

Fowler, Robert Booth. *The Greening of Protestant Thought.* Chapel Hill: University of North Carolina Press, 1995.

Fox, Stephen. *The American Conservation Movement: John Muir and His Legacy.* Madison: University of Wisconsin Press, 1985.

Fradkin, Philip L. *A River No More: The Colorado River and the West.* New York: Alfred A. Knopf, 1981.

Frazier, Terry W. "The Green Alternative to Classical Liberal Property Theory." *Vermont Law Review* 20 (1995) 299–371.

———. "Protecting Ecological Integrity Within the Balancing Function of Property Law." *Environmental Law* 28 (1998) 53–112.

Freyfogle, Eric T. "Land Use and the Study of Early American History." *Yale Law Journal* 94 (1985): 717–742.

———. "*Lux v. Haggin* and the Common Law Burdens of Modern Water Law." *University of Colorado Law Review* 57 (1986): 485–525.

———. "Context and Accommodation in Modern Property Law." *Stanford Law Review* 41 (1989): 1529–1556.

———. "The Land Ethic and Pilgrim Leopold." *University of Colorado Law Review* 61 (1990): 217–256.

———. "The Evolution of Property Rights: California Water Law as a Case Study." In M. H. Hoeflich and P. Hay, eds. *Property Law and Legal Education: Essays in Honor of John E. Cribbet,* 73–107. Urbana: University of Illinois Press, 1988.

———. *Justice and the Earth: Images for Our Planetary Survival.* New York: Free Press, 1993.

———. "Ownership and Ecology." *Case Western Reserve Law Review* 43 (1993) 1269–1297.

———. "The Owning and Taking of Sensitive Lands." *UCLA Law Review* 43 (1995): 77–138.

———. "Ethics, Community, and Private Land." *Ecology Law Quarterly* 26 (1996) 631–661.

———. "Water Rights and the Common Wealth." *Environmental Law* 26 (1996) 27–51.

———. *Bounded People, Boundless Lands: Envisioning a New Land Ethic.* Washington, D.C.: Island Press, 1998.

———. "Owning the Land: Four Contemporary Narratives." *Land Use and Environment Law Review* 13 (1998): 279–307.

———. "*A Sand County Almanac* at 50: Leopold in the New Century." *Environmental Law Reporter* 30 (2000): 10058–10068.

———. "Regulatory Takings, Methodically." *Environmental Law Reporter* 31 (2001): 10313–10321.

———. "Private Lands Made (Too) Simple." *Environmental Law Reporter* 33 (2003): 10155–10169.

———. "Conservation and the Four Faces of Resistance." In B. Mineer and R. Manning, eds. *Reconstructing Conservation: History, Values, and Practice.* Washington, D.C.: Island Press. Forthcoming.

Friedman, Lawrence M. *A History of American Law.* 2d ed. New York: Simon and Schuster, 1985.

Gale, Richard P., and Sheila M. Cordray. "Making Sense of Sustainability: Nine Answers to 'What Should Be Sustained?'" *Rural Sociology* 59 (1994): 311–332.

George, Henry. *Progress and Poverty: An Inquiry into the Cause of Industrial Depressions and of Increase of Want with Increase of Wealth.* New York: Modern Library, 1929.

George, Henry. *A Perplexed Philosopher.* New York: Robert Schalkenbach Foundation ed., 1946.

Gies, Frances, and Joseph Gies. *Life in a Medieval Village.* New York: Harper & Row, 1990.

Glanz, James. *Saving Our Soil: Solutions for Sustaining Earth's Vital Resource.* Boulder, CO: Johnson Books, 1995.

Glendon, Mary Ann. *Rights Talk: The Impoverishment of Political Discourse.* New York: Free Press, 1991.

Glennon, Robert. *Water Follies: Groundwater Pumping and the Fate of America's Fresh Waters.* Washington, D.C.: Island Press, 2002.

Goble, Dale D., and Eric T. Freyfogle. *Wildlife Law: Cases and Materials.* New York: Foundation Press, 2002.

Goble, Dale D., and Paul W. Hirt. *Northwest Lands, Northwest Peoples: Readings in Environmental History.* Seattle: University of Washington Press, 1999.

Goldstein, Robert J. "Green Wood in the Bundle of Sticks: Fitting Environmental Ethics and Ecology into Real Property Law." *Boston College Environmental Affairs Law Review* 25 (1998): 347–430.

Goodwyn, Lawrence. *The Populist Revolt: A Short History of the Agrarian Revolt in America.* New York: Oxford University Press, 1978.

Gottlieb, Robert. *Forcing the Spring: The Transformation of the Environmental Movement.* Washington, D.C.: Island Press, 1993.

Graham, Edward H. *The Land and Wildlife.* New York: Oxford University Press, 1947.

Graham, Frank, Jr. *Man's Dominion: The Story of Conservation in America.* New York: M. Evans and Co., 1971.

Greven, Philip. *Four Generations: Population, Land, and Family in Colonial Andover, Massachusetts.* Ithaca, N.Y.: Cornell University Press, 1970.

Grumbine, R. Edward. "What is Ecosystem Management?" *Conservation Biology* 8 (March 1994): 27–38.

———, ed. *Environmental Policy and Biodiversity.* Washington, D.C.: Island Press, 1994.

Gunningham, Neil, and Michael D. Young. "Toward Optimal Environmental Policy: The Case of Biodiversity Conservation." *Ecology Law Quarterly* 24 (1997): 243–298.

Hall, Kermit L. *The Magic Mirror: Law in American History.* New York: Oxford University Press, 1989.

Halper, Louise A. "Nuisance, Courts and Markets in the New York Court of Appeals, 1850–1915." *Albany Law Review* 54 (1990): 301–357.

———. "Why the Nuisance Knot Can't Undo the Takings Muddle." *Indiana Law Review* 28 (1995): 329–352.

———. "Untangling the Nuisance Knot." *Boston College Environmental Affairs Law Review* 26 (1998): 89–130.

Hanawalt, Barbara. *The Ties that Bound: Peasant Families in Medieval England.* New York: Oxford University Press, 1986.

Hanna, Susan, ed. *Rights to Nature: Ecological, Economic, Cultural, and Political Principles of Institutions for the Environment.* Washington, D.C.: Island Press, 1996.

Hanna, Susan, and Mohan Munasinge, eds. *Property Rights and the Environment: Social and Ecological Issues.* Washington, D.C.: Beijer International Institute, 1995.

Hannum, Hildegarde, ed. *People, Land, and Community.* New Haven: Yale University Press, 1997.

Hanson, Victor Davis. *Fields Without Dreams: Defending the Agrarian Idea.* New York: Free Press, 1996.

—————. *The Land Was Everything: Letters from an American Farmer.* New York: Free Press, 2000.

Hart, John F. "The Maryland Mill Act, 1669-1766: Economic Policy and the Confiscatory Redistribution of Private Property." *American Journal of Legal History* 39 (1995): 1–24.

—————. "Colonial Land Use Law and Its Significance for Modern Takings Doctrine." *Harvard Law Review* 109 (1996):1252-1300.

—————. "Takings and Compensation in Early America: The Colonial Highway Acts in Social Context." *American Journal of Legal History* 40 (1996): 253–306.

—————. "Forfeiture of Unimproved Land in the Early Republic." *University of Illinois Law Review* (1997): 435–451.

—————. "Property Rights, Costs, and Welfare: Delaware Water Mill Legislation, 1719–1859." *Journal of Legal Studies* 27 (1998): 455–471.

—————. "Land Use Law in the Early Republic and the Original Meaning of the Takings Clause." *Northwestern University Law Review* 94 (2000): 1099–1156.

—————. "'A Less Proportion of Idle Proprietors': Madison, Property Rights, and the Abolition of Fee Tail." *Washington and Lee Law Review* 58 (2001): 167–194.

Hartz, Louis. *The Liberal Tradition in America.* New York: Harcourt Brace & Co., 1955.

Hays, Samuel P. *Conservation and the Gospel of Efficiency: The Progressive Conservation Movement, 1890–1920.* Cambridge: Harvard University Press, 1959.

—————. *Beauty, Health, and Permanence: Environmental Politics in the United States, 1955–1985.* Cambridge: Cambridge University Press, 1987.

—————. *The Response to Industrialism, 1885–1914.* 2d ed. Chicago: University of Chicago Press, 1995.

—————. *A History of Environmental Politics Since 1945.* Pittsburgh: University of Pittsburgh Press, 2000.

Heller, Michael A. "The Tragedy of the Anticommons: Property in the Transition from Marx to Markets." *Harvard Law Review* 111 (1998): 621–688.

Helvarg, David. *The War Against the Greens: The "Wise Use" Movement, the New Right, and Anti-Environmental Violence.* San Francisco: Sierra Club Books, 1994.

Herndl, Carl G., and Stuart C. Brown, eds. *Green Culture: Environmental Rhetoric in Contemporary Culture*. Madison: University of Wisconsin Press, 1996.

Hiss, Tony. *The Experience of Place: A New Way of Looking at and Dealing with Our Radically Changing Cities and Countryside*. New York: Alfred Knopf, 1990.

Hoffer, Peter Charles. *Law and People in Colonial America*. Baltimore: Johns Hopkins University Press, 1992.

Hofstadter, Richard. *The Age of Reform: From Bryan to F.D.R.* New York: Vintage Books, 1955.

———. *Social Darwinism in American Thought*. Boston: Beacon Press, 1992.

Honore, Anthony. "Ownership." In A. G. Guest, ed. *Oxford Essays in Jurisprudence*, 107–147. Oxford: Oxford University Press, 1961.

Horn, James. *Adapting to the New World: English Society in the Seventeenth Century Chesapeake*. Chapel Hill: University of North Carolina Press, 1994.

Horwitz, Morton J. *The Transformation of American Law 1780–1860*. Cambridge: Harvard University Press, 1977.

———. *The Transformation of American Law 1870–1960*. Cambridge: Harvard University Press, 1992.

Houck, Oliver A. "Why Do We Protect Endangered Species, and What Does That Say About Whether Restrictions on Private Property to Protect Them Constitute 'Takings'?" *Iowa Law Review* 80 (1995): 297–332 .

Hovenkamp, Herbert. *Enterprise and American Law, 1836–1937*. Cambridge: Harvard University Press, 1991.

Howard, Sir Albert. *The Soil and Health: A Study of Organic Agriculture*. New York: Devin-Adair, 1947.

Humbach, John A. "Evolving Thresholds of Nuisance and the Takings Clause." *Columbia Journal of Environmental Law* 18 (1993): 1–29.

Hundley, Norris. *The Great Thirst: Californians and Water, 1770s–1990s*. Berkeley: University of California Press, 1992.

Hunter, David B. "An Ecological Perspective on Property: A Call for Judicial Protection of the Public's Interest in Environmentally Critical Resources." *Harvard Environmental Law Review* 12 (1988): 311–383.

Hurst, James Willard. *Law and the Conditions of Freedom in the Nineteenth-Century United States*. Madison: University of Wisconsin Press, 1956.

Isaac, Rhys. *The Transformation of Virginia, 1740–1790.* Chapel Hill: University of North Carolina Press, 1982.

Jackson, J. B. *The Necessity for Ruins and Other Topics.* Amherst: University of Massachusetts Press, 1980.

Jackson, Kenneth T. *Crabgrass Frontier: The Suburbanization of the United States.* New York: Oxford University Press, 1985.

Jackson, Wes. *New Roots for Agriculture.* Lincoln: University of Nebraska Press 1985.

———. *Altars of Unhewn Stone: Science and the Earth.* San Francisco: North Point Press, 1987.

———. *Becoming Native to this Place.* Lexington: University of Kentucky Press, 1994.

Jacobs, Harvey M., ed. *Who Owns America? Social Conflict Over Property Rights.* Madison: University of Wisconsin Press, 1998.

John, DeWitt. *Civic Environmentalism: Alternatives to Regulation in States and Communities.* Washington: Congressional Quarterly Inc., 1994.

Johnson, Hildegard Binder. *Order Upon the Land: The U.S. Rectangular Land Survey and the Upper Mississippi Country.* New York: Oxford University Press, 1976.

Josephson, Paul R. *Industrialized Nature: Brute Force Technology and the Transformation of the Natural World.* Washington, D.C.: Island Press, 2002.

Judd, Richard W. *Common Lands, Common People: The Origins of Conservation in Northern New England.* Cambridge: Harvard University Press, 1997.

Kahn, Alfred. "The Tyranny of Small Decisions: Market Failures, Imperfections, and the Limits of Economics." *Kyklos* 19 (1966): 23–47.

Kammen, Michael. *Spheres of Liberty: Changing Perceptions of Liberty in American Culture.* Madison: University of Wisconsin Press, 1986.

Kanazawa, Mark T. "Efficiency in Western Water Law: The Development of the California Doctrine, 1850–1911." *Journal of Legal Studies* 27 (1998): 159–184.

Kaplow, Louis, and Steven Shavell. "Property Rules Versus Liability Rules: An Economic Analysis." *Harvard Law Review* 109 (1996): 713–790.

Karp, James P. "Aldo Leopold's Land Ethic: Is an Ecological Conscience Evolving in Land Development Law?" *Environmental Law* 19 (1989): 737–765.

Katz, Stanley N. "Thomas Jefferson and the Right to Property in Revolutionary America." *Journal of Law and Economics* 19 (1976): 467–488.

Keiter, Robert B. "Beyond the Boundary Line: Constructing a Law of Ecosystem Management." *University of Colorado Law Review* 65 (1994): 293–333.

———. "Conservation Biology and the Law: Assessing the Challenge Ahead." *Chicago-Kent Law Review* 69 (1994): 911–933.

Kemmis, Daniel. *Community and the Politics of Place.* Norman: University of Oklahoma Press, 1990.

———. *The Good City and the Good Life: Renewing the Sense of Community.* Boston: Houghton Mifflin, 1995.

Kempton, Willett, James S. Boster, and Jennifer A. Hartley. *Environmental Values in American Culture.* Cambridge: MIT Press, 1995.

Kinney, J. P. *Forest Legislation in America Prior to March 4, 1789.* Bulletin 370. Ithaca, N.Y.: Cornell University Agricultural Experiment Station, February 1916.

Kittredge, William. *Owning it All.* St. Paul: Graywolf Press, 1987.

Klein, Maury. *The Flowering of the Third America: The Making of an Organizational Society, 1850–1920.* Chicago: Ivan R. Dee, 1993.

Kmiec, Douglas W. "The Original Understanding of the Taking Clause is Neither Weak Nor Obtuse." *Columbia Law Review* 88 (1988): 1630–1666.

———. "The Coherence of the Natural Law of Property." *Valparaiso Law Review* 26 (1991): 367–384.

Knight, Richard L., and Peter B. Landres. *Stewardship Across Boundaries.* Washington, D.C.: Island Press, 1998.

Knight, Richard L., and Sarah F. Bates, eds. *A New Century for Natural Resources Management.* Washington, D.C.: Island Press, 1995.

Knight, Richard L., and Suzanne Riedel, eds. *Aldo Leopold and the Ecological Conscience.* New York: Oxford University Press, 2002.

Kohak, Erazim V. "Possessing, Owning, Belonging." In Irving Howe, ed. *Beyond the Welfare State.* New York: Schocken Books, 1982.

Korngold, Gerald. "The Emergence of Private Land Use Controls in Large-Scale Subdivisions: The Companion Story to *Village of Euclid v. Ambler Realty Co.*" *Case Western Reserve Law Review* 51 (2001): 617–643.

Kulikoff, Alan. *The Agrarian Origins of American Capitalism.* Charlottesville: University Press of Virginia, 1992.

Kunstler, James Howard. *The Geography of Nowhere: The Rise and Decline of America's Man Made Landscape.* New York: Simon and Schuster, 1993.

Kurtz, Paul M. "Nineteenth Century Anti-Entrepreneurial Nuisance

Injunctions: Avoiding the Chancellor." *William and Mary Law Review* 17 (1976): 621–670.

Kutler, Stanley I. *Privilege and Creative Destruction: The Charles River Bridge Case.* New York: J. B. Lippincott, 1971.

Large, Donald W. "This Land is Whose Land? Changing Concepts of Land as Property." *Wisconsin Law Review* (1973): 1039–1083.

Larkin, Paschal. *Property in the Eighteenth Century.* London: Longman's, 1930.

Lasch, Christopher. *The True and Only Heaven: Progress and Its Critics.* New York: W. W. Norton, 1991.

———. *The Revolt of the Elites and the Betrayal of Democracy.* New York: W. W. Norton, 1995.

Lears, T. J. Jackson. *No Place of Grace: Antimodernism and the Transformation of American Culture, 1880–1920.* Chicago: University of Chicago Press, 1981.

Lee, Kai N. *Compass and Gyroscope: Integrating Science and Politics for the Environment.* Washington, D.C.: Island Press, 1993.

Lees, Martha A. "Preserving Property Values? Preserving Proper Homes? Preserving Privilege?: the Pre-*Euclid* Debate over Zoning for Exclusively Private Residential Areas, 1916–1926." *University of Pittsburgh Law Review* 56 (1994): 367–439.

Lehman, Tim. *Public Values, Private Lands: Farmland Preservation Policy, 1933–85.* Chapel Hill: University of North Carolina Press, 1995.

Leopold, Aldo. *A Sand County Almanac and Sketches Here and There.* New York: Oxford University Press, 1949.

———. *For the Health of the Land: Previously Unpublished Essays and Other Writings.* Callicott, J. Baird, and Eric T. Freyfogle, eds. Washington, D.C.: Island Press, 1999.

Levy, Leonard. *The Law of the Commonwealth and Chief Justice Shaw.* New York: Oxford University Press, 1957.

Light, Walter. *Industrializing America: The Nineteenth Century.* Baltimore: Johns Hopkins University Press, 1995.

Limerick, Patricia Nelson. *The Legacy of Conquest: The Unbroken Past of the American West.* New York: W. W. Norton, 1987.

———. *Something in the Soil: Legacies and Reckonings in the New West.* New York: W. W. Norton, 2000.

Little, Charles E. *The Dying of the Trees: The Pandemic of America's Forests.* New York: Viking, 1995.

Locke, John. *Two Treatises of Government.* Cambridge: Cambridge University Press: Peter Laslett, ed., 1988.

Lockridge, Kenneth A. *A New England Town: The First Hundred Years.* 2d ed. New York: W. W. Norton, 1985.

Logsdon, Gene. *The Contrary Farmer.* Post Mills, Vt.: Chelsea Green, 1993.

———. *At Nature's Pace: Farming and the American Dream.* New York: Pantheon, 1994.

Lowenthal, David. *George Perkins Marsh: Prophet of Conservation.* Seattle: University of Washington Press, 2000.

Luccarelli, Mark. *Lewis Mumford and the Ecological Region: The Politics of Planning.* New York: Guilford Press, 1995.

Lund, Thomas A. *American Wildlife Law.* Berkeley: University of California Press, 1980.

McConnell, Grant. *Private Power and American Democracy.* New York: Alfred A. Knopf, 1966.

McCoy, Drew. *Elusive Republic: Political Economy in Jeffersonian America.* Chapel Hill: University of North Carolina Press, 1980.

McElfish, James M., Jr. "Property Rights, Property Roots: Rediscovering the Legal Protection of the Environment." *Environmental Law Reporter* 24 (1994): 10231–10249.

McEvoy, Arthur F. *The Fisherman's Problem: Ecology and Law in the California Fisheries.* Cambridge, England: Cambridge University Press, 1986.

McGovern, George, ed. *Agricultural Thought in the Twentieth Century.* Indianapolis: Bobbs-Merrill, 1967.

McInerney, Thomas F. III. "Common Ground: Reconciling Rights and Communal Concerns in Real Property Law." *Boston College Environmental Affairs Law Review* 25 (1998): 831–861.

MacKaye, Benton, ed. *The New Exploration: A Philosophy of Regional Planning.* Urbana: University of Illinois Press, 1962.

MacNeill, Jim, Pieter Winsemius, and Taizo Yakushiji. *Beyond Interdependence: The Meshing of the World's Economy and the Earth's Ecology.* New York: Oxford University Press, 1991.

McPhee, John. *The Pine Barrens.* New York: Farrar, Straus, and Giroux, 1968.

———. *The Control of Nature.* New York: Farrar, Straus, and Giroux, 1989.

MacPherson, C. B., ed. *Property: Mainstream and Critical Positions.* Toronto: University of Toronto Press, 1978.

Maier, Pauline. *American Scripture: Making the Declaration of Independence.* New York: Vintage Books, 1998.

Mandelker, Daniel R. "Controlling Non-point Source Water Pollution: Can It Be Done?" *Chicago-Kent Law Review* 65 (1989): 479–502.

———. "Managing Space to Manage Growth." *William and Mary Environmental Law & Policy Review* 23 (1999): 801–824.

Manes, Christopher. *Green Rage: Radical Environmentalism and the Unmaking of Civilization.* Boston: Little, Brown, 1990.

Marks, Stuart A. *Southern Hunting in Black and White: Nature, History, and Ritual in a Carolina Community.* Princeton: Princeton University Press, 1991.

May, Dean L. *Three Frontiers: Family, Land, and Society in the American West.* Cambridge: Cambridge University Press, 1994.

Meine, Curt. *Aldo Leopold: Life and Work.* Madison: University of Wisconsin Press, 1988.

Mensch, Elizabeth V. "The Colonial Origins of Liberal Property Rights." *Buffalo Law Review* 31 (1982): 635–735.

Merchant, Carolyn. *The Death of Nature.* New York: Harper & Row, 1980.

———. *The Columbia Guide to American Environmental History.* New York: Columbia University Press, 2002.

Merrill, Thomas W. "The Landscape of Constitutional Property." *Virginia Law Review* 86 (2000): 885–999.

Milbrath, Lester W. *Envisioning a Sustainable Society: Learning Our Way Out.* Albany: State University of New York Press, 1989.

Miller, Char. *Gifford Pinchot and the Making of Modern Environmentalism.* Washington, D.C.: Island Press, 2001.

Miller, Donald. *Lewis Mumford: A Life.* New York: Weidenfeld & Nicholson, 1989.

Mills, Stephanie. *In Service of the Wild: Restoring and Reinhabiting Damaged Land.* Boston: Beacon Press, 1995.

Milsom, S. F. C. *Historical Foundations of the Common Law.* Toronto: Butterworths, 2d ed., 1981.

Mitchell, John Hanson. *Trespassing: An Inquiry into the Private Ownership of Land.* Reading, Mass.: Addison-Wesley, 1998.

Montmarquet, James A. *The Idea of Agrarianism: From Hunter-Gatherer to*

Agrarian Radical in Western Culture. Moscow: University of Idaho Press, 1989.

More, Thomas. *Utopia*. New Haven: Yale University Press, Edward Surtz, ed., 1964.

Morgan, Edmund S. *From Slavery to Freedom: The Ordeal of Colonial Virginia*. New York: W. W. Norton, 1975.

Morrison, Roy. *Ecological Democracy*. Boston: South End Press, 1995.

Moynihan, Cornelius J., and Sheldon F. Kurtz. *Introduction to the Law of Real Property*. 3d ed. St. Paul: West Publishing Co., 2002.

Munzer, Stephen R. *A Theory of Property*. Cambridge: Cambridge University Press, 1990.

———. "The Acquisition of Property Rights." *Notre Dame Law Review* 66 (1991): 661–686.

———, ed. *New Essays in Legal and Political Theory of Property*. Cambridge: Cambridge University Press, 2001.

Nabhan, Gary Paul. *Cultures of Habitat: On Nature, Culture, and Story*. Washington, D.C.: Counterpoint Press, 1997.

Nash, Roderick Frazier. *The Rights of Nature: A History of Environmental Ethics*. Madison: University of Wisconsin Press, 1989.

———. *Wilderness and the American Mind*. 4th ed. New Haven: Yale University Press, 2001.

Nedelsky, Jennifer. *Private Property and the Limits of American Constitutionalism: The Madisonian Framework and Its Legacy*. Chicago: University of Chicago Press, 1990.

Nelson, Robert H. *Zoning and Property Rights: An Analysis of the American System of Land Use Regulation*. Cambridge: MIT Press, 1977.

Nelson, William E. *The Americanization of the Common Law: The Impact of Legal Change on Massachusetts Society, 1760–1830*. Cambridge: Harvard University Press, 1975.

Neuman, Janet C. "Beneficial Use, Waste, and Forfeiture: The Inefficient Search for Efficiency in Western Water Law." *Environmental Law* 28 (1998): 919–996.

Norton, Bryan G. *Why Preserve Natural Variety?* Princeton: Princeton University Press, 1987.

———. *Toward Unity Among Environmentalists*. New York: Oxford University Press, 1991.

Norton, Bryan G., ed. *The Preservation of Species: The Value of Biological Diversity.* Princeton: Princeton University Press, 1986.

Noss, Reed F., and Allen Y. Cooperrider. *Saving Nature's Legacy: Protecting and Restoring Biodiversity.* Washington, D.C.: Island Press, 1994.

Novak, William J. *The People's Welfare: Law & Regulation in Nineteenth-Century America.* Chapel Hill: University of North Carolina Press, 1996.

O'Brien, Dan. *Buffalo for the Broken Heart: Restoring Life to a Black Hills Ranch.* New York: Random House, 2001.

Odum, William E. "Environmental Degradation and the Tyranny of Small Decisions." *BioScience* 32 (1982): 728–729.

Oksanen, Markku. *"Nature as Property: Environmental Ethics and the Institution of Ownership."* Ph.D. diss., University of Turku, Finland, 1998.

Opie, John. *Nature's Nation: An Environmental History of the United States.* Fort Worth, Tex.: Harcourt Brace, 1998.

Orr, David W. *Ecological Literacy: Education and the Transition to a Postmodern World.* Albany: State University of New York Press, 1992.

———. *Earth in Mind: On Education, Environment, and the Human Prospect.* Washington, D.C.: Island Press, 1994.

———. *The Nature of Design: Ecology, Culture, and Human Intention.* New York: Oxford University Press, 2002.

Ostrom, Elinor. *Governing the Commons: The Evolution of Institutions for Collective Action.* Cambridge: Cambridge University Press, 1990.

Parenteau, Patrick A. "Unreasonable Expectations: Why *Palazzolo* Has No Right to Turn a Silk Purse into a Sow's Ear." *Boston College Environmental Affairs Law Review* 30 (2002): 101–135.

Partridge, Ernest, ed. *Responsibilities to Future Generations: Environmental Ethics.* Buffalo, N.Y.: Prometheus Books, 1981.

Paul, Ellen Frankel, Fred D. Miller, Jr., and Jeffrey Paul, eds. *Property Rights.* Cambridge: Cambridge University Press, 1994.

Pells, Richard H. *Radical Visions and American Dreams: Culture and Social Thought in the Depression Years.* Urbana: University of Illinois Press ed., 1998.

Penner, James E. *The Idea of Property in Law.* New York: Oxford University Press, 1997.

Pennock, J. Roland, and John W. Chapman, eds. *Nomos XXII: Property.* New York: New York University Press, 1980.

Philbrick, Francis S. "Changing Conceptions of Property in Law." *University of Pennsylvania Law Review* 86 (1938): 691–732.

Pimm, Stuart L. *The Balance of Nature? Ecological Issues in the Conservation of Species and Communities.* Chicago: University of Chicago Press, 1991.

Pirenne, Henri. *Economic and Social History of Medieval Europe.* New York: Harcourt, Brace & World, Inc., 1937.

Poirer, Marc. "Property, Environment, Community." *Journal of Environmental Law and Litigation* 12 (1997): 43–86.

———. "The Virtue of Vagueness in Takings Doctrine." *Cardozo Law Review* 24 (2002): 93–191.

Polanyi, Karl. *The Great Transformation: The Political and Economic Origins of Our Time.* Boston: Beacon Press, 1957.

Pole, J. R. *Paths to the American Past.* New York: Oxford University Press, 1979.

Pomfret, John E. *Founding the American Colonies, 1583–1660.* New York: Harper & Row, 1970.

Popper, Frank J. *The Politics of Land-Use Reform.* Madison: University of Wisconsin Press, 1981.

Posner, Richard. *Economic Analysis of Law.* 3d ed. Boston: Little, Brown, 1986.

Powell, Sumner Chilton. *Puritan Village: The Formation of a New England Town.* Middletown, Conn.: Wesleyan University Press, 1963.

President's Council on Sustainable Development. *Towards a Sustainable America: Advancing Prosperity, Opportunity, and a Healthy Environment for the 21st Century.* Washington, D.C., 1999.

Radin, Margaret Jane. *Reinterpreting Property.* Chicago: University of Chicago Press, 1993.

Rajan, Vithal, ed. *Rebuilding Communities: Experiences and Experiments in Europe.* Darlington, England: Green Books Ltd., 1993.

Raymond, Leigh, and Sally K. Fairfax. "The 'Shift to Privatization' in Land Conservation: A Cautionary Essay." *Natural Resources Journal* 41 (2002): 599–639.

Reeve, Andrew. *Property.* Atlantic Highlands, N.J.: Humanities Press International, 1986.

Reiger, John F. *American Sportsmen and the Origins of Conservation.* 3d ed. Corvallis: Oregon State University Press, 2001.

Reisner, Marc, and Sarah Bates. *Overtapped Oasis: Reform or Revolution in Western Water.* Washington, D.C.: Island Press, 1990.

Rome, Adam. *The Bulldozer in the Countryside: Suburban Sprawl and the Rise of American Environmentalism.* Cambridge: Cambridge University Press, 2001.

Rose, Carol M. " 'Enough and as Good' of What?" *Northwestern University Law Review* 81 (1987): 417–442.

———— "Property Rights, Regulatory Regimes and the New Takings Jurisprudence–An Evolutionary Approach." *Tennessee Law Review* 57 (1990): 577–594.

————. *Property and Persuasion: Essays on the History, Theory, and Rhetoric of Ownership.* Boulder, Colo.: Westview Press, 1994.

————. "Property as the Keystone Right?" *Notre Dame Law Review* 71 (1996): 329–365.

————. "Takings, Federalism, Norms." *Yale Law Journal* 105 (1996): 1121–1152.

————. "Property and Expropriation: Themes and Variations in American Law." *Utah Law Review* 2000: 1–38.

Rösener, Werner. *Peasants in the Middle Ages.* Urbana: University of Illinois Press ed., 1992.

Ryan, Alan J. *Property and Political Theory.* New York: Blackwell, 1984.

————. *Property.* Minneapolis: University of Minnesota Press, 1987.

Rypkema, Donovan D. "Property Rights/Property Values: The Economic Misunderstandings of the 'Property Rights' Movement." *The Responsive Community* (Summer 1993): 28–37.

Sack, Robert David. *Human Territoriality: Its Theory and History.* Cambridge: Cambridge University Press, 1986.

Sagoff, Mark. *The Economy of the Earth: Philosophy, Law, and the Environment.* Cambridge: Cambridge University Press, 1988.

Salamon, Marylynn. *Women and the Law of Property in Early America.* Chapel Hill: University of North Carolina Press, 1986.

Salamon, Sonya. *Prairie Patrimony: Family, Farming, and Community in the Midwest.* Chapel Hill: University of North Carolina Press, 1992.

Sale, Kirkpatrick. *Dwellers in the Land: The Bioregional Vision.* San Francisco: Sierra Club, 1985.

Sandel, Michael J. *Democracy's Discontent: America in Search of a Public Philosophy.* Cambridge: Harvard University Press, 1996.

Sanders, Scott Russell. *Secrets of the Universe: Scenes from the Journey Home.* Boston: Beacon Press, 1991.

———. *Staying Put: Making a Home in a Restless World*. Boston: Beacon Press, 1993.

———. *Writing from the Center*. Bloomington: Indiana University Press, 1995.

Sax, Joseph. "The Public Trust Doctrine in Natural Resources Law: Effective Judicial Intervention." *Michigan Law Review* 68 (1970): 471–566.

———. "Takings, Private Property and Public Rights." *Yale Law Journal* 81 (1971): 149–186.

———. "Liberating the Public Trust Doctrine from Its Historical Shackles." *University of California Davis Law Review* 14 (1980): 185–194.

———. "Some Thoughts on the Decline of Private Property." *Washington Law Review* 58 (1983): 481–496.

———. "Takings." *University of Chicago Law Review* 53 (1986): 279–293.

———. "The Limits of Private Rights in Public Waters." *Environmental Law* 19 (1989): 473–483.

———. "Property Rights and the Economy of Nature: Understanding *Lucas v. South Carolina Coastal Council*." *Stanford Law Review* 45 (1993): 1433–1455.

———. "Using Property Rights to Attack Environmental Protection." *Pace Environmental Law Review* 14 (1996) 1–14.

———. *Playing Darts with a Rembrandt: Public and Private Rights in Cultural Treasures*. Ann Arbor: University of Michigan Press, 1999.

Schlatter, Richard. *Private Property: The History of an Idea*. London: Russell & Russell, 1973.

Schreiber, Harry. "The Road to *Munn*: Eminent Domain and the Concept of Public Purpose in the State Courts." In Donald Fleming and Bernard Bailyn, eds. *Law in American History*, 329–402. Cambridge: Harvard University Press, 1971.

———. "Property Law, Expropriation, and Resource Allocation by Government: The United States, 1789–1910." *Journal of Economic History* 33 (1973): 232–251.

———. "Public Rights and the Rule of Law in American Legal History." *California Law Review* 72 (1984): 217–251.

———. "Instrumentalism and Property Rights: A Reconsideration of American 'Styles of Judicial Reasoning' in the Nineteenth Century." *Wisconsin Law Review* (1985): 1–18.

Schultz, David. "Political Theory and Legal History: Conflicting Depictions of Property in the American Political Founding." *American Journal of Legal History* 37 (1993): 464–495.

Schumpeter, Joseph A. *Capitalism, Socialism and Democracy.* New York: Harper & Bros., 1942.

Scott, William B. *In Pursuit of Happiness: American Conceptions of Property from the Seventeenth Century to the Twentieth Century.* Bloomington: Indiana University Press, 1977.

Sears, Paul B. *Deserts on the March.* Norman: University of Oklahoma Press, 1935.

Sen, Amartya. *On Ethics and Economics.* Oxford: Basil Blackwell, 1987.

Shabecoff, Philip. *A Fierce Green Fire: The American Environmental Movement.* New York: Hill & Wang, 1993.

Shoard, Marion. *A Right to Roam.* Oxford: Oxford University Press, 1999.

Singer, Joseph William. "Sovereignty and Property." *Northwestern University Law Review* 86 (1991): 1–56.

———. "No Right to Exclude: Public Accommodations and Private Property." *Northwestern University Law Review* 90 (1996): 1283–1495.

———. *The Edges of the Field: Lessons on the Obligations of Ownership.* Boston: Beacon Press, 2000.

———. *Entitlement: The Paradoxes of Property.* New Haven: Yale University Press, 2000.

———. *Introduction to Property.* Boston: Aspen Law & Business, 2001.

Singer, Joseph William, and Jack M. Beerman. "The Social Origins of Property." *Canadian Journal of Law and Jurisprudence* 6 (1993): 217–248.

Sitarz, Daniel, ed. *Agenda 21: The Earth Summit Strategy to Save Our Planet.* Boulder, Colo.: EarthPress, 1993.

Smith, Henry E. "Semicommon Property Rights and Scattering in the Open Fields." *Journal of Legal Studies* 29 (2000): 131–169.

Smith, Henry Nash. *Virgin Land: The American West as Symbol and Myth.* Cambridge: Harvard University Press, 1950.

Soule, Judith D., and John K. Piper, *Farming in Nature's Image: An Ecological Approach to Agriculture.* Washington, D.C.: Island Press, 1992.

Sprankling, John. "The Antiwilderness Bias in American Property Law." *University of Chicago Law Review* 63 (1996): 519–590.

Sproat, John G. *"The Best Men": Liberal Reformers of the Gilded Age.* New York: Oxford University Press, 1968.

Sreenivasan, Gopal. *The Limits of Lockean Rights in Property*. New York: Oxford University Press, 1995.

Steinberg, Theodore. *Nature Incorporated: Industrialization and the Waters of New England*. New York: Cambridge University Press, 1991.

———. *Slide Mountain, or the Folly of Owning Nature*. Berkeley: University California Press, 1995.

———. *Down to Earth: Nature's Role in American History*. New York: Oxford University Press, 2002.

Stilgoe, John R. *Common Landscape of America, 1580–1845*. New Haven: Yale University Press, 1982.

Stiverson, Gregory A. *Poverty in a Land of Plenty: Tenancy in Eighteenth Century Maryland*. Baltimore: Johns Hopkins University Press, 1977.

Stone, Christopher. *Earth and Other Ethics: The Case for Moral Pluralism*. New York: Harper & Row, 1987.

Strong, Ann L. *Private Property and the Public Interest: The Brandywine Experience*. Baltimore: Johns Hopkins University Press, 1975.

Sunstein, Cass. "On the Expressive Function of Law." *University of Pennsylvania Law Review* 144 (1996): 2021–2053.

Sutter, Paul S. *Driven Wild: How the Fight Against Automobiles Launched the Modern Wilderness Movement*. Seattle: University of Washington Press, 2002.

Swaney, James A. "Common Property, Reciprocity, and Community." *Journal of Economic Issues* 24 (1990): 451–461.

Tarlock, A. Dan. "The Changing Meaning of Water Conservation in the West." *Nebraska Law Review* 66 (1987): 145–174.

———. "Local Government Protection of Biodiversity: What Is Its Niche?" *University of Chicago Law Review* 60 (1993): 555–613.

———. "The Potential Role of Local Governments in Watershed Management." *Environmental Law Reporter* 32 (2002):11273–11283.

———. *Law of Water Rights and Resources*. New York: Clark Boardman, 1988, 2002 supp.

Tate, Thad W., and David L. Ammerman, eds. *The Chesapeake in the Seventeenth Century: Essays on Anglo-American Society and Politics*. New York: W. W. Norton, 1979.

Taylor, Alan. *American Colonies*. New York: Viking, 2001.

Taylor, John. *Arator: Being a Series of Agricultural Essays*. Indianapolis: Liberty Classics, 1977.

Thiel, Jo. *"Land Communities, Land Ethics, and Private Land."* Master's thesis, Colorado State University, 2001.

Thomas, John L. *Alternative America: Henry George, Edward Bellamy, Henry Demarest Lloyd and the Adversary Tradition.* Cambridge: Harvard University Press, 1983.

Thomashow, Mitchell. *Ecological Identity: Becoming a Reflective Environmentalist.* Cambridge: MIT Press, 1995.

Thompson, Barton. "Markets for Nature." *William and Mary Environmental Law and Policy Review* 25 (2000): 261–316.

Thompson, E. P. *Customs in Common: Studies in Traditional Popular Culture.* New York: New Press, 1991.

Tideman, T. Nicolaus. "Takings, Moral Evolution, and Justice." *Columbia Law Review* 88 (1988): 1714–1730.

Tober, James A. *Who Owns Wildlife? The Political Economy of Conservation in Nineteenth-Century America.* Westport, Conn.: Greenwood Press, 1981.

Treanor, William Michael. "The Original Understanding of the Takings Clause and the Political Process." *Columbia Law Review* 95 (1995): 782–887.

Trefethen, James B. *An American Crusade for Wildlife.* New York: Winchester Press, 1975.

Twelve Southerners. *I'll Take My Stand: The South and the Agrarian Tradition.* Baton Rouge: Louisiana State University Press, 1977.

Underkuffler, Laura S. "On Property: An Essay." *Yale Law Journal* 100 (1990): 127–148.

Underkuffler-Freund, Laura S. "Takings and the Nature of Property." *Canadian Journal of Law and Jurisprudence* 9 (1996) 161–205.

Urofsky, Melvin I. "State Courts and Protective Legislation during the Progressive Era: A Reevaluation." *Journal of American History* 72 (1985): 63–91.

Van Hise, Charles R. *The Conservation of Natural Resources in the United States.* New York: Macmillian Co., 1910.

Vandevelde, Kenneth J. "The New Property in the Nineteenth Century: The Development of the Modern Conception of Property." *Buffalo Law Review* 29 (1980): 325–367.

Veblen, Thorstein. *Absentee Ownership and Business Enterprise in Recent Times: The Case of America.* Boston: Beacon Press, 1967.

Vileisis, Ann. *Discovering the Unknown Landscape: A History of America's Wetlands.* Washington, D.C.: Island Press, 1997.

Vitek, William, and Wes Jackson, eds. *Rooted in the Land: Essays on Community and Place.* New Haven: Yale University Press, 1996.

Votteler, Todd H. "Raiders of the Lost Aquifer? Or, the Beginning of the End to Fifty Years of Confllict Over the Texas Aquifer." *Tulane Environmental Law Journal* 15 (2002): 257–321.

Waldron, Jeremy. *The Right to Private Property.* New York: Oxford University Press, 1988.

———. "Property, Justification and Need." *Canadian Journal of Law and Jurisprudence* 6 (1993): 185–215.

Wallach, Bret. *At Odds with Progress: Americans and Conservation.* Tucson: University of Arizona Press, 1991.

Warren, Louis S. *The Hunter's Game: Poachers and Conservationists in Twentieth-Century America.* New Haven: Yale University Press, 1997.

Washburn, Wilcomb E. "The Moral and Legal Justification for Dispossessing the Indians." In James Morton Smith, ed., *Seventeenth-Century America: Essays in Colonial History,* 15–32. New York: W. W. Norton, 1972.

Weeks, W. William. *Beyond the Ark: Tools for an Ecosystem Approach to Conservation.* Washington, D.C.: Island Press, 1997.

Wenz, Peter. *Environmental Ethics Today.* New York: Oxford University Press, 2001.

———. *Environmental Justice.* Albany: State University of New York Press, 1988.

Western, David, and R. Michael Wright, eds. *Natural Connections: Perspectives in Community-based Conservation.* Washington, D.C.: Island Press, 1994.

Westra, Laura, and John Lemons, eds. *Perspectives in Ecological Integrity.* Dordrecht, Netherlands: Kluwer, 1995.

White, G. Edward. *Patterns of American Legal Thought.* Charlottesville, Va.: Michie Co., 1978.

White, Richard. *Land Use, Environment, and Social Change: The Shaping of Island County, Washington.* Seattle: University of Washington Press, 1980.

———. *The Organic Machine: The Remaking of the Columbia River.* New York: Hill and Wang, 1995.

Wiebe, Robert H. *The Search for Order, 1877–1920.* New York: Hill and Wang, 1967.

———. *Self-Rule: A Cultural History of American Democracy.* Chicago: University of Chicago Press, 1995.

Wilcove, David S. *The Condor's Shadow: The Loss and Recovery of Wildlife in America*. New York: W. H. Freeman, 1999.

Wilkinson, Charles F. *Crossing the Next Meridian: Land, Water, and the Future of the West*. Washington, D.C.: Island Press, 1992.

Williams, Joan. "The Rhetoric of Property." *Iowa Law Review* 83 (1998): 277–361.

Wood, Gordon S. *The Creation of the American Republic, 1776–1787*. Chapel Hill: University of North Carolina Press, 1969.

———. *The Radicalism of the American Revolution*. New York: Vintage, 1991.

World Commission on Environment and Development. *Our Common Future*. New York: Oxford University Press, 1987.

Worster, Donald. *Dust Bowl: The Southern Plains in the 1930s*. New York: Oxford University Press, 1979.

———. *Rivers of Empire: Water, Aridity, and the Growth of the American West*. New York: Pantheon Books, 1985.

———. *The Wealth of Nature: Environmental History and the Ecological Imagination*. New York: Oxford University Press, 1993.

———. *An Unsettled Country: Changing Landscapes of the American West*. Albuquerque: University of New Mexico Press, 1994.

———. *A River Running West: The Life of John Wesley Powell*. New York: Oxford University Press, 2001.

Wuthnow, Robert, ed. *Rethinking Materialism: Perspectives on the Spiritual Dimension of Economic Behavior*. Grand Rapids, Mich.: Eerdmans Publishing Co., 1995.

Portions of Chapters 5, 6, and 10 appeared in the *Environmental Law Reporter,* and I am grateful to its able editor, John Turner, for giving me such freedom to develop my thought. Chapter 6 was also delivered as the annual law review lecture at Valparaiso Law School; I thank the student editors who arranged my visit and made it so enjoyable. An early version of Chapter 7 appeared in *Dissent* and was improved by its talented editors, Jim Rule and Michael Walzer. Portions of Chapter 10 were also delivered at the University of California, Berkeley, and appeared as "The Particulars of Owning" in the *Ecology Law Quarterly*; again I thank the students who brought me to their campus. Many of my historical interpretations were included in "Community and the Market in Modern American Property Law," in *Land, Property, and the Environment*; I thank the volume's editor, John F. Richards, as well as the other contributors to the book who met over a period of years to discuss the complex links between property rights and environmental change. Helpful comments on portions of the manuscript were offered by Chris Elmendorf, Richard McAdams, Curt Meine, Julianne Newton, Jim Pfander, Steve Ross, Scott Russell Sanders, and Todd Wildermuth. My greatest debt is owed my editor and friend, Jonathan Cobb, who helped me clarify my thought and words. Helen Whybrow and Diana Siemens provided skilled text editing, and I thank them for it.